D1611661

THE NEW JERSEY FEDERALISTS

THE
NEW JERSEY
FEDERALISTS

Rudolph J. Pasler
and
Margaret C. Pasler

Rutherford • Madison • Teaneck
Fairleigh Dickinson University Press
London: Associated University Presses

37488

© 1975 by Associated University Presses, Inc.

Associated University Presses, Inc.
Cranbury, New Jersey 08512

Associated University Presses
108 New Bond Street
London W1Y OQX, England

Library of Congress Cataloging in Publication Data

Pasler, Rudolph J
The New Jersey Federalists.

Bibliography: p.
1. Federal Party. New Jersey. 2. New Jersey—
Politics and government—1775–1865. I. Pasler, Margaret
C., 1939–   joint author. II. Title.
JK2308.N5 1790b   329'.1'009749   73–22570
ISBN 0–8386–1525–2

PRINTED IN THE UNITED STATES OF AMERICA

PREFACE

The interpretation of the Federalist party in New Jersey that emerges from this study is one that is compatible with many aspects of the current revisionist views of that party whose leadership was drawn from the elite and possessed elitist beliefs. Certainly it is clear that those elements of the New Jersey party which offered serious and persistent rivalry to their opposition were, in contrast to the standard view of the Federalists, energetic, flexible, and effective in their response to the Jeffersonians. Moreover, largely as a concomitant of this posture, the New Jersey Federalist party became significant in the ongoing development of political and social democratization,[1] the major trend of the age. Because the Federalists offered the Jeffersonian Republicans long-term close competition for popular support, intense party rivalry occurred, and this party interaction in turn resulted in the swell in voter participation in New Jersey elections during the Jeffersonian era.[2] Too, as the Federalists increasingly emulated Jeffersonian electioneering techniques and rhetoric regarding the common man, the dominant Republicans were driven ever further in the direction of total democratization, further than they might otherwise have gone, in an effort to differentiate clearly between their position and that of the Federalists.

That the Federalist party in New Jersey was indeed tenacious is evident from its survival until the mid-1820s, long after Federalism in many areas of the nation had ceased to exist.[3] Therefore, in an effort to explore fully the history of the Federalists in New Jersey, this study begins with the rudimentary origins of the party and extends through the party's disintegration to its realignment during the formation of the second party system.

NOTES

1. "The process of political democratization may be specified . . . as the expansion of voter participation within an increasingly open and free electoral process." David Hackett Fischer, *The Revolution of American Conservatism* (New York: Harper & Row, 1965), p. xi. In New Jersey, Federalists throughout their history vigorously initiated, from a benevolent paternal position, a variety of successful social reform movements.

2. Richard P. McCormick, *The History of Voting in New Jersey: A Study of the Development of Election Machinery, 1664–1911* (New Brunswick: Rutgers University Press, 1953), p. 121. "It will be noted that the expansion of popular participation [during the Jeffersonian era] is apparent in state elections. The Jacksonian era may have been a period of expanded voter participation in presidential contests, but not in the electoral process." Fischer, *The Revolution of American Conservatism*, p. xv.

3. Rudolph J. Pasler and Margaret C. Pasler, "Federalist Tenacity in Burlington County, 1810–1824," *New Jersey History* LXXXVII (Winter, 1969): passim.

ACKNOWLEDGMENTS

Many debts have been incurred during the formulation, research, and writing of this study. Unfortunately, more space than is available would be required to acknowledge fully the numerous contributions of colleagues, archivists, and other scholars.

Certain contributions, however, cannot pass unnoticed, for they have been invaluable. These include the contributions of the late Harold F. Wilson, John A. Munroe, Richard P. McCormick, Carl E. Prince, William C. Wright, and James Broussard.

Furthermore, we are indebted to the collections of many libraries and archives, which provided the material for this study. Principal among these are the special collections departments of Rutgers and Princeton Universities, the New Jersey Historical Society, the Historical Society of Pennsylvania, Morristown (New Jersey) National Historical Park, and the New-York Historical Society.

At all of these institutions, and the many that must go unmentioned, the staff invariably aided our research. Still, the Rutgers University Special Collection Department staff, headed by Director Donald A. Sinclair, must receive special mention in this regard. Thanks also are due here to Mrs. Carol McCollough of the New Jersey Historical Society.

The completion of this study would have been impossible, financially speaking, had it not been for assistance from the

9

Noyes Foundation of Smithville, New Jersey, and the New Jersey State Historical Commission. At critical points in the preparation of this work, these agencies provided not only generous grants but vital encouragement.

THE NEW JERSEY FEDERALISTS

1

ROOTS IN THE PAST

Entrenched Federalism characterized the New Jersey political scene of the early 1790s. Within a decade a legion of forces would combine to uproot Federalist hegemony, but these forces had yet to make themselves keenly felt.[1] For a time, then, the present leadership group would continue supreme. No stranger to the reins of power, this group, for the most part, was composed of the same families, or even the same people, who had figured largely as leaders of New Jersey in earlier eras.[2]

In some cases, individuals holding official power in the early 1790s had also been leaders in earlier periods of New Jersey history. For example, James Kinsey, of Burlington County, Chief Justice of the New Jersey Supreme Court from the ratification of the federal Constitution in 1789 until 1803, had been a member of the Assembly during the Colonial period (1772 to 1776). Also, John Outwater, of Bergen County, who had served in the legislature during the American Revolution continued there during the Federalist period of the 1790s.

More often, however, the Federalist leaders of the early 1790s and later, while not themselves in the forefront of power during earlier periods, had close relatives who had been leaders then. Jonathan Dayton, for instance, was one of those members of the early 1790s leadership cadre whose father also had been a political leader. The younger Dayton in 1791 began an eight-year tenure as a United States Congressman, becoming Speaker of the House of Representatives in 1795 for the next four years.

Earlier, his father, Elias Dayton, had served in the state legislature. Then, too, there was Richard Stockton, Jr., of Princeton, a member of the United States Senate from 1796 to 1797 whose father, a Justice of the New Jersey Supreme Court in the Colonial period, had been a signer of the Declaration of Independence.[3] These are far from isolated examples but rather representative of the majority of Federalist leaders, for, as Carl Prince stated,

> In New Jersey, the fathers of most Federalist leaders, themselves wielded significant political and economic power in their day. . . .[4]

Kinship ties between Federalist leaders of the early 1790s and leaders of earlier periods of New Jersey history were not confined to father-son relationships, however. Erkuries Beatty, for example, who held several Hunterdon County posts in the early 1790s and who later would be a member of the New Jersey legislature almost continually from 1801 to his death in 1823, was the younger brother of John Beatty, whose political career began in 1781, when he was elected to the Council, and who in later decades held many county and federal elective and appointive posts.[5]

A further example, one of an uncle-nephew relationship between two very prominent Federalist leaders, was that between William Griffith and his uncle Elias Boudinot, under whom he had studied law. After Griffith had completed his studies, Boudinot advised him to leave East Jersey for the

> . . . Western Counties [which] promise the most success in . . . [the] profession.[6]

Among Griffith's activities in the 1790s was the authorship of *Eumenes,* a polemic urging the revision of the 1776 New Jersey Constitution.[7] His equally prominent uncle, Elias Boudinot, numbered among his earlier offices that of President of the Continental Congress from 1782 to 1783.

The relationship between William Griffith and Elias Boudinot was created not by blood, as in all of the previous examples, but by marriage. However, among the Federalists of the 1790s, kinship created by marriage was just as common as that created by blood since for generations there had been intermarriage among New Jersey's leading families. And these marriages sometimes extended beyond New Jersey county, sectional, and state borders, particularly in the case of families of the New Jersey "Progressive Strip,"[8] the counties of Somerset, Middlesex, Hunterdon, Essex, and Burlington, which provided a land bridge between Philadelphia and New York City.

For example, the Stockton family of Hunterdon County was related by marriage to the Bayard family of Middlesex County, while a Frelinghuysen of Somerset married a Mercer of Hunterdon. Also, an Essex County, East Jersey, Dayton married a Cumberland County, West Jersey, Giles. Furthermore, a New Jersey Boudinot married one of the New York Pintards, and a West Jersey Davenport married into the family of Philadelphia's Benjamin Franklin. Too, the New Jersey Bayards were related to those in Delaware and Maryland.[9] Marriage ties between New Jersey Federalist families and those of national prominence were, however, rare. One example is the marriage of Elias Boudinot's daughter to United States Attorney General William Bradford.

In addition to being joined by kinship, based on birth and marriage, members of the New Jersey leadership group were further intertwined by ties of friendship which resulted in widening circles of influence for these dominant families of New Jersey in the 1790s with their roots in the past. Manuscripts furnish a source from which information may be gleaned to construct a rudimentary sociogram.

For example, the calendar of the Garret D. Wall papers reveals the sum of Wall's correspondents, with whom he discussed personal as well as business and political matters, to have constituted a virtual who's who of the New Jersey Federalist party, including as it does the name of almost every important New Jersey Federalist of the time.[10] Also, individual letters from other collections reveal the ties between New Jersey Federal-

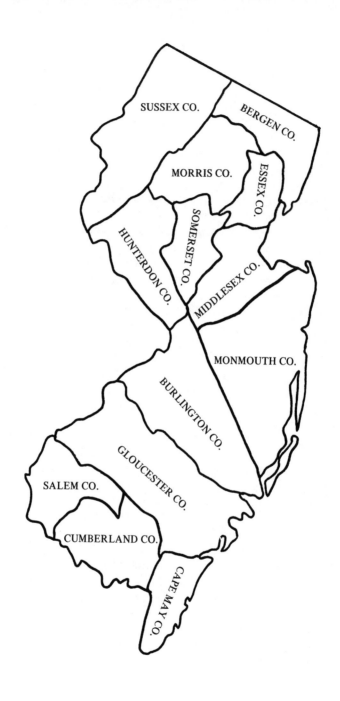

SUSSEX CO.

BERGEN CO.

MORRIS CO.

ESSEX CO.

SOMERSET CO.

HUNTERDON CO.

MIDDLESEX CO.

MONMOUTH CO.

BURLINGTON CO.

GLOUCESTER CO.

SALEM CO.

CUMBERLAND CO.

CAPE MAY CO.

Prominent New Jersey Federalist Surnames Listed by Home County

SUSSEX COUNTY
RUTHERFURD
THOMSON

MORRIS COUNTY
FORD

HUNTERDON COUNTY
BAYARD
BEATTY
EWING
MERCER
SHERMAN
SMITH
STOCKTON
WOODRUFF

MIDDLESEX COUNTY
BAYARD
BELL
BLAUVELT
HARDENBURG
NEILSON
PARKER
PATERSON
SCHUREMAN
WHITE

BURLINGTON COUNTY
BOUDINOT
COXE
GRIFFITH
KINSEY
LACEY
PEARSON
WALL
WALLACE

SALEM COUNTY
JOHNSON
SINNICKSON

CAPE MAY COUNTY
HAND
HUGHES
LEAMING
WHILLDIN
WILLETTS

BERGEN COUNTY
BLAUVELT
COLEFAX
OUTWATER
WARD

ESSEX COUNTY
BOUDINOT
CHETWOOD
CUMMING
DAYTON
HORNBLOWER
OGDEN
WILLIAMSON

SOMERSET COUNTY
FRELINGHUYSEN
SCOTT
STRYKER
VROOM

MONMOUTH COUNTY
IMLAY
LLOYD
RHEA

GLOUCESTER COUNTY
CLARK
DAVENPORT
WHITE

CUMBERLAND COUNTY
ELMER
EWING
WHITE

ists Richard Stockton and Aaron Ogden and the nationally prominent Federalist Alexander Hamilton. Hamilton also was a correspondent of Elias Boudinot and Elisha Boudinot, whose less political and pragmatic letters reveal their close friendship with such other national figures as John Jay and Rufus King.

In addition, Hamilton and Jay were guests of the Federalist Bayard-Kirkpatrick family of New Brunswick, as were George Washington and New Jersey's William Paterson, according to the diary of Jane Bayard Kirkpatrick, wife of New Jersey Chief Justice Andrew Kirkpatrick and daughter of Colonel John Bayard. This source reveals the highly developed social life that existed among the state's Federalist families and that played a large role in keeping the Federalist party intact.[11]

These Jerseymen and others like them, dominant in the 1790s as, for the most part, their fathers before them had been, joined into a network by ties of kinship (conferred by birth and marriage) and friendship, began in New Jersey to call themselves Federalists by 1792.

Continuity between the earlier eras of New Jersey history and the early 1790s (in addition to that already seen in the composition of the leadership group) was also present in the form of a common main basis of political alignment, the sectional cleavage between East Jersey and West Jersey. Originally two disparate colonies, the joining of the two in 1702 had not erased their distinctiveness. Afterward, as before, there were two Jerseys

> . . . split into two rival geographic divisions by historical, religious, economic and cultural factors. . . .[12]

Although the whole of this small,[13] markedly rural state appeared a veritable patchwork of diverse ethnic and religious groups compared with Connecticut or Massachusetts, West Jersey was more homogeneous than East Jersey. Owned and settled as a colony by English Quakers, it is not surprising, given the additional elements of geography, that of the two major cities the pull of neighboring Quaker Philadelphia, homogeneous and conservative, was stronger on West Jersey, while a similar attraction developed between the two heterogeneous, neighboring areas of East Jersey and New York City.

This attraction exerted on New Jersey by New York City on the east and Philadelphia on the west (besides in general leading to polarization and disunity between the two sections of the state) had a profound effect on the life of New Jersey.[14] A contemporary writer declared,

> The people of West Jersey trade to Philadelphia, and of course imitate their fashions, and imbibe their manners. The inhabitants of East Jersey trade to New York and regulate their fashions and manners according to those of New York.[15]

Furthermore, New Jersey's bond to Philadelphia and New York was evident on an individual basis as well. Philadelphians found in West Jersey a suitable location for retirement from the city; likewise, New Yorkers found East Jersey convenient as a site for a country home. In addition, many of the leading New Jersey Federalists themselves had ties to one of these great cities. For instance, Garret D. Wall had studied law in New York, while Jonathan Elmer, the Rutherfurds, and the Bayards either had received their education in one of these cities or had been active in New York or Philadelphia politics. Also, certain entrepreneurs, such as the Wallaces, Richards, and Laceys of Philadelphia moved to West Jersey to develop the bog iron resources of its most important county, Burlington. Conversely, New Yorkers such as the Ogdens allied with New Jersey relatives, like Aaron Ogden, of Essex County, to promote various profit-making ventures.

As the two cities of New York and Philadelphia grew in importance, New Jersey assumed her role as a highway between them. Indeed, the state's highways provided the sole direct land route from New York and New England to Philadelphia and points south. One of the most heavily traveled sections in the nation, the narrow New Jersey corridor between New York City and Philadelphia constituted the most populous and thriving area of the state. Beside accommodating the main roads,

NEW JERSEY IN 1790

SUSSEX CO.

BERGEN CO.

MORRIS CO.

ESSEX CO.

New York City

HUNTERDON CO.

SOMERSET CO.

MIDDLESEX CO.

MONMOUTH CO.

Philadelphia

BURLINGTON CO.

GLOUCESTER CO.

SALEM CO.

CUMBERLAND CO.

CAPE MAY CO.

——— = Former dividing line between East and West Jersey
(Keith's Line run in 1687)
- - - = Progressive Strip

this progressive strip contained the only stage lines, the leading church buildings, most of the post offices, libraries, bookstores, schools and colleges (College of New Jersey, now Princeton University, and Queen's College, now Rutgers–The State University), and the principal towns—Newark, Elizabeth, Perth Amboy (capital of colonial East Jersey), and New Brunswick in East Jersey and Trenton and Burlington City (capital of colonial West Jersey) in West Jersey.[16]

Elizabeth, the social and cultural center of East Jersey, boasted an unusually large professional and mercantile class. As one scholar has noted,

> In its background, its society, and its contributions to its state and nation Elizabethtown was New Jersey's most sophisticated city.[17]

Newark, with which Elizabeth had a keen rivalry for New York trade, for stage lines, and for road construction, was the state's center for light industry and manufacturing. As exemplified by the following letter from one New Jersey Federalist, a resident of Newark, to another, the citizens of each town beheld their municipality with particular esteem:

> ... how I regret the friends and pleasures of Newark—a place in which above all others I could wish to live and indeed where my heart constantly is—. . . .[18]

The area north of the southern boundary of the progressive strip claimed the bulk of New Jersey's prosperity. Although in 1790 it contained less than one-half of the total land area, it possessed three-fifths of the Caucasian population and three-fourths of the slaves and paid three-fifths of the state tax. Also, it included

2/3 of the grist mills
4/5 of the forges
1/2 of the iron furnaces
1/2 of the tan yards
almost 1/2 of the fulleries[19]

East Jersey, which constituted the bulk of this area north of the strip's southern "boundary," was, in contrast to West Jersey (the more homogeneous section in every respect), divided into geographically diverse regions, settled by several ethnic and religious groups with different economic interests.

The prosperity of this northern area resulted partially from the superb valley farmlands of Bergen, northern Essex, Hunterdon, and Middlesex counties. And mountainous Morris and Sussex counties, in addition to valuable grazing lands, had rich iron ore and limestone deposits as well as facilities for processing and manufacturing.

The six counties of West Jersey, most of which lay in the state's southern plain, which runs from the Atlantic to the Delaware River, contained more than half of the total land area.[20] Bordering the Delaware River and Bay lay a fertile ten-mile wide stretch of desirable farmland. The sections of Cumberland, Salem, Gloucester, and Burlington counties that fronted on the Delaware were quite prosperous, and the life style of the people was equal to that in the northern areas of the state, but, excepting Burlington City, the towns were only pale shadows of those in East Jersey. Further inland, much of the western counties of New Jersey consisted of areas where the soil was extremely poor and scrub pine and marsh land abounded. Along the Atlantic coast, the soil was sandy.

If not small farmers, most West Jerseyans in the first half of the nineteenth century were small-scale fishermen or worked in the scattered, small industries—primarily iron, glass, or timber works. In 1789, West Jersey contained

4 of the state's 8 iron furnaces
30 of the state's 41 fisheries[21]

Ethnically and religiously, a contrast between East Jersey and West Jersey similar to that seen already in the case of geography and economic resources presented itself, West Jersey being again the more homogeneous area. In 1790 the population of West Jersey was almost entirely English, and most of them were members of the religious Society of Friends (Quakers). The following shows the high percentage of Quakers in West Jersey:

> Our Quakers of West Jersey . . . are seven eights of the body of the people, Cumberland and Cape May excepted.[22]

Also from among the English-speaking citizens of the southern portion of the state[23] probably came the majority of the adherents of Methodism, which had gained its first roots in New Jersey in the 1770s.

The Lutheran Swedes, who formed only a small percentage of the total New Jersey population, also were concentrated in the south and west of the state. Despite their small numbers, they constituted the second largest stock in West Jersey.[24] Their New Jersey center first had been in Gloucester County. Later they expanded along the Delaware River banks and the coast of the Bay into Burlington, Salem, Cumberland, and Cape May counties.

Virtually a Protestant state,[25] New Jersey in 1790 contained few Catholics. However, some Catholics were located in the Bordentown-Trenton area of West Jersey and probably a some-

TABLE 1.1
Estimated Number and Percentage of Caucasians of Various Stocks in New Jersey in 1790*

	Number	Per Cent
English	79,878	47.0
Scotch	13,087	7.7
Irish—Ulster	10,707	6.3
Irish—Free State	5,439	3.2
German	15,636	9.2
Dutch	28,250	16.6
French	4,000	2.4
Swedish	6,650	3.9
Unassigned	6,307	3.7
Total Caucasian Population	169,954	100.0

*American Council of Learned Societies, *Surnames in the United States Census of 1790* (Baltimore: Genealogical Publishing Company, 1969), pp. 124–25.

what larger number resided in Newark and in Elizabeth, East Jersey. Most, at this time, were from Santo Domingo in the West Indies.[26] Indeed, as a whole, New Jersey's national groups were several generations removed from Europe.[27]

Residing generally in the towns (and therefore by extrapolation primarily in East Jersey) were a handful of deists, professed atheists, and agnostics. Also, here were centered the small number of Episcopalians who still clung to their denomination despite the stigma attached to it as a result of the Revolution. From this small body of communicants, however, came a large percentage of the state's prominent citizens.

Ethnically English, Scotch, or Scotch-Irish, the Presbyterians[28] were distributed throughout the state. Not unnaturally, the density of the Presbyterians, whose religious denomination ranked first in New Jersey, coincided for the most part with the distribution of the population in general; that is, they were most numerous in the northern counties, especially near New York City, and followed the strip which stretched across central New Jersey to Philadelphia. This church by now had absorbed the Congregational churches brought down from New England by the early settlers. (Unlike West Jersey, which drew its early population directly from Britain, East Jersey, particularly Essex County, was settled largely by emigrants from New England.) Still, however, Gerlach notes,

. . . ethnocentricity remained a powerful force—towns, townships and even counties took on a distinctive ethnic character.[29]

For example, the following Essex Countians who, like the majority of local citizens, were descendants of New England Puritans, attributed to themselves certain superior characteristics on that basis:

. . . Judge Pennington . . . and William Tuttle . . . a few years since . . . actually were heading . . . [toward] one of the Newark Taverns and claiming weight of character from the circumstances of their being descendants of Connecticut ancestors. . . .[30]

The Dutch of East Jersey, numerically the second most important stock in the state, had emigrated primarily from New York. By 1790 northern New Jersey was as completely Dutch as any part of New York state. Centered in rural Bergen, Middlesex, Somerset, and Hunterdon, where the valleys of the Raritan, the Hackensack, and the Passaic offered rich land to these agriculturists of the Reformed church, the Dutch, holding fast to their customs and language, placed their stamp upon these areas.[31]

Because the Dutch owned more slaves than the English, it was in the areas of New Jersey where they predominated that the majority of slaves were found (and the majority of Blacks for that matter since four-fifths of the New Jersey Blacks were slaves). Furthermore, largely as a result of the Dutch practice in this regard, New Jersey in the early 1800s had more slaves, excepting New York, than any other northern state. However, in West Jersey, while the three Quaker counties of Burlington, Gloucester, and Salem accounted for 23 percent of the state's total population, they contained only 3 percent of its slave population, a testament to the abolitionist sentiments of this religious sect.[32]

The Germans, largely products of an eighteenth-century eastward migration from Pennsylvania to East Jersey, were especially numerous in Sussex and Hunterdon counties, although Germans were also to be found working in the iron mines of Morris County and even in the glass industry of Salem County in West Jersey. Usually Protestants, they were admired for their industry and their agricultural productivity.[33]

The division between the two sections of East Jersey and West Jersey, shown above in geographic, economic, religious, and ethnic terms, expressed itself in the New Jersey legislature in the form of political alignments.[34] East Jersey and West Jersey, had battled to achieve hegemony over the state since its inception, but neither section had been successful in doing so.

Then, in 1785, over the issue of monetary policy, a long-standing one which now came to a climax, the soft money faction of East Jersey, the section which had suffered the greatest disruption and dislocation of trade during the Revolution and

Confederation (because of the stagnation of trade and the pro-
longed drain on specie),[35] gained control of the legislature for
the next three years, defeating the conservative West Jersey-
hard money faction.

Led by lawyer and land speculator Abraham Clark, of Essex
County, who championed the state's inflationary cause, the victorious forces in the legislature created large amounts of loan-
office currency, made the loan-bills legal tender, and exempted
debtors from interest payments on the bills for one year.[36] That
at least the leading supporters of the inflationary movement,
like Clark and his fellow Essex County Assemblyman Daniel
Marsh, were not themselves debtors is evident.[37] In addition,
certain other members of the so-called "creditor class" supported for a time the soft-money East Jerseyans, although in
truth, they were protesters against inflation. They did so because as slaveholders, the Dutch Frelinghuysens, Strykers,
Vrooms, and others found the anti-slavery agitation of the West
Jerseyans threatening.[38]

Three years later, however, a revitalized West Jersey rose to
dominate the Assembly by a narrow margin. Not a little of West
Jersey's success in 1788 (when several East Jersey members in
each house of the legislature were first won over to the West
Jersey-hard money side) may be traced to the stimulation West
Jersey felt from the adoption of the federal Constitution, with
its promise to protect property rights buoying up the heretofore disheartened conservatives. Overcoming sectionalism
temporarily,[39] this East-West coalition joined to pass legislative
measures which initiated a mild deflation. It cancelled the loan-
office bills, adopted a new tax to remove paper money from
circulation, and required that future debts and contracts be
paid in gold or silver coin.[40] The laws for the relief of insolvent
debtors were repealed. As a result, the economic ills of the state
were somewhat alleviated, causing propertied men such as
Walter Rutherfurd to exclaim that the state would "no longer
[be] ranked with Rhode Island."[41]

Capitalizing upon their power base in the legislature, the
conservative forces led by West Jersey politicians fought to

extend their power in the federal Congressional election of 1789, the first of its kind and the first New Jersey state-wide general election. That this election was to be conducted on a general basis and not on a district one also shows the influence of the western alliance, for that group had favored the former method. Most importantly, however, the Western dominance in the legislature secured the Assembly's nomination for the United States Congressional ticket backed by this group, which became known as the "West Jersey ticket" or the "Junto ticket."

Composed of Elias Boudinot, of Elizabeth, James Schureman, of New Brunswick, Lambert Cadwalader, of Trenton, and Thomas Sinnickson, of Salem, all future Federalists,[42] the ticket was as popular in the West as it was unpopular in the East. Unlike the West, which united behind this one ticket (its relative homogeneity noted above greatly contributed to this stance[43]), East Jersey (the more heterogeneous area) was unable to unite and nominated many tickets, though they almost all bore the names of Abraham Clark and Jonathan Dayton.

To see the anti-Junto group as the opposition to the Constitution (Clark's early, short-lived lukewarm reaction to the document notwithstanding, New Jersey's response to the Constitution was almost universally favorable[44]), or as the debtor group, or as the nucleus of the future New Jersey Jeffersonian party would be to err. Hardly debtors, the members of the anti-Junto group, like their opposition, belonged to the landed, business, and professional groups which had long dominated New Jersey politics, and Dayton, as well as some of his supporters, the Ogdens and John Cumming for example, became Federalists.[45] Instead, the Junto–anti-Junto contest constituted a sectional battle, characteristic of New Jersey, between two factions of the ruling political class.[46]

The United States Congressional campaign of 1789 was not waged over any clearly defined issues but consisted mainly of appeals to sectionalism (which will be detailed later) and personal attacks. For example, Elias Boudinot, the Junto ticket leader, was denounced for having taken, while President of the Continental Congress,

. . . many thousands of dollars out of the public treasury to decorate his palace, profusely furnish his table, and clatter through the streets in a chariot. . . .[47]

while anti-Junto candidate Abraham Clark was vilified as an enemy of the Constitution.

Under the direction of its "Generalissimo Col. [Joseph] Ellis" whose "Embryo" the ticket was said to have been,[48] the Junto machinery, exhibiting a no-holds-barred spirit, worked to turn out, in the words of the opposition,

. . . every one without exception—and indeed, the Blind . . . and even decrepit old age. . . .[49]

Better organized than its opposition, the Junto employed herculean efforts to amass every possible ballot in West Jersey[50] to counter the expected anti-Junto majority in the East, recognizing the largely sectional appeal of each ticket.[51] For example, the West Jersey election officials were chosen for their partiality to the Junto ticket. One even was related to "Generalissimo" Ellis himself. Also, completed ballots were tampered with by Junto pollwatchers and collected at places not mentioned in the election laws.[52]

In addition, the West Jersey managers kept in daily touch, via Boudinot and John Chetwood, with election proceedings in the north. When these managers received, late in February, 1789, the final East Jersey returns, excepting those of Essex County, where the poll had not closed (no closing date had been set for the election), they scrapped their plans to close the Burlington poll on the twenty-first and the Gloucester one on the twenty-third. Instead, they continued the election with the goal of exceeding the showing already made by the anti-Junto ticket in East Jersey to such an extent that the withheld returns of Essex County too would be offset.

Later, on March 3, when the Governor's Privy Council met to count the ballots, it had the returns of only seven counties; Essex in the north was still out, as were the five southern counties. Had the election been decided on the basis of the partial returns then reported, at least three of the Congressional seats would have gone to anti-Junto candidates.[53] But West Jersey had seen to it that it was fully represented at the meeting so that it could press with all possible force for a decision advantageous to its ticket,[54] so, although the anti-Junto supporters proposed that the election be decided on the basis of the returns at hand, Governor Livingston, a close friend of Junto leader Elias Boudinot postponed any decision.

By March 18, when the Governor's Privy Council met for the second time, not only were the returns of all the counties except Essex at hand but the entire Junto ticket now had enough votes to be victorious. The absence of the Essex returns was ignored.[55]

Besides being less well-organized than the Junto, the anti-Junto group had shown itself to be less politically astute. Joseph Bloomfield, a prominent Dayton backer who lived in Burlington City, New Jersey's Quaker capital, no less, made a serious miscalculation regarding the Quakers. Writing on February 23, 1789 Bloomfield said,

> Notwithstanding the exertions intended to be made, I believe the rigid Quakers will not turn out. . . .[56]

Less than a week later, Bloomfield's next letter to Dayton included the text of the successful propaganda which the Junto was directing at the Quakers:

> . . . Come Friend, go to the Election and vote for the West-Jersey-ticket, the Quakers [sic] ticket. . . . Come, turn out, oppose the Prysbeterian [sic] Ticket. The Prysbeterians want another War. . . . [If] You don't feel a Freedom [to vote]. You will lose your freedom, Your Liberty and Your Property, nay more, Your Religion. . . .[57]

The outcome of the events of 1789 found in control of the New Jersey government a group of individuals who, in a few short years, would call themselves Federalists. These would include not only the elected United States Congressmen from New Jersey and the dominant group in the state legislature but also appointed officials—United States Senators William Paterson of East Jersey and Jonathan Elmer of West Jersey, New Jersey Chief Justice James Kinsey of West Jersey and presidential electors John Neilson, John Rutherfurd, and Matthias Ogden of East Jersey, and David Brearly, James Kinsey, and David Moore of West Jersey.[58]

Indeed, the politically astute Junto constituted the embryo of the New Jersey Federalist party to which it would contribute its political acumen. That this 1789 group aimed to maintain its unity for the achievement of more ambitious goals is indicated by the comment of one Junto backer, ". . . our views are extended beyond the present election,"[59] when urging a friend to preserve the alliances made and strengthened during the 1789 Congressional election.

NOTES

1. New Jersey lagged behind many states (even adjacent ones like New York and Pennsylvania) in challenging Federalist authority. Carl Prince, "New Jersey's Democratic-Republicans, 1790–1817: A Study in Early Party Machinery" (Ph.D. diss., Rutgers University, 1963), p. 17.

2. Ruth Keesey generalizes regarding Federalist Bergen county, ". . . often the same people carried on county and local affairs after the war as they had before and during the Revolution." Ruth Keesey, "Loyalty and Reprisal: The Loyalists of Bergen County, New Jersey and Their Estates (Ph.D. diss., Rutgers University, 1957), p. 232.

3. Alfred Hoyt Bill, *A House Called Morven* (Princeton: Princeton University Press, 1954), pp. 18–88, passim.

4. Carl Prince, "The Leadership of New Jersey's First Party System" (paper presented at the Second Annual New Jersey History Symposium, Trenton, New Jersey, December 5, 1970), p. 7.

5. Harry Weiss and Grace Zeigler, *Colonel Erkuries Beatty* (Trenton, New Jersey: Past Times Press, 1958), pp. 3–104, passim.

6. John Griffith to Joshua Wallace, December 7, 1789, Wallace Papers, Historical Society of Pennsylvania.

7. William Griffith, *Eumenes* (Trenton, 1799), passim.

8. Harold F. Wilson, *The Jersey Shore: A Social and Economic History of the Counties of Atlantic, Cape May, Monmouth and Ocean* (New York: Lewis Historical Publishing Company, 1953), p. 51.

9. Uncommon, however, were New Jersey marriage ties to New England and the South.

10. These friendships dating from 1807 were to prove invaluable in young Wall's rapid rise to the fore of New Jersey political life after the War of 1812. Large collections of Garret D. Wall papers are located at Rutgers University Library, Princeton University Library, and the New Jersey Historical Society.

11. The sole Republican welcomed in many elegant Federalist homes was Governor Joseph Bloomfield, who simultaneously was castigated by the Federalist press for his defection from the Federalist party. There is strong evidence to indicate that the Republicans never fully trusted and accepted Bloomfield. David Thompson, Jr. to Samuel Southard, October 4, 1811, Samuel Southard Papers, Princeton University Library; Jane Bayard Kirkpatrick, MS. Diary, Rutgers University Library.

12. Richard McCormick, *Experiment in Independence: New Jersey in the Critical Period, 1781–1789* (New Brunswick: Rutgers University Press, 1950), p. viii.

13. In 1810 only five of the seventeen states were smaller than New Jersey. Joseph Bloomfield, ed., *Laws of the State of New Jersey Compiled and Published Under the Authority of the Legislature* (Trenton: James J. Wilson, 1821), p. 350.

14. Even though New Jersey had proportionately the longest coastline of any of the other original colonies, except Rhode Island, its ports had soon been surpassed by those of New York City and Philadelphia, and little incentive evolved in New Jersey to develop port facilities. Also, New York and Philadelphia remained New Jersey's chief markets. Because of stable and longer term credit and better prices on established markets, New Jersey did not develop her own markets. Carl R. Woodward, *Agriculture in New Jersey* (New York: American Historical Society), p. 43.

15. Jedidiah Morse, *The American Geography* (Elizabeth Town: Shepard Kollock, 1789), p. 292.

16. Julia Sabine, "Antecedents of the Newark Public Library" (Ph.D. diss., University of Chicago, 1946), p. 33, passim.

17. Marilynn Ann Johnson, "Clockmakers and Cabinetmakers of Elizabethtown, New Jersey in the Federal Period" (M.A. thesis, University of Delaware, 1963), p. 3; Theodore Thayer, *As We Were: The Story of Old Elizabethtown* (Newark, New Jersey: New Jersey Historical Society, 1964), passim.

18. Elisha Boudinot to William Griffith, March 17, 1790, Stimson-Boudinot Collection, Princeton University Library.

19. Walter Fee, *The Transition from Aristocracy to Democracy in New Jersey, 1789–1826* (Somerville: Somerset Press, 1933), p. 6; "An Estimate of the Rateables in the State of New Jersey, Taken by the Legislature, January 25, 1794," broadside.

20. Starting about 1790 this area began to lose its position as the most thickly settled part of the state to the rapidly developing northern counties.

21. Fee, *The Transition from Aristocracy to Democracy,* p. 6.

22. Joseph Bloomfield to Colonel Jonathan Dayton, February 7, 1789, Ely Collection, New Jersey Historical Society.

23. Wilson, *The Jersey Shore*, p. 284.

24. American Council of Learned Studies, *Surnames in the United States Census of 1790* (Baltimore: Genealogical Publishing Company, 1969), p. 122. In 1790 New Jersey had the largest number of Swedes of any state in the nation.

25. Unlike New England, however, no one group had ever been strong enough to institute an established church.

26. Walter C. Hartridge, "The St. Domingan Refugees in New Jersey," *Proceedings of the New Jersey/Historical Society* LXII (October, 1941): 197–206. Later more French Catholics would settle in the state because of the political turmoil in France. While their numbers continued to be small, their attachment to their faith and their minority political positions created tension in New Jersey political life of the later 1790s.

27. At the end of the period under consideration in this study, the mid-1820s, only about 1 percent of the population would consist of nonnaturalized foreigners. Except for Gloucester County, which would rank third in the state for aliens, most of these individuals would be concentrated in the northern counties. Bloomfield, *Laws of the State of New Jersey*, pp. 342–52.

28. ". . . The Scotch and Scotch-Irish . . . were [mostly] latecomers, although some were descendants of the earliest settlers in East Jersey, and were to be found principally on the poorer lands in the north central part of the state." McCormick, *Experiment in Independence*, p. 41.

29. Larry R. Gerlach, "Quaker Politics in Eighteenth Century New Jersey: A Documentary Account," *The Journal of the Rutgers University Library* XXXIV (December, 1970): 2.

30. *Federalist*, May 10, 1810.

31. "Until 1800 the use of the Holland language was general." American Council of Learned Studies, *Surnames in the United States Census of 1790*, p. 372; Frederick B. Hanson, "The Interior Architecture and Household Furnishings of Bergen County, New Jersey, 1800–1810" (M.A. thesis, University of Delaware, 1959), p. 19, notes that in Bergen County forty-eight Dutch Bibles were listed in inventories of wills in the early nineteenth century as opposed to three English-language Bibles.

32. McCormick, *Experiment in Independence*, p. 41; D. H. Gardner, "The Emancipation of Slaves in New Jersey," *Proceedings of the New Jersey Historical Society* IX (January, 1924): 18.

33. Two groups which were scattered throughout the state were the Irish and the Baptists. Although some Irishmen were located in nearly every county, in none did they account for more than 10 percent of the population. In about a decade they would begin to migrate to the towns, first appearing in Newark in the late 1790s. Richard Purcell, "Irish Settlers in Early New Jersey," *New Jersey Genesis* VI (April, 1959): 227; Frank J. Urquhart, *A History of the City of Newark, New Jersey* I (New York: Lewis Historical Publishing Company, 1913), p. 440. The Baptists, on the other hand, while scattered from northernmost to southernmost New Jersey, did not appear in the towns. McCormick, *Experiment in Independence*, p. 53.

34. Richard Hofstadter, *The Idea of a Party System: The Rise of Legitimate Opposition in the United States, 1780–1840* (Berkeley: The University of California Press, 1970), pp. 1–30; Michael Wallace, "Changing Concepts of Party in the United States: New York, 1815–1828," *American Historical Review* LXXXIV (December, 1968): 453–91.

35. One writer eloquently declared, "the cloven foot of large European importations begins to appear—our merchants are precipated into a labyrinth, from which nothing short of bankruptcy will extricate them." *New Jersey Journal*, January 24, 1787.

36. *Elizabeth Town Political Intelligencer*, May 17, 1786; *Acts of the General Assembly of the State of New Jersey*, 10th Session, 3rd Sitting (May 26, 1786).

37. In 1783 Abraham Clark, a member of an old and well-established family, owned ninety acres of land in Essex County. *County Tax Ratables, 1778–1832*, New Jersey Historical Society.

38. Joshua Wallace to Elias Boudinot, October 1, 1786, Charles Roberts Autograph Collection, Haverford College.

39. Earlier, over the question of the ratification of the Constitution, sectionalism, or any significant division for that matter, simply had been absent in New Jersey. The state had long advocated revision of the Articles of Confederation and thus unanimity had been the order of the day on December 18, 1787, when the elected New Jersey delegates ratified the Constitution after only four days of deliberation. Richard McCormick, "The Unanimous State," *The Journal of the Rutgers University Library* XXIII (December, 1958): 4–8.

40. McCormick, *Experiment in Independence*, pp. 285–86; *Acts of the General Assembly*, 14th Session, 1st Sitting (November 30, 1789).

41. Walter Rutherfud to John Stevens, Sr., December 17, 1789, Stevens Papers, New Jersey Historical Society.

42. Like these men, the areas they represented would become Federalist. Particularly interesting in this connection are the cases of Elizabeth, which would become a Federalist enclave in Jeffersonian Essex County, and Trenton, which often would be decisive in delivering Hunterdon County for the Federalist side.

43. The Junto faction showed itself capable of political compromise, ". . . if by uniting and voting for the whole [four], we get our choice as to three we do well indeed—. . . ." Franklin Davenport to Ebenezer Elmer, February 9, 1789, Gratz Collection, Historical Society of Pennsylvania.

44. Richard McCormick, "New Jersey's First Congressional Election, 1789: A Case Study in Political Skulduggery," *William and Mary Quarterly*, Third Series VI (April, 1949): 240–41; Carl Prince, *New Jersey's Jeffersonian Republicans: The Genesis of an Early Party Machine, 1789–1817* (Chapel Hill: University of North Carolina, 1967), p. 11; George Schmidt, "The First Congressional Election in New Jersey," *Journal of the Rutgers University Library* IV (June, 1941): 45–50.

45. Clark died in 1794 before the New Jersey Jeffersonian party truly took shape. Prince, "New Jersey's Democratic-Republicans," p. 17.

46. Clark's courting of the discontented elements in society does not indicate control by small farmers, tenants, and artisans.

47. *New Jersey Journal*, February 11, 1789.

48. Joseph Bloomfield to Jonathan Dayton, February 28, 1789, Miscellaneous Manuscripts, Rutgers University Library.

49. Ibid.

50. West Jersey was aided in this effort by a new law providing for a threefold increase in the section's polling facilities. McCormick, *Experiment in Independence*, p. 288.

51. Joseph Bloomfield to Jonathan Dayton, February 7, 1789, Ely Collection, New Jersey Historical Society.

52. Joseph Bloomfield to Jonathan Dayton, February 28, 1789, Miscellaneous Manuscripts, Rutgers University Library.

53. McCormick, *Experiment in Independence*, pp. 298–99.

54. James Kinsey to Elias Boudinot, n.d. This letter has been dated between February 18 and March 3, 1789 by Richard McCormick. *Journal of the Rutgers University Library* XXI (December, 1957): 38.

55. "For the state as a whole, nearly one-half of the adult white males voted. In Burlington and Essex, where the election fever was highest, the percentage of white males voting was seventy-eight per cent and ninety per cent respectively. These fantastically large figures indicate that when votes were needed and the election officials were amenable, the property qualification was an unimportant barrier. It is significant that in the state election held in October, 1787 the total vote in Burlington was only 258." In the Congressional election of 1789 it was 2,826. McCormick, "New Jersey's First Congressional Election, 1789," pp. 244–45, 247. Certain East Jersey counties would take to the House of Representatives their demand that the Junto men be unseated. After much delay and uncertain deliberation on the part of that body, however, East Jersey's attempt proved unavailing, for the House, too, declared the New Jersey Congressmen to have been "duly elected." *Annals of Congress*, vol. I, September 10, 1789, pp. 756–57, 834, 836; U. S., Congress, House, *An Historical and Legal Digest of all the Contested Election Cases in the House of Representatives of the United States from the First to the Fifty-Sixth Congress, 1789–1901*, House Document 510, 56th Congress, 2nd Session (Washington: Government Printing Office, 1901), p. 38.

56. Joseph Bloomfield to Jonathan Dayton, February 23, 1789, Gratz Collection, Historical Society of Pennsylvania.

57. Joseph Bloomfield to Jonathan, Dayton, February 28, 1789, Miscellaneous Manuscripts, Rutgers University Library.

58. MSS, Minutes of the Governor's Privy Council, vol. I, January 7, 1789, New Jersey State Library. The Junto captains and lieutenants supporting the ticket also would become Federalists. They were joined together and with the ticket members by social and family ties. For example, Richard Stockton was a nephew of ticket leader Elias Boudinot, whose brother Elisha Boudinot and

business associates Joshua Wallace and James Kinsey were important Junto leaders, too.

59. Joshua Maddox Wallace to Elias Boudinot, March 6, 1789, Wallace Papers, Historical Society of Pennsylvania.

2

THE NEW JERSEY FEDERALIST PARTY AND THE STATE CONSTITUTION

Adopted in 1776, New Jersey's constitution survived for nearly seventy years to span the birth, development, and demise in the mid-1820s of the state's Federalist party. Constituting the basic legal environment of the New Jersey Federalist party during the whole of its existence, the state constitution so affected the party that the latter cannot be understood apart from its life-long relationship with the New Jersey instrument.[1]

Under the New Jersey Constitution of 1776 the popularly elected state legislature was far and away the most powerful New Jersey governmental branch; it was lost almost permanently by the Federalists in 1801. In contrast there was the position of governor, held primarily by Federalists or ex-Federalists during the entire first party system period, which was weak. Commenting on the near powerlessness of the executive, the *Federalist* characterized a New Jersey governor as ". . . a man of straw."[2]

This lack of significant executive power was keenly felt, for example, by long-term governor Isaac Williamson, an ex-Federalist who held the office for twelve one-year terms. Like the other governors who served during the long existence of the New Jersey Constitution of 1776, Williamson possessed no legislative veto and few appointive powers.[3] Moreover, he was dependent upon the legislature for his tenure in office. Out of the

36

feeling of helplessness this situation bred, Governor Williamson was known to

> . . . lament, almost with tears in his eyes, that he had been so foolish [as] . . . to place himself in a position from which he was liable at any time to be removed [and in which] his salary . . . [depended upon] a new law every year. . . .[4]

Lacking significant intrinsic authority,[5] a New Jersey governor's greatest potential sources of executive power were extrinsic ones, for example, his noteworthy personal attributes and the extent of his prestige and influence. Together with his skill in bringing them to bear, such characteristics largely determined whether he would be effective.[6]

One source of personal power possessed by all but one of the New Jersey governors who served between 1776 and 1829 was a result of their patrician class standing, for a pattern of deference toward the elite, while diminishing, had not yet disappeared. Members, for the most part, of wealthy and established families, the majority of governors during this period were either Federalists or ex-Federalists. Moreover, collectively, the terms of office of these present and past Federalist party members constituted 93 percent of the period in question.[7]

Only lately separated from the Federalist party when they assumed office, the ex-Federalist governors never fully severed their previous ties.[8] For instance, often they lobbied to retain Federalists in government positions and, with their limited powers, even appointed a few former fellow party members to office, as ex-Federalist Joseph Bloomfield, the first Republican governor of New Jersey, did.[9]

In turn, the Federalists exhibited a decided affinity for these ex-party members, compared to their reaction toward firm Republicans. For example, they consistently chose to support ex-Federalist candidates for governor over thoroughgoing Republicans.[10]

In Governor Bloomfield's case, the Federalist organ even went so far as to state,

For ourselves we can boast for having given Mr. Bloomfield his office.[11]

In truth the *Federalist* had taken Bloomfield almost as its own, vociferously calling for his election in 1804. Bloomfield, it stated on that occasion, was sorely needed as governor, being not a rabid radical or one given to excess, but a propertied man who was friendly to education (he was a trustee of the College of New Jersey).[12] Then, when he was elected, the *Federalist* ". . . rejoice[d] that a worse man has not been appointed."[13]

These continuing bonds with their former party associates made the Republicans view the ex-Federalists as objects of distrust. Isaac Williamson, for example, was termed, shortly before the first of his twelve consecutive elections to the governorship, a "Federalist in disguise" by the Republican organ the *True American*.[14]

Another source of extrinsic power possessed by New Jersey governors of the period was that derived from their high standing in their political party. All of them, Federalists and Republicans alike, were ranking party leaders, but some were higher in their party's echelon than others. Governors William Paterson (Federalist, 1790–1792), Aaron Ogden (Federalist, 1812–1813), William Pennington (Republican, 1813–1815), and Mahlon Dickerson (Republican, 1815–1817), all of whom fell into this higher ranking category, remained in office for only one or two terms, leaving, with one exception, as a result of their own resignations.[15] Perhaps because these men were accustomed to a good deal of power in another sphere of life, they experienced even more keenly the frustration caused by the restrictions upon executive authority under which all holders of the New Jersey gubernatorial office labored.

Truly, as a committee of the Council stated regarding the office of governor under the Constitution of 1776, the executive office was merely

. . . an *addendum* requiring but little time or attention. . . . In reality, the judicial office [was] the only important one.[16]

These judicial functions of the governor were indeed varied and exacting, for they included acting as Surrogate-general, as Chancellor, hearing in this capacity appeals from cases tried in equity, a comparable function to that of Chief Justice, who heard cases arising out of contested wills, and as presiding Judge of the Court of Errors and Appeals, the highest appellate court in New Jersey.[17]

That these functions, for their proper exercise, required the governor to have an extensive background in law was recognized, for every governor appointed under the Constitution of 1776 was trained in the law.[18] The fact that very few Republicans of the day were lawyers, legal education and the structure of the profession

... powerfully disposing the legal practitioner toward Federalism,[19]

lent impetus, once the Republicans came to control the legislature, to their appointment as governor of Republicans who formerly were Federalists.

The dominant Republicans were confronted with a comparable situation in making judiciary appointments, which like the governorship, required legal training. When the Republicans came to power, they desired to remove Federalist judges at all levels, but often they lacked qualified Republicans with whom to replace them. Hence, frequently they had no choice but to retain many Federalists in office, especially at the upper levels of the judiciary system.

At length, it was the entrenched, Federalist-controlled New Jersey judiciary which labored to check the power of the Legislature, Republican-controlled after 1801, by establishing the principle of judicial review. By 1804 the judiciary had met its goal, but only on a theoretical level, for action indicating the omnipotence of the legislature did not cease, but at least the principle of judicial review, adopted in New Jersey under the influence of the federal Constitution, was never seriously questioned after 1804, when it was authoritatively stated by Federalist New Jersey Chief Justice Andrew Kirkpatrick:[20]

> I will take the liberty to say, that the Legislature of New Jersey themselves, have, by solemn act, impliedly decided the question. To all judges, before they enter upon the execution of their offices, they have prescribed this oath, "I do solemnly promise and swear, that I will administer justice ... agreeably *to the constitution and laws* of the State of New Jersey." This I take to amount to a legislative determination, clearly declaring constitutional as well as legal rights and questions to be the proper subjects of judicial investigation and decision.[21]

That the Republicans viewed the court versus legislature contest over the establishment of the power of judicial review as a Federalist-Republican one was clearly indicated by the following 1807 Republican exclamations:

> A federal [i.e. Federalist] court undertaking to annul a law of a republican legislature!—The Judiciary trampling upon the acts of . . . the Legislature![22]

New Jersey's Assembly, the lower house of its legislature, at first was composed of three representatives from each of the thirteen counties.[23] But this was a travesty upon the Constitution in unevenly populated New Jersey, for the instrument called for the size of each county's Assembly delegation to be based upon the "principle of population," continuously reflecting the number of inhabitants in that county.[24] Later, exercising its constitutional power, the legislature did reallocate the number of Assembly seats assigned each county. In fact, to speak only of the years 1797–1844, the period from the firm establishment of the two-party system in New Jersey to the end of the life of the 1776 New Jersey Constitution, the legislature did so some ten times.[25]

However, the particular adjustments in representation effected by the legislature often were not the result of objective attempts at making a county's delegation truly proportionate to its population. Rather, being unhampered by the existence of a population ratio formula regulating the allowance of representatives and having early grasped the political significance of the size of particular counties' delegations, legislators of both parties frequently assumed their stands on a proposed change in the strength of a county's delegation on the basis of their partisan interests.

For example, in spite of southern New Jersey's loss of the population advantage to northern New Jersey, Federalist legislators fought hard to avoid both an increase in Republican North Jersey's representation and a decrease in Federalist South Jersey's seats. So it was in 1813, for instance, when the *Centinel of Freedom* noted regarding the legislative proceedings over a Republican-sponsored resolution to reduce the delegation of the least populated county in the state, Cape May in South Jersey, and to increase that of the most heavily populated one, Essex County in North Jersey,

> When the population of Essex shall be as thirty to one of Cape-May, this latter county will be more unwilling to equalize the representation, than now, when it is only about ten to one. . . .[26]

Besides the adjustment in the representation of counties in the legislature, two other notably partisan questions, both of which revolved about federal offices, engaged the attention of the New Jersey Legislature starting with the Adams administration. These were (1) whether a particular Congressional election would be held by the district or general election plan and (2) the manner in which presidential electors would be chosen.[27]

On the first of these issues, the district versus the general election plan, there were no stable, party-sponsored stances. As it had been in the first United States Congressional election, it also was thereafter the policy of the dominant political group to support whichever method it, the majority contingent, believed would deliver to it the advantage on the occasion at hand.[28]

In contrast to the first issue, a legislator's position on the second one, the way in which presidential electors should be selected, usually bore a definite and stable relationship to his party affiliation. Federalists, in general, always voted in favor of presidential electors being appointed by the legislature, while Republicans desired them to be popularly and directly elected. The Federalists' wish prevailed until 1804, when presidential electors first were required by the legislature to run for office, a practice which the dominant Republicans initiated at their first opportunity and continued until their brief ouster in 1812. The ascendant Federalists then immediately repealed the 1804 law and returned the office of presidential elector to appointive status.[29] In turn, the Republicans, upon their restoration to power the following year, once again, in 1813, designated the office an elective one.

To exercise its appointive powers, the legislature annually, at the beginning of its term, convened in joint meeting, the Legislative Council and the General Assembly sitting together.[30] Its wide powers of appointment on this occasion included both the executive and judicial branches of the government and extended from the state level to the local one.

Beginning with the state officials of the executive branch, the joint meeting appointed, for example, the state's chief executive, the governor,[31] his attorney general and even his chief military aid, the quartermaster general. It then filled a considerable number of county and local level executive offices, such as the mayorship of some of the principal towns. Finally, the legislature elected the whole of the judiciary, from the bench of the supreme court down to the justices of the peace. In sum, it was nothing less than the bulk of the entire state's patronage that was dispensed at joint meeting.

Thus, to lose the state legislature in New Jersey was to lose not that body alone but also a very great deal more, to which the Federalist experience after 1801 bore bitter witness. For example, with the coming of a Republican legislature, that newly dominant parly quickly put its revenue power to partisan use. As Federalist William Coxe, Jr., for one, lamented,

. . . we see daily attempts to remove good men [Federalists] from the Executive and Judicial Departments by diminishing their salaries and so starve them out.[32]

A further testament to the broad powers of the legislature was the Federalists' ability, after having been for eleven years the minority party, to rapidly regain control of the state after once again winning legislative dominance in 1812. Within a week of the new legislative session, the Federalists, in this presidential election year, were able to leave their mark upon not only the state scene,

Col. Ogden will tomorrow be elected Governor—Mr. Pearson Speaker,

but on the national scene as well:

. . . a bill will be brot [sic] in for the appointment of Electors in Joint Meeting this afternoon. It will pass the houses tomorrow and our friends in every state may be aprized [sic] that New Jersey will give eight votes for Mr. Clinton and Mr. Ingersol [as President and Vice-President of the United States, respectively.][33]

Because of the very vastness of the legislature's power, it was required by the Constitution of 1776 to stand for election annually. As Erdman states,

. . . annual elections [alone] . . . were believed to safeguard individual rights

against this all-powerful body.[34] Required to join legislators in facing the voters yearly were all New Jersey officials below the federal level.[35] County officials, such as sheriffs and coroners, stood for election every October along with legislators. Local officials—mayors not appointed by the legislature, tax collectors, and election clerks—were elected in April. And, until 1807, alternate years usually saw the conducting of a third election, the federal one, for only in 1792, 1798, and 1806 were state and federal officials elected simultaneously.[36]

Apparently an effort to gain political advantage thereby accounted for state and federal elections being held separately and for the variability in the date of the federal election in New Jersey, set biennially on an individual basis for a number of years. Federalist William Paterson explained,

> The reason is simply this, that some of our law makers wish to be candidates for the state legislature, and also for Congress, which could not be the case with any tolerable chance of succeeding in either if the election was held on the same day for both.[37]

Furthermore, the cause of the continual change in federal election dates lay, Paterson later revealed, in the "convenience of parties."[38]

With two or three elections occurring a year, the matter easily could become boring for the average voter. Therefore, the possession of effective motivation-building techniques on the part of a political party could mean a great deal to the outcome of the election. Also, considering the number and frequency of elections in the state, a political organization, like the Republican one, which operated year around and moved quickly, was, under the circumstances, a decided asset in New Jersey.

The theoretical defects of the 1776 New Jersey Constitution, such as those which have been touched upon in other connections above—the omnipotence of the legislature, the impotence of the executive, and the dependence of the judiciary upon the legislature—together with the violation of the doctrine of the separation of powers[39] brought forth calls for constitutional conventions to revise the instrument. Arising amidst a spirit of constitutional reform, which in several other states resulted in new constitutions by 1800, the long-futile drive for reform in New Jersey[40] began under the leadership of prominent Federalists.

At first William Coxe, Jr. was the outstanding individual in this regard. In 1797 it was he who introduced in the Assembly the bill to revise the Constitution that eventually led to the question of revision being placed before the voters in 1800.[41]

Then, in 1798, after a second resolution for a constitutional convention was defeated in the legislature,[42] William Griffith, a brilliant lawyer who led the powerful Burlington County wing of the Federalist party, lent his legal and literary talents to the cause, writing a series of articles, the most valuable extant criticism of the 1776 New Jersey Constitution, which appeared serially in the *New Jersey Gazette*. Later, in October, 1799, in anticipation of the third legislative vote on the question of revision, the previously published "Eumenes" articles were quickly combined with others that had yet to appear and together the total of fifty-three articles were issued as a monograph.

Taken the following month, November, 1799, this third vote in the Assembly showed a ratio of 1.1 to 1 against revision, by far the narrowest defeat the revisionists had suffered to date. (In 1798 the ratio had been 3 to 1 against them and earlier, in 1797, 6 to 1.[43]) There the situation would have rested but for the action of some Republicans.

Henry Southard, a Republican, rose to successfully amend the bill, substituting for the provision that the matter be handled within the legislature another that stipulated that the question of revision or no revision be put to the electorate. Added to Southard's own vote for this amended bill, beyond those of the proponents of the original one, were seven other Republican votes, and the bill passed because of them.

However, less than a year after Republican votes had revived the moribund constitutional revision question and had seen to it that it was brought to the electorate, apparently deeming it worthy of the voters' consideration, the Republican party, in its organs, appended "NO REVISION" to its list of candidates for the October, 1800, state legislative election.[44] And during the campaign the Republicans labored to divest themselves of identification with constitutional revision on the basis of expediency.

Believing they were close to winning the legislature (which, as has been seen, was tantamount to dominating the state under the Constitution of 1776), the Republicans did not wish the strength of the nearly omnipotent body they were about to control to be weakened through a redistribution of power among the branches of the government. Surely the Republicans felt, the concomitant of such a redistribution of power in which the legislature was to be weakened through a new constitution, probably to be written by Federalist lawyers, such as William Griffith, William Coxe, Jr., and Richard Stockton, would be not only the creation of an independent executive but also the establishment of a more powerful judiciary, Federalist in persuasion, which would constitute a threat to Republican power.

Even William Griffith, that most ardent Federalist fighter for constitutional revision, had turned against the movement by the month before the October, 1800, referendum, believing that a moment when party strife was rampant was not favorable for the undertaking of a revision of the fundamental law of the state. Speaking for the Federalist party, Griffith, like the Republicans, urged the electorate to vote against revision,[45] which it did.

Because the resounding "No," which defeated constitutional revision in 1800 would be repeated until 1844, the 1776 New Jersey Constitution's influence on the state's Federalist party would endure to the end of the party's history.

NOTES

1. Richard McCormick has stated, "[Political parties] are profoundly affected by the constitutional and legal environment. . . ." Richard P. McCormick, *The Second American Party System: Party Formation in the Jacksonian Era* (Chapel Hill: University of North Carolina Press, 1966), p. 4.

2. *Federalist,* October 29, 1804.

3. In stating qualifications for the office of governor, the framers of the Constitution were even more brief than in allocating powers to it. They simply required that the governor be ". . . some fit person." Neither an age, sex, residence, property nor citizenship requirement was stipulated, leading Federalist William Griffith to observe later, ". . . a child, a bankrupt, an alien or a criminal convict . . . [may be appointed] governor of New Jersey." Griffith, *Eumenes,* p. 55.

4. Elmer, *The Constitution and Government of the Province and State of New Jersey,* pp. 175–76.

5. One executive power which the Constitution did confer upon the governor was that of ". . . captain-general and commander in chief of all the militia and other military force. . . ." Elmer, *The Constitution and Government of the Province and State of New Jersey*, p. 33. Some governors were more active in this area of responsibility than were others, partly as a function of their personalities and the thrust of events during their tenure. For example, Federalist Governor Richard Howell, on the occasion of the Whiskey Rebellion, personally led the New Jersey militia into Pennsylvania in order to help crush it. Likewise, later, ex-Federalist Joseph Bloomfield, governor during the early part of the War of 1812, reorganized the state militia in preparation for British attack. Also, Bloomfield's Federalist successor, Aaron Ogden, a man, like Howell and Bloomfield, with military experience, continued to prepare the state for possible invasion. On the other hand, Republican Governor William Pennington, who came into office while the War of 1812 was still being waged, did not personally take part in military activities. He did, however, warn the legislature of the exposed and vulnerable conditions of the coastline, as a result of which it requested him to tour the area and make recommendations for its defense. Duane Lockard, *The New Jersey Governor: A Study in Political Power*, The New Jersey Historical Series, vol. XIV (Princeton: D. Van Nostrand Company, 1964), p. 36.

6. Herbert Ershkowitz, "New Jersey Politics During the Era of Andrew Jackson, 1820–1837" (Ph.D. diss., New York University, 1965), p. 3; Prince, *New Jersey's Jeffersonian Republicans*, p. 5; Lockard, p. 37.

7. Furthermore, viewed on an individual governor basis, a similar pattern in length of term emerges. While both the firm Republicans served only two terms each, only one-half of the firm Federalists served so short a time. The other Federalists served from nine to twelve years each, and the ex-Federalist governors closely approximated their former fellow party members in length of gubernatorial tenure enjoyed.

8. *Guardian*, October 31, 1811.

9. *Federalist*, October 8, 1804.

10. Federalist support probably accounts; in part, for the long terms enjoyed by ex-Federalist governors, for at no time during their life as a minority party did the strength of Federalists in the legislature, the electing body, fall below 23 percent.

11. *Federalist*, October 29, 1804.

12. *Federalist*, October 1, 10, 1804.

13. *Federalist*, October 29, 1804. Being the minority party in the legislature, the most the Federalists could hope to achieve in the gubernatorial election was a victory for a Republican who formerly had been a Federalist.

14. *True American*, October 5, 1817.

15. The exception was Aaron Ogden, who was ousted from office when the Republicans won the legislature in October, 1813.

16. Erdman, *The New Jersey Constitution of 1776*, p. 63.

48   THE NEW JERSEY FEDERALISTS

17. Thomas F. Gordon, *A Gazetteer of the State of New Jersey*. . . . (Trenton, New Jersey: Daniel Fenton, 1834), pp. 72–73.

18. Although William Pennington had only read law on his own, he was recognized as a legal authority by the New Jersey bar.

19. James M. Banner, *To the Hartford Convention: The Federalists and the Origins of Party Politics in Massachusetts, 1789–1815* (New York: Alfred Knopf, 1970), p. 184. Often, the local Republicans referred to the New Jersey Federalist party as the lawyer party.

20. Perhaps it may be said that although the New Jersey Legislature had accepted the theory of constitutional supremacy, only in time would this acceptance result in more than lip service. Ershkowitz, "New Jersey Politics During the Era of Andrew Jackson," p. 6. Witness, for example, the legislature's defense of the enactment of the attacked election law of 1807, which undoubtedly did change the Constitution. Impliedly recognizing the theory of constitutional supremacy, the legislature denied that the law had altered the Constitution and maintained the legal fiction that it merely explained its ". . . true sense and meaning. . . ." Erdman, *The New Jersey Constitution of 1776*, pp. 81, 87–88.

21. State v. Parkhurst, 9 Halsted (New Jersey), pp. 443, 445.

22. *True American*, November 30, 1807.

23. Relatively high property qualifications, which the Republicans, despite their democratic image, never moved to reduce, were stipulated for membership in the legislature. Assemblymen had to be freeholders for one year in the county they represented and be worth 500 pounds real and personal estate. Councillors had to be worth twice that amount, 1,000 pounds. Although there is evidence that men of less property than that required by law held legislative office, nevertheless, legislators necessarily had to be men of substance, for the low salaries paid them demanded they have other sources of income. Essex, Middlesex, Cape May County Tax Records, 1785–1810; *Federalist*, September 19, 1808. Witness the fact that in 1810 a legislator received $2.00 a day, while an unskilled laborer received fifty cents and a skilled craftsman earned about $1.50. What is more, a legislator's expense for room and board while in the capital could not have been less than $2.00 per week. Robert R. Beckwith, "Mahlon Dickerson of New Jersey, 1770–1853" (Ph.D. diss., Columbia University, 1964), p. 84.

24. Erdman, *The New Jersey Constitution of 1776*, p. 51. In the Legislative Council, the upper house, the counties were equally represented.

25. Ernest C. Reock, *Population Inequality Among Counties in the New Jersey Legislature, 1791–1962* (New Brunswick: Bureau of Government Research, Rutgers University, 1963), pp. 13–20. The minimum number of representatives was, however, set by the 1776 Constitution at thirty-nine. *New Jersey Constitution*, July 2, 1776, Article III.

26. *Centinel of Freedom*, November 2, 1813.

27. Pole, "Jeffersonian Democracy and the Federalist Dilemma in New Jersey," p. 271.

28. William Rossell to Samuel Southard, February 1, 1819, Southard Papers, Princeton University Library.

29. William Griffith to Joshua Wallace, October 17, 1812, Wallace Papers, Volume 7, Historical Society of Pennsylvania. One of the earliest Republican protests against the appointing of electors appeared in the broadside *To the People of New Jersey,* September 30, 1800.

30. The upper house of the New Jersey Legislature, the Legislative Council, had full legislative powers excepting in the field of financial matters, it being the Assembly's function alone to initiate revenue bills. *New Jersey Constitution of 1776,* July 2, 1776, Article VI.

31. Six other states (Pennsylvania, Maryland, Virginia, North Carolina, Georgia, and Delaware) also adopted this method of selecting their governor.

32. Griffith, *Eumenes.* Notes by William Coxe, Jr. in his personal copy of the work at Princeton University Library.

33. William Griffith to Joshua Wallace, October 27, 1812, Wallace Papers, Historical Society of Pennsylvania.

34. Erdman, *The New Jersey Constitution of 1776,* p. 90.

35. "One dictum of nineteenth century political life declared that the degree of democracy in a state was measured by the number of elections held." Ershkowitz, "New Jersey Politics During the Era of Andrew Jackson," p. 8.

36. Between 1807 and 1842 federal elections and state elections generally occurred simultaneously, except in presidential election years because the timing of the choosing of the presidential electors was set by federal statute.

37. William Paterson, "Hortensius," No. 1 [1797] William Paterson Papers, Rutgers University Library.

38. Paterson, "Hortensius," No. 3 [1797] William Paterson Papers, Rutgers University Library.

39. *Trenton State Gazette,* February 13, 1844. Theoretically, both the Council and the governor possessed roles in all three branches of the government. Therefore, not a separation of powers but a union of them existed in these cases. For example, the Council served as a judicial body when it was the final court of appeals, as an executive body when it was the governor's cabinet, and as a legislative body when it was the upper house of the bicameral New Jersey legislature. Similarly, the governor, in addition to his executive and judicial duties, was president of the upper house of the Legislature, in which he possessed a tie-breaking vote.

40. Before and during the Federalist tenure, the movement to revise the Constitution of 1776 was defeated in the legislature in 1790, 1797, and 1798 and by a popular vote in 1800. At the end of its life in 1844, New Jersey's Constitution was one of the oldest ones in the nation.

41. *Votes and Proceedings of the General Assembly of the State of New Jersey,* 21st Session, 2nd Sitting (February 11, 1797).

42. *Votes and Proceedings of the General Assembly of the State of New Jersey,* 22nd Session, 2nd Sitting (March 1, 1798).

43. *Votes and Proceedings of the General Assembly of the State of New Jersey,* 21st Session, 2nd Sitting (March 5, 1797); 22nd Session, 2nd Sitting (March 6, 1798); 23rd Session, 1st Sitting (November 14, 1799).

44. *Centinel of Freedom,* October 14, 1800.

45. *Address to the Federal-Republicans of Burlington County,* Trenton, New Jersey, August 30, 1800, p. 7.

3

RISE OF THE NEW JERSEY FEDERALIST PARTY

The New Jersey Federalist party evolved from the statewide Junto faction, which had won the first Congressional election in 1789.[1] Following the lead of Secretary of the Treasury Hamilton at the nation's capital in nearby Philadelphia, the Junto gradually developed into the New Jersey Federalist party.[2]

The national party's leader, Alexander Hamilton, had unusually close ties with Jerseyans and their state. Therefore he had no difficulty in drawing together the nucleus of a machine to advance his economic program from among his own contacts enlarged by those of President Washington. Indeed, only in creating the New York contingent of the national structure was Hamilton's task easier, for his relationship with New Jersey was second in intimacy only to that which he enjoyed with New York.[3]

Elizabeth, New Jersey, was Hamilton's first home in the United States. It was a Jerseyan, the Rev. Hugh Knox, who saw to it that Hamilton was brought to the United States for an education. In answer to Knox's appeal in behalf of the unknown Hamilton, offers of assistance followed, notably from William Livingston, with whom Hamilton went to live, and from Elias Boudinot, a trustee of Francis Barber's Academy in Elizabeth. Together, Boudinot and Livingston stood as the young man's sponsors during his student days at Barber's Academy. During this time, Hamilton formed friendships with the prominent

New Jersey families in the Livingston and Boudinot circles which he maintained throughout his life.[4]

After his appointment to Washington's cabinet, Hamilton's former mentors in New Jersey became his firm political allies, Livingston as governor of New Jersey during the first years of Hamilton's tenure as Secretary of the Treasury and Boudinot as a United States Congressman for the whole of Hamilton's term of service.

Like Hamilton, Washington enjoyed a long-standing friendship with the Boudinots. During his encampment west of Elizabeth in 1778 and 1779, Washington had found time to visit the town on special occasions, such as for the wedding of Elisha Boudinot.[5] With the latter's brother, Elias Boudinot, the President maintained a correspondence partially devoted to a discussion of scientific agricultural methods, a mutual interest of the two men.[6]

Washington's first trips through New Jersey as president found him cementing ties with some of his old friends in the state. On the way to his first inauguration, Washington paused in Elizabeth for dinner, received a committee of Congressmen at the home of Elias Boudinot, and continued to New York in Boudinot's company.[7] Earlier, Washington had been met at the New Jersey state capital by Richard Howell, whom he had singled out for special intelligence tasks during the Revolution.[8]

Later, traveling from New York to Mount Vernon as president for the first time, Washington dined in New Jersey with another old friend, Colonel John Bayard, of New Brunswick. The two men's recollections of their Delaware River crossing and of Bayard's bringing food and clothing to the destitute men of Valley Forge probably entered their conversation as frequently was the case.[9]

During the Early National period Congressman Elias Boudinot, Judge Elisha Boudinot, Governor Richard Howell,[10] Col. John Bayard, and other Jerseyans possessing long-standing ties to Hamilton and Washington[11] were important members of the New Jersey Federalist party leadership. This nucleus of the future New Jersey party had drawn in other participants, largely their relations and friends, and the party's leadership took form.

As a whole, the leadership of the mature party was less personally attached to its national chiefs than its precursor had been, but it also was primarily drawn from the ranks of the well-to-do, educated, and long-established segments of society.[12] A statistical comparison between the New Jersey Federalist leadership and the leadership of New Jersey Republicans reveals that the Federalist leadership possessed the higher social status.

To a greater extent than its opposition, the Federalist leadership was composed of men with Revolutionary War service, usually in the officer corps, old-stock family origins, membership in established religious groups, college degrees at a time when college graduates were rare, relations among the other leaders of the Federalist party in New Jersey and perhaps in neighboring states as well, high status occupations, such as the law, and involvement in manufacturing and transportation projects.

These members of the established elite, who claimed the Revolution and Constitution as their own, believed that their possession of education, experience, and property marked them as best fitted to govern their fellows.[13] For the public good, gentlemen of their stamp must stand for office as a guard against the election of lesser men, the Federalists felt.[14] In the manner of noblesse oblige, this "natural aristocracy" expected its members to make the sacrifice believed by many to be entailed in the acceptance of public office.[15] And once in office the incumbents should not give way for the purpose of office rotation, as demanded in 1791 by their opponents, for such a move would mitigate against experience in government.[16] Even after the transition from faction to party had taken place, the Federalist theme remained the same: keep government in the hands of the tried and proven.[17]

In the generally conservative ideological theme of the New Jersey Federalists, government was the mainstay of "Heaven's first law," order.[18] Dubbing themselves the "friends of order"

THE NEW JERSEY FEDERALISTS

TABLE 3.1

Characteristics of Top-Echelon Party Leaders in New Jersey, 1796–1815

	Federalists	Republicans
Born before 1750	32%	24%*
Born 1750–1775	48%	42%*
Born after 1775	20%	34%*
Old-stock family origins	92%	68%
Immigrant or the son of an immigrant	8%	32%
Revolutionary War service	73%	60%*
College graduate	66%	15%*
Father held public appointive or elective office	74%	12%*
Related to other leaders of the New Jersey party	91%	37%*
Related to party leaders in Pennsylvania, New York, Maryland, and/or Delaware	28%	0%
Land speculator	40%	31%
Farmer	10%	18%*
Lawyer	14%	6%
Merchant	49%	64%
Clergyman	.02%	.06%
Physician	.04%	.03%
Artisan	.02%	26%*
Printer and/or editor	0%	10%
Engaged in manufacturing and/or transportation enterprises	68%	27%*
Episcopalian	20%	9%*
Quaker	14%	12%
Dutch Reformed	16%	3.4%
Presbyterian	48%	40%*
Methodist	.4%	16%
Baptist	.02%	12%
Unknown and other	14%	7.2%

*Carl, Prince, "The Leadership of New Jersey's First Party System, Paper presented at the Second Annual New Jersey History Symposium, Trenton, New Jersey, December 5, 1970.

Note: Figures in occupational section add up to more than 100 per cent because men of the time often pursued several occupations simultaneously.

the New Jersey Federalists attacked the Republicans for being disorganizers. With the Republicans' unabashed appeals to the masses, the Federalists feared their opposition would bring about a democratic regime like that of the French Republic, which "would be fatal to property and order."[19]

Republicans' irreligion alone branded them as dangerous, for, to the New Jersey Federalists, the maintenance of the "peace and order of society" depended upon organized religion.[20] To their minds, honesty in government could only occur when public officials possessed faith in a revealed religion as they, the Federalists, did.[21]

New Jersey's Federalist legislators believed that as the elite they were more qualified to discern what action was in the populace's best interests than the people themselves were.[22] Thus, they found ludicrous the Republican resolution that, after their election, the legislators should be given time to consult their constituencies before reporting for the session. A proper legislator, the Federalists countered, did not require instruction from the people; he did not need to go around on a pilgrimage to learn what should be done and how to do it.[23]

Federalists always placed more confidence in the representatives of the people than in the people themselves.[24] This attitude was revealed in their opposition to the popular election of presidential electors. New Jersey's presidential electors must continue to be chosen by the legislature, Federalist Speaker of the Assembly William Coxe declared in 1798, for the representatives

. . . operate[d] as a strainer of popular feelings and attachments, ensuring the best chance of a wise and virtuous choice.[25]

Along with their conception of a natural aristocracy, most New Jersey Federalists possessed a belief in the basic principles of popular sovereignty.[26] In a state where widespread manhood suffrage already existed,[27] New Jersey Federalist party theoretician William Griffith in 1799 argued thusly for the removal of even the nominal monetary worth requirement:

The poor man's freedom is, perhaps, his sweetest enjoyment; ought not he then to be consulted in the choice of those, who have the power to infringe it? . . . Ought he not to participate in electing those who assess him?

The rich and powerful will take care of themselves; the least privilege which the poor should enjoy is that of giving a solitary vote for their rulers.[28]

The Federalists attempted to operate under a system that included a measure of equality in political rights but stopped short of equalitarianism.[29] Said they,

> We're not attached to *monarchy,*
> Nor are we friends to *anarchy,*
> Neither to *aristocracy,*
> Nor what is call'd *democracy,*
> But to a *System* of our own,
> Where all their virtues join'd in one,
> Form what is stil'd republican.[30]

The belief on the part of the New Jersey Federalists that the electorate would "generally . . . [vote] in favor of the most deserving character," bolstered their conviction that the suffrage should be nearly universal. They were convinced that given "fair play" men of talents would prevail at the polls.[31] In line with the spirit of deference, the electorate surely would recognize the superiority of the elite by consenting to be ruled by it.[32]

The New Jersey Federalists and their precursors were eager to obtain the public offices to which, as members of the elite, they felt entitled.[33] This was particularly true in the case of appointive offices.

Because they were allies of the Washington and Adams administrations, federal patronage was available to the New Jersey Federalists during these years. And from the first session of Congress, the importunities of Jerseyans contributed to the general "rage for [appointive] office" at the nation's capital.[34] Among the positions to be filled were those of federal circuit and district judge, supervisor of the revenue, United States attorney, United States marshall, port collector, and postmaster.

To their basic qualifications for a federal position, some Jerseymen like Jonathan Dayton could add the weight of

. . . being personally known to you [President Washington] and many of the members of the present Congress. . . .[35]

Dayton's mention of Congressmen indicates his recognition of the influence of Congress on federal appointments, an influence that increased with time.[36] Less than a year later, John Noble Cumming sent his application to the President through Congressman Elias Boudinot.[37]

At the state level, the New Jersey Federalists and their forerunners were the patronage dispensers. By far the bulk of the appointments to public office lay in the hands of the legislature, and throughout the period this body used its appointive powers to entrench its partisans in the government.

[By] oppos[ing] the appointment of men to whatever office, who . . . [were] not entirely enlisted under the banners of federalism,[38]

the Federalist legislature created a militia and a judiciary whose political sentiments agreed with the legislature's own.

Down to the last Federalist-dominated New Jersey legislature of the era, Assembly Speaker William Coxe maintained that only Federalists must be appointed to the judiciary. The judiciary's ideological composition must be retained, he continued, for it would be "improper to have on the same bench . . . men of different principles."[39]

The Federalists were quite successful in their attempt to bar Republicans from the New Jersey judiciary. Even in the early Republican stronghold of Essex County, which began to send Republicans to the legislature in 1796, no Republican except Federalist defector Daniel Marsh gained an Essex County judicial office before 1798.

From the early days, the Federalist legislature concentrated its judicial and militia appointments among prominent party members. By way of illustration some 78 percent of the major

Federalist leaders received militia appointments at one time or another during the era. Most of the appointments went to the officeholding elite, a large porportion of them being allocated to present and former members of the state legislature. In a single session, atypical because of the passage of a new militia law, the legislature conferred upon its members four major generalships, one brigadier generalship, and three lieutenant colonelcies in the state militia. Two additional brigadier generalships were conferred upon former members of the Assembly and one upon a United States Congressman.[40]

Judicial appointments, too, were concentrated among the Federalist officeholding elite. However, for some Federalists who went on to hold elective office at the state level, a judicial appointment had constituted their first public office, an avenue to the legislature which was then closed to Republicans, who rose to the legislature through local elective office.

A judiciary appointment, even a county one, could be as rewarding monetarily as the most important elective offices in the state. Often the fees of the office were more weighty than the salary. That judicial fees were indeed high is indicated by the reply of a Federalist Associate Justice of the United States Supreme Court, William Paterson, to several leading Essex County party members, who requested that he use his influence to enact a bill raising and enlarging the fee structure of the state Supreme Court and Court of Common Pleas. He refused, explaining,

I have been informed that the bills of cost of some practitioners [already] have been swelled to an enormous size.[41]

The profit involved in a prospective appointment was an important consideration for Federalist and future Federalist applicants.[42] Other reasons they sought appointments were for their relative security compared to elective office and for the honor and prestige involved in holding any public office.

Normally, the Federalists applied quite indirectly for the appointive positions dispensed primarily by the state legislature.

William Griffith, for example, asked that Elisha Boudinot influence Governor Paterson in his behalf.[43] Since Paterson himself did not possess the power to appoint Griffith to a judicial position, he would need to contact still others in order to effect the appointment. In pleading a friend's or relative's case, an intermediary might cite the applicant's need and imply that the contactor himself would return the favor on demand.[44]

Those who lent their good offices to the cause of another's appointment did not always do so purely in the name of filial feeling or friendship. Rather often they expected assistance in return.[45]

The New Jersey Federalist party never used the patronage at its disposal to increase the depth of the party's apparatus to any significant extent. Federalist candidates received appointments largely because of their connections and not because of conspicuous service to the party, a Republican qualification for patronage that the New Jersey Federalists derided.[46]

To signify their likemindedness with the federal administration, the state's political leaders and other Jerseymen began to call themselves Federalists after 1792.[47] New Jersey's pro-government course of action that eventually placed her in the "truly federal"[48] camp started with strong support for Secretary's Hamilton's nascent economic program.

Congressman Elias Boudinot became one of the staunchest supporters of the program, which had met with his approval from the first.[49] Along with other representatives in the United States House close to Hamilton, Boudinot was responsibile for pushing through the Funding Act in the form Hamilton wanted.[50] New Jersey's delegation, unlike the delegations from neighboring New York and Pennsylvania, voted unanimously in favor of the funding measure.[51]

From the homefront, Jerseyans such as Federalist-to-be William Peartree Smith signaled their approval of the financial plan that aimed to wed the creditor interests to the government.[52] "Public credit is established," exclaimed the *Brunswick Gazette and Weekly Monitor.*[53] And, speaking for all those who believed the plan to be

... an act of great wisdom in the establishment of the nation's financial stability,

"Veritas" called for the reelection of the representatives who had supported Hamilton's economic policy.[54]

To the national bank question the people of New Jersey gave comparatively little attention.[55] However, a New Jersey Revolutionary War officer's organization, dominated by future Federalists,[56] early evinced their confidence in it. When the bank was established, this New Jersey chapter of the Society of Cincinnati instructed their treasurer

... to subscribe the whole of that part of the funds of this Society which bears a present interest of six per cent to the Bank of the United States.

Further, if unavailable from any other source, the Society authorized the buying of bank shares from individuals, even if this required the payment of a premium for them.[57]

As a member of the first United States Senate, future New Jersey Federalist leader William Paterson strongly endorsed Hamilton's financial program.[58] In token of his pro-government stance, Senator William Maclay numbered Paterson among the "gladiatorial band retained by the Secretary" [Alexander Hamilton].[59]

Later, in the capacity of governor of New Jersey, Paterson helped Hamilton implement his program to encourage manufacturing as outlined in the latter's "Report on Manufactures."[60] That report had called for the establishment of a national manufacturing center and proposed New Jersey as the location.[61] It was the Governor who helped steer the enabling legislation through the New Jersey legislature, a task which did not prove difficult. Dominated by future Federalists, the legislature gave the bill to incorporate the Society for the Establishing of Useful Manufactures (SUM) a very favorable reception, and within three weeks the bill became law. The articulate New Jersey citizenry apparently approved of the legislature's action.[62]

The extremely liberal act of incorporation signed by Gover-

nor Paterson on November 22, 1791, revealed that the New
Jersey legislature had afforded the corporation extensive tax
privileges, a municipal charter to found a town to be named in
honor of the Governor, and the power to build canals, construct
roads, and operate lotteries.[63] Shortly after the passage of the
charter, the State of New Jersey itself purchased 100 shares of
its first business corporation, leading a contemporary observer
to note,

> . . . [the] legislature [of New Jersey] patronizes the undertak-
> ing.[64]

Of the individual New Jersey stockholders of the SUM, nearly
all would become Federalists. In fact, a number of them, including the first Vice Chairman of the Board of Directors, John
Bayard, would rank among the top echelon of the state party's
leadership.[65]

Publicity on the subject of the "New National Manufactory"
appeared in New York, New Jersey, and Philadelphia newspapers. In Newark John Woods printed broadside advertisements
to promote the SUM and changed the name of his newspaper,
later a Federalist sheet, to *Woods' Newark Gazette and Paterson Advertiser.*[66]

In May of 1793 the word "Paterson" disappeared from
Woods' masthead, foreshadowing the fate of the SUM. Later
that year a desperate Elisha Boudinot vainly petitioned Hamilton not to ". . . let anything draw [his] attention from this great
object [the SUM]."[67]

But, understandably, Hamilton could not give his undivided
attention to the problems of the New Jersey corporation.
Among the other matters that demanded application on his
part was the handling of the adverse reaction to the excise tax.

When opposition to the tax culminated in the July, 1794,
Whiskey Rebellion in western Pennsylvania, New Jersey again
rallied to the support of the federal administration.[68] Governor
Howell, commander-in-chief of the state's militia, immediately
took steps to comply with President Washington's order that

the New Jersey militia be called out and sent to help suppress the rebellion.[69]

Howell's preparations were not hampered by a major protest on the part of the citizenry as was the case in the other three states where the militia were activated.[70] And when the expedition left Trenton in September of 1794, the local inhabitants gave them an enthusiastic send-off.[71]

Nearly all of New Jersey's militia officers were prominent Federalists,[72] but none was more zealous in suppressing the insurgents than Governor Howell or General Anthony Walton White, Commander of the New Jersey Cavalry. While the Governor urged the troops to "... push home your steel,"[73] White assured Howell,

> We will never sheath ... [our swords] tell we have subdued or extirpated the hydra of discord from among us.[74]

The callousness of such New Jersey Federalist leaders as Howell and, in particular, White[75] alienated many men and probably helped effect at least several desertions from the party. For instance, Captain Abraham Kinney, the subject of a court-martial for refusing to obey White's orders, became a Republican. So did General Joseph Bloomfield, later the first Republican governor of the state, and Mahlon Dickerson. Both men testified for defendant Kinney at his trial.[76]

If the debate over the components of Hamilton's economic policy constituted the initial stimulus for party formation, the contention over European politics constituted the crystallizing force. The ideology and emotional ties that emerged in the face of the series of foreign policy issues that presented themselves after 1793 effected the transition from a Federalist faction to a New Jersey Federalist party. Thereafter Federalists were Anglomen, and Washington was a Federalist symbol.[77]

New Jersey Federalists began to evince an anti-French attitude after that country's Reign of Terror started. The trial and execution of Louis XVI was denounced locally by the friends of order,[78] but opposition to France, the United States's old ally, was not yet a Federalist faith. Witness the Federalists' early approbation of the new French Republic's first minister to the United States, Citizen Edmond Genêt.[79]

A few months later, however, New Jersey Federalism's opposition to the French Republic stiffened. France's representative had defied the revered Washington!

In response, Federalists all over New Jersey rallied to the President's side. Led by such prominent partisans as Elias Dayton, Aaron Ogden, John Bayard, and Elias Boudinot, public meetings expressing support for Washington were held in at least six New Jersey towns, Trenton, Newark, New Brunswick, Burlington, Morristown, and Princeton.[80] The first of these meetings was held in the state capital some two weeks after Genêt had disobeyed Washington's orders in mid-July. Although all the delegates were from the Trenton area, the gathering declared that, to the best of its knowledge, the state as a whole approved of the President's stance.[81]

The other five meetings occurred before mid-September. Some sent memorials to the President. All signified satisfaction with Washington's neutral position and affirmed the constitutionality of his action.[82]

Of the pro-Washington meetings, including those held in neighboring states, only the New Brunswick, New Jersey, meeting mentioned Genêt's defiance of Washington, the act which actually had precipitated the meetings.[83] The rest followed the pattern set by the resolutions of the New York Chamber of Commerce.[84]

Two of the six pro-Washington meetings in New Jersey were held above the local level. Burlington's was a county meeting; New Brunswick's was a bi-county meeting.[85] Details are available regarding the latter. In preparation for it, a New Brunswick committee sent a circular letter to the various townships in Middlesex and Somerset counties advertising an August 30 New Brunswick meeting to consider the neutrality proclamation. Forty delegates arrived representing "the commercial, agricultural and mechanical interest." Therefore, the meeting felt qualified to observe that in regard to the federal administration

... an entire satisfaction ... [prevailed] among all classes of citizens in the state.[86]

Federalist expressions of the state's unanimity in supporting Washington's neutral stance and in condemning Genêt's action represented wishful thinking.[87] By November, 1793 New Jersey Federalists publicly recognized that there were those

> ... who countenance and justify ... [Genêt's] conduct ... [and Washington's calumniation]. They call themselves Republicans. ...[88]

The opposite was implied regarding the Federalists: they were anti-Genêt and pro-Washington.

After the Jay Treaty issue, Federalists were defined as being pro-British as well. Supporters of the federal administration's stand on the treaty were automatically judged to be friends of England.

Although the New Jersey Federalists finally rallied to the position of the federal government, as a group they were never enthusiastic about the Jay Treaty.[89] Their campaign to elicit local support started later than did that of their opponents, and it was conducted on a considerably smaller scale.

One of the Jerseyans' first expressions of support for the treaty constituted the only spirited act of the entire Federalist campaign. In late July, 1795 a Flemington meeting set ablaze a petition in circulation against the treaty to the accompaniment of ". . . general Huzas from the multitude."[90]

But the action of the Flemington Federalists did not set back the Republican campaign significantly. By the time of the Flemington meeting, July 23, the Republicans already had obtained ". . . thousands of [West Jersey] signatures" to petitions forming a Grand Remonstrance addressed to the President.[91]

Made early in the campaign, "Candor's" newspaper appeal illustrated the inclination of the Federalist propagandists to rely upon Washington's prestige to garner support for the government's position.[92]

Fear not, . . . my countrymen, the protecting arm of a Washington is extended between us and the danger, if there be any—. . . .[93]

The comparative hesitancy of most New Jersey Federalists to take a public stand on the treaty while it was awaiting Washington's signature may be accounted for in part by their belief that the President's decision must not be influenced by the pressure of public opinion.[94] Republicans, on the other hand, had no such qualms about sending resolutions to the President. In fact, several such anti-treaty addresses from West Jersey locations— Bordentown, Crosswicks, Black Horse, and Reckless Town— were judged by him to be "too rude to merit" a reply.[95]

Once the President had indicated he would sign the Jay Treaty, the New Jersey Federalists became more active in attempting to marshal public opinion. Their success was limited, however, especially in the state capital. There, despite two meetings held on consecutive days, the Federalists were forced to accept commitments to the public officials involved in place of approval for the treaty itself.

Senator Frederick Frelinghuysen spoke before the first of the two meetings. It was held at the state house on August 13. Frelinghuysen's appearance was precipitated by a resolution of an anti-treaty meeting implying that in voting for the treaty the Senator suffered from "a want of independence, integrity and patriotism."[96]

Chaired by Federalist State Attorney General Aaron Woodruff, the meeting acquitted Frolinghuysen of these charges, but it did not express support for the treaty. After the Senator had given his opinion on the treaty, support was sought for a resolution which could have been construed as approval of the treaty as well as of Senator Frelinghuysen's motives in voting for it. The resolution was immediately objected to, notably by State Treasurer Mott, later a Republican. Gershom Craft echoed Richard Stockton's previous statement that a vote for the resolution was not inconsistent with a position against the treaty. In fact, Craft himself was prepared to vote for the resolution although General Frelinghuysen had not convinced him that he, Craft, was wrong in opposing the treaty.

Thus reinforced, Stockton insisted the original resolution be placed before the meeting. It "lost by a very large majority." The consent of the meeting was only obtained by inserting in the resolution the qualification that it was "without reference to the merits of the said treaty."[97]

The second Trenton meeting, held the next day was dominated by Federalists. Yet, again, the most that could be obtained was a declaration of

> . . . entire satisfaction and confidence in the constituted authorities of our country [and because of this] a determination to acquiesce in such measures as have been or may be finally adopted relative to the said treaty by such constituted authorities.[98]

An October 13, 1795, election day publication of the Republicans urged that the voters carefully consider a candidate's stand on the Jay Treaty and reject those who had objected to the public's probing into government measures and the holding of anti-treaty meetings.[99] But the Republican attempt to channel the anti-treaty feeling into action against the Federalists at the polls failed.[100] As the Federalists correctly had observed the previous month,

> . . . proceedings on the subject of the Treaty . . . [had] become stale.[101]

Unlike the Republicans, the Federalists made no attempt to turn the Jay Treaty into an election issue. Instead, they confined themselves to rallying support on the basis of their connection with the "FATHER OF HIS COUNTRY," and they won once again.[102]

NOTES

1. Prince, *New Jersey's Jeffersonian Republicans*, p. 9.

2. William Nisbet Chambers, *Political Parties in a New Nation: The American Experience, 1776–1809* (New York: Oxford University Press, 1963), p. 1.

3. Broadus Mitchell, "Alexander Hamilton in New Jersey," *Proceedings of the New Jersey Historical Society* LXXVI (April, 1958): 84; John Miller, *Alexander Hamilton: Portrait in Paradox* (New York: Harper & Row, 1959), p. 7.

4. Stryker, "Elias Boudinot," p. 191; Mitchell, "Alexander Hamilton in New Jersey," pp. 88, 111; Johnson, "Clockmakers and Cabinetmakers of Elizabethtown," p. 2; Paul Sher, "Party Battles in Middlesex County, 1789–1824" (M.A. thesis, Rutgers University, 1937), p. 20; John P. Wall, *History of Middlesex County, New Jersey, 1664–1920*, vol. I (New York: Lewis Historical Publishing Company, 1912), p. 117.

5. Johnson, "Clockmakers and Cabinetmakers of Elizabethtown," p. 2.

6. Jane Boudinot, ed., *The Life, Public Service, Addresses, and Letters of Elias Boudinot*, vol. II (Boston: Houghton Mifflin and Company, 1896), p. 23.

7. Stryker, "Elias Boudinot," pp. 191–93.

8. Elmer, *The Constitution and Government of the Province and State of New Jersey*, p. 107.

9. William Benedict, *New Brunswick in History* (New Brunswick, New Jersey: By the Author, 1925), p. 53.

10. Richard Howell was elected governor by the joint meeting of the legislature in 1793 over his opponents, fellow Federalists Frederick Frelinghuysen and John Rutherfurd, by a margin of some fourteen votes in each case. Elmer, *The Constitution and Government of the Province and State of New Jersey*, p. 109. Since both of his opponents possessed substantial qualifications as civil officeholders whereas Howell had only served as a clerk of the Supreme Court, it is likely that his connection with Washington was partly responsible for his election and reelection to the governorship until 1801, when the Federalists lost the state.

11. William Colefax, former officer in Washington's personal guard, is another example of a top echelon New Jersey Federalist party leader who had longstanding ties to the President. William Nelson, "Biographical Sketch of William Colefax," *Proceedings of the New Jersey Historical Society* IV (1876, no. 3): 145–52.

12. National studies have arrived at a similiar conclusion. See Paul Goodman, "Social Status of Party Leadership: The House of Representatives, 1797–1802," *William and Mary Quarterly* XXV (July, 1968): 465–74 and David Hackett Fischer, *The Revolution of American Conservatism: The Federalist Party in the Era of Jeffersonian Democracy* (New York: Harper & Row, 1965).

13. *New Brunswick Guardian*, October 10, 1797; Griffith, *Eumenes*, p. 426; William B. Paterson, Princeton College Copybook, n.d., William B. Paterson Papers, Princeton University Library.

14. *Federalist*, September 30, 1799; *New Jersey Journal*, September 17, 1794.

15. George A. Boyd, *Elias Boudinot: Patriot and Statesman, 1740–1821* (Princeton: Princeton University Press, 1952), pp. 150–64.

16. *Brunswick Gazette and Weekly Monitor*, January 4, 1791.

17. *Address to the Federal Republicans of the State of New Jersey* (Trenton: Sherman, Mershon, and Thomas, November 13, 1800), p. 12.

18. Chambers, *Political Parties in a New Nation*, p. 102; Banner, *To the Hartford Convention*, p. 22; Leonard Rosenberg, "The Political Thought of William Paterson" (Ph.D. diss., New School for Social Research, 1967), pp. 34, 44; Paterson, charge to a grand jury, c. 1798, Rutgers University Library. Paterson used the expression ". . . order, Heaven's first law . . ." on several occasions.

19. Hofstadter, *The Idea of a Party System*, p. 85. "The Trenton *Federalist* attacked the 'impudent pretentions of the *democrats* to republicanism'." J. R. Pole, "The Reform of Suffrage and Representation in New Jersey, 1774–1844" (Ph.D. diss., Princeton University, 1953), p. 191.

20. *Federalist; New Jersey Gazette*, September 30, 1800; Harold Thatcher, "The Political Ideas of New Jersey's First Governor," *Proceedings of the New Jersey Historical Society* LX (July, 1942): pp. 190–99.

21. Fee, *The Transition from Aristocracy to Democracy*, pp. 111–12; Banner, *To the Hartford Convention*, p. 19; William B. Paterson, "Necessity of Religion to a Stable Government," c. 1800, William B. Paterson Papers, Princeton University Library. New Jersey's Federalists stressed that Republicanism was allied ". . . with vice and atheism . . . [while] Federalism . . . [stood] with virtue and religion. . . ." *State Gazette and New Jersey Advertiser*, May 27, 1799.

22. Fee, *The Transition from Aristocracy to Democracy*, p. 105.

23. Sher, "Party Battles in Middlesex County," p. 114.

24. Pole, "Jeffersonian Democracy and the Federalist Dilemma in New Jersey," p. 286.

25. *State Gazette and New Jersey Advertiser*, November 12, 19, 1798.

26. Leonard Rosenberg, "William Paterson: New Jersey's Nation-Maker," *New Jersey History* LXXXV (Spring, 1967): p. 34; Rosenberg, "The Political Thought of William Paterson," p. 63; Pole, "The Reform of Suffrage and Representation in New Jersey," p. 202; Pole, "Jeffersonian Democracy and the Federalist Dilemma in New Jersey," p. 285; Fischer, *The Revolution of American Conservatism*, p. 22; Griffith, *Eumenes*, p. 113.

27. Possibly 70 percent of New Jersey's adult white males voted in 1790. Chilton Williamson, *American Suffrage: From Property to Democracy, 1760–1860* (Princeton: Princeton University Press, 1960), p. 179.

28. Griffith, *Eumenes*, pp. 46–48.

29. Pole, "Jeffersonian Democracy and the Federalist Dilemma in New Jersey," p. 289.

30. *Newark Gazette*, November 8, 1797.

31. Paterson, "Hortensius," No. 39, William Paterson Papers, Rutgers University Library.

32. Pole, "Jeffersonian Democracy and the Federalist Dilemma in New Jersey," p. 286; Fischer, *The Revolution of American Conservatism*, p. 17.

33. Banner, *To the Hartford Convention*, p. 126.

34. Elias Boudinot to Mrs. Boudinot, April 2, 1789, Stimson-Boudinot Letters, Princeton University Library.

35. Jonathan Dayton to George Washington, June 22, 1790, Jonathan Dayton Papers, Rutgers University Library.

36. Leonard D. White, *The Federalists: A Study in Administrative History, 1789-1801* (New York: The Free Press, 1948), p. 83.

37. Elias Boudinot to Elisha Boudinot, March 15, 1791, Boudinot Papers, Historical Society of Pennsylvania.

38. *Centinel of Freedom*, March 5, 1799.

39. *Centinel of Freedom*, November 4, 1800.

40. Fee, *The Transition from Aristocracy to Democracy*, p. 30; *Minutes of the Joint Meeting*, 18th Session (June 5, 1793), p. 20; *Woods' Newark Gazette*, June 12, 1793. Eleven years as a minority party did not bring about a change in this pattern. In 1812 the Federalist New Jersey legislature again allocated most of its appointments to current and former legislators, some 75 percent in fact. *Minutes of the Joint Meeting*, 37th Session, 1st and 2nd Sittings (October 29, 1812, February 19, 1813), pp. 245-71.

41. William Paterson to Matthias Williamson, Aaron Ogden, Alexander MacWhorter, and David Ogden, March 16, 1799, William Paterson Papers, Rutgers University Library. Some examples of the fees available to holders of offices ranging from town constable to governor might be illustrative. A justice of the peace could expect to receive $.30 for each summons he drew up, while the governor charged $3.00 for every license he issued to a new counselor-at-law. The state attorney general collected $15.00 for each guilty verdict he obtained. Bloomfield, *Laws of the State of New Jersey*, pp. 352, 481, 486.

42. William Griffith to Elias Boudinot, August 8, 1790; Jonathan Dayton to George Washington, June 22, 1790; William Griffith to Elisha Boudinot, June 27, 1790; Elias Boudinot to Elisha Boudinot, March 15, 1791; William B. Paterson, Princeton College Copybook, n.d., William B. Paterson Papers, Princeton University Library.

43. William Griffith to Elisha Boudinot, August 8, 1790. At the time, Associate Chief Justice Elisha Boudinot was one of the three men who, informally, possessed influence over judicial appointments. The other two were Chief Justice James Kinsey and New Jersey Attorney General Joseph Bloomfield. William Griffith to Elisha Boudinot, June 27, 1790.

44. William Griffith to Elisha Boudinot, August 8, 1790; L. H. Stockton to Ebenezer Elmer, August 7, 1794; William Griffith to Elisha Boudinot, June 27, 1790; Richard Howell to Richard Stockton, February 20, 1795; Jonathan Dayton to Aaron Ogden, January 21, 1801; Richard Stockton to Aaron Ogden, November 6, 1800; L. H. Stockton to Elisha Boudinot, March 16, 1796; Elisha Boudinot to Elias Boudinot, June 13, 1790.

70 THE NEW JERSEY FEDERALISTS

45. David Brearly to Jonathan Dayton, September 24, 1789.

46. Elias Boudinot to Samuel Bayard, October 17, 1795, Elias Boudinot Collection, Princeton University Library; *New Brunswick Guardian*, January 10, 1805.

47. Prince, "New Jersey's Democratic Republicans," p. 7. "Much of the impetus for the crystallization of party formation in New Jersey was national in origin." Prince, *New Jersey's Jeffersonian Republicans*, p. 40. Also, to an unusual extent, New Jersey election campaigns of the Early Republic period were conducted on the basis of national issues.

48. *New Jersey Journal*, July 20, 1796.

49. Elias Boudinot to Mrs. Boudinot, January 14, 1790; Fee, *The Transition from Aristocracy to Democracy*, p. 20; *Annals of Congress*, I: 1139, 1238–39.

50. Joseph Charles, *The Origins of the American Party System* (Williamsburg, Virginia: Institute of Early American History and Culture, 1956), p. 15.

51. Ibid., p. 23; Fee, *The Transition from Aristocracy to Democracy*, p. 21; *Annals of Congress*, II: 1753.

52. William P. Smith to Elias Boudinot, March 14, 1790. Smith kept abreast of proceedings at the capital via John Fenno's *Gazette of the United States*.

53. *Brunswick Gazette & Weekly Monitor*, January 18, 1791. Later, Federalist sheets would attribute the state's and nation's prosperity to the funding system. *Newark Gazette*, October 15, 1794; December 30, 1795.

54. *Burlington Advertiser*, January 25, 1791.

55. Fee, *The Transition from Aristocracy to Democracy*, p. 29.

56. Meetings of the New Jersey chapter of the Society of Cincinnati were virtually gatherings of New Jersey Federalist party leaders. Of the 101 original members, only two would become early Republicans. Neither of them ever entered the Society's leadership ranks. "Roster of Members of Society of Cincinnati in New Jersey," 1791, New Jersey State Library; *New Jersey Journal*, July 14, 1790; July 8, 1795; July 10, 1798; *Emporium*, July 10, 1824.

57. Walter Fee, "The Effect of Hamilton's Financial Policy Upon Public Opinion in New Jersey," *Proceedings of the New Jersey Historical Society* L (January, 1932): 43.

58. Rosenberg, "The Political Thought of William Paterson," pp. 81–82; William Paterson to Euphemia Paterson, August 1, 1790, *Somerset County Historical Quarterly* II (1913): 273.

59. William Maclay, *Sketches of Debate in the First Senate of the United States, 1789–1791* (Harrisburg, Pennsylvania: Hart Company, 1880), p. 94. William Paterson's close link with Hamilton, forged in the early 1790s may have cost him the chief justiceship of the United States in 1801. In view of President Adams' great animosity for Hamilton by that date, Paterson's close association with the latter may have been one reason the President rejected him. Rosenberg, "William Paterson: New Jersey's Nation-Maker," p. 33; Jonathan Dayton to Aaron Ogden, January 21, 1801.

60. About this time some Burlingtonians also evinced an interest in encourag-

ing manufacturing by founding the Burlington Society for the Promotion of Agriculture and Domestic Manufactures. The organization, headed by future Federalist leader William Coxe, Jr., consisted primarily of other future New Jersey Federalist party members. Pasler, "The Federalist Party in Burlington County, New Jersey," p. 19.

61. Mitchell, "Alexander Hamilton in New Jersey," p. 109; Robert T. Thompson, *Colonel James Neilson: A Businessman of the Early Machine Age in New Jersey, 1784–1862* (New Brunswick: Rutgers University Press, 1940), p. 217.

62. John W. Cadman, *The Corporation in New Jersey: Business and Politics, 1791–1875* (Cambridge: Harvard University Press, 1949), pp. 33, 54.

63. Rosenberg, "The Political Thought of William Paterson," p. 38; Rosenberg, "William Paterson: New Jersey's Nation-Maker," p. 106; L. R. Trumbull, *A History of Industrial Paterson* (Paterson, New Jersey: Carleton M. Herrick Company, 1882), p. 31; W. Woodford Clayton, *History of Bergon and Passaic Counties, New Jersey* (Philadelphia: Everts and Peck, 1882), pp. 403–5.

64. Cadman, *The Corporation in New Jersey*, p. 110; Fred Shelley, "Travel Contrasts: Chancellor Kent's Impressions of New Jersey, 1793–1821," *Proceedings of the New Jersey Historical Society* LXXVI (October, 1955): 303.

65. William Nelson, "The Founding of Paterson," *Proceedings of the New Jersey Historical Society*, Second Series IX (1883, no. 3): 182, 187. Other SUM stockholders who would become prominent New Jersey Federalists were Elias Boudinot, Elisha Boudinot, James Parker, John N. Cumming, John Neilson, Elias Dayton, Jonathan Dayton, and Richard Stockton. Boyd, *Elias Boudinot: Patriot and Statesman*, pp. 193–96; *New Brunswick Guardian*, February 2, 1794; Trumbell, *A History of Industrial Paterson*, p. 37.

66. Nelson, "The Founding of Paterson," p. 103; Sabine, "Antecedents of the Newark Public Library," p. 37.

67. Nelson, "The Founding of Paterson," pp. 189–90.

68. Thayer, *As We Were: The Story of Old Elizabethtown*, p. 194. Even the recently formed democratic society of Newark decried the violence in Pennsylvania. *Woods' Newark Gazette*, September 24, 1794; Urquhart, *A History of the City of Newark, New Jersey*, I: 452.

69. Richard D. Howell to Joseph Bloomfield, September 16, 1794. The extensive collection of White Papers at Rutgers University Library details the New Jersey militia's preparation for and participation in the Whiskey Rebellion.

70. Leland Baldwin, *Whiskey Rebels: The Story of a Frontier Uprising* (Pittsburgh, Pennsylvania: University of Pittsburgh Press, 1939), p. 222.

71. Mahlon Dickerson, MS. Diary, September 27, October 2, 1794, New Jersey Historical Society.

72. Beckwith, "Mahlon Dickerson of New Jersey," p. 74; Thayer, *As We Were: The Story of Old Elizabethtown*, p. 194; Fee, *The Transition from Aristocracy to Democracy*, p. 56; *New Jersey State Gazette*, September 17, 1794; Frederick Frelinghuysen to Jonathan Dayton, November 15, 1794, Gratz Collection, Historical Society of Pennsylvania; Charles D. Deshler, "New Jersey and the Whis-

key Rebellion," unpublished paper presented at the New Brunswick Historical Club, New Brunswick, New Jersey, October 25, 1894.

73. *New Brunswick Guardian*, December 18, 1794; Deshler, "New Jersey and the Whiskey Rebellion."

74. Anthony Walton White to Richard Howell, September 16, 1794, White Papers, Rutgers University Library.

75. Two incidents may serve to illustrate why White emerged from the Whiskey Rebellion with a reputation for brutality. First, under White's command the cavalry detachment rode into a small western Pennsylvania settlement, dragged forty suspects from their beds, tied them by twos, back to back, and left them in a cellar without food or water. Also, White marched prisoners on foot between mounted soldiers with drawn swords, who had orders to decapitate the prisoners if a rescue attempt was made or if the men tried to escape on their own. Baldwin, *Whiskey Rebels: The Story of a Frontier Uprising*, pp. 247, 257.

76. "Within months after the close of the Expedition [Dickerson] displayed unmistakeable Republican leanings." Beckwith, "Mahlon Dickerson of New Jersey," pp. 48, 83; William Leddel, MS. Diary, September 26, 29, 1794; William Leddel to A. W. White, December 13, 1794, William Leddel Papers, New Jersey Historical Society.

77. Chambers, *Political Parties in a New Nation*, pp. 11, 76; William N. Chambers, "Nation Building and the Rise of Parties," in *The Federalists vs. the Jeffersonian Republicans*, ed. by Paul Goodman (New York: Holt, Rinehart and Winston, 1967), pp. 27, 29–30; Charles, *The Origins of the American Party System*, p. 91; Hofstadter, *The Idea of a Party System*, pp. xi, 88.

78. Sher, "Party Battles in Middlesex County," p. 45; *New Brunswick Guardian*, March 27, April 10, 1793.

79. *New Brunswick Guardian*, May 22, 1793. On May 18, President Washington had received Genêt, thereby recognizing the French Republic.

80. Harry Ammon, "The Genet Mission and the Development of American Political Parties," *Journal of American History* LII (March, 1966): 730; Thayer, *As We Were: The Story of Old Elizabethtown*, p. 194.

81. Fee, *The Transition from Aristocracy to Democracy*, p. 35; *New Jersey Journal*, July 13, 1793.

82. *New Jersey Journal*, July 31, August 21, 28, 1793; *Woods' Newark Gazette*, August 14, 21, September 4, 18, 1793; Prince, *New Jersey's Jeffersonian Republicans*, p. 14; *New Jersey State Gazette*, September 11, 1793; Fee, *The Transition from Aristocracy to Democracy*, pp. 35–36.

83. ". . . for any minister to threaten an appeal from the constituted authority of this country, to the people at large, is an act of the highest insolence and injustice and an insult not only to the Executive authority . . . but to the whole people of the United States." *New Brunswick Guardian*, September 4, 1793; Sher, "Party Battles in Middlesex County," p. 46.

84. Ammon, "The Genet Mission and the Development of American Political

Parties," p. 730; *Gazette of the United States,* August 21, 28, September 4, 11, 1793.

85. Later, it was in the counties of Middlesex and Burlington that the New Jersey Federalists evinced the best organization. McCormick, *The Second American Party System,* p. 127.

86. Woods' *Newark Gazette,* September 4, 11, 1793; *New Jersey Journal,* September 4, 1793; Fee, *The Transition from Aristocracy to Democracy,* pp. 35–36.

87. Thayer, *As We Were: The Story of Old Elizabethtown,* p. 194; Fee, *The Transition from Aristocracy to Democracy,* p. 36; Sher, "Party Battles in Middlesex County," p. 47; *New Brunswick Gazette,* November 19, 1793; *New Jersey Journal,* August 17, 1793; *Woods' Newark Gazette,* August 14, 1793; Charles Nisbet to Joshua Wallace, December 19, 1793.

88. *Arnett's New Jersey Federalist,* November 12, 1793.

89. Even that staunch supporter of the federal administration, Elias Boudinot, the then Director of the Mint, "submitted" to the treaty largely because it had been enacted by the constituted authorities. Elias Boudinot to Samuel Bayard, October 17, 1795, Stockton Papers, New Jersey Historical Society; David Sterling, "A Federalist Opposes the Jay Treaty: The Letters of Samuel Bayard," *William and Mary Quarterly,* Third Series XVIII (July, 1961): 409.

90. Moore Furman to Benjamin Guild, July 28, 1795; *Genius of Liberty and New Brunswick Advertiser,* August 24, September 14, December 14, 1795; *New Jersey State Gazette,* August 4, 1795.

91. *Jersey Chronicle,* July 25, 1795; Fee, *The Transition from Aristocracy to Democracy,* pp. 59, 62. The Republican campaign had begun in the spring. May 2 found Philip Freneau rallying support against the treaty with Great Britain regardless of what the yet undisclosed provisions might prove to be. Prince, *New Jersey's Jeffersonian Republicans,* p. 16; *Jersey Chronicle,* May 2, 1795; *New Jersey Journal,* July 15, 1795.

92. Miller, *Alexander Hamilton: Portrait in Paradox,* p. 168.

93. *Woods' Newark Gazette and New Jersey Advertiser,* July 22, 1795; Fee, *The Transition from Aristocracy to Democracy,* p. 66.

94. Charles, *The Origins of the American Party System,* p. 103; Jerald Combs, *The Jay Treaty* (Berkeley: University of California Press, 1970), p. 163.

95. John C. Fitzpatrick, ed., *The Writings of George Washington,* vol.XXXV (Washington, D. C.: United States Printing Office, 1940), p. 254.

96. *New Brunswick Guardian,* September 1, 1795.

97. Ibid., *Genius of Liberty and New Brunswick Advertiser,* August 24, 1795; *New Jersey State Gazette,* August 8, 1795; *Woods' Newark Gazette and New Jersey Advertiser,* August 26, 1795.

98. "Three or four persons . . . totally disapproved of the . . . proceedings." *Genius of Liberty and New Brunswick Advertiser,* August 24, 1795.

99. *New Jersey State Gazette,* October 13, 1795.

100. Prince, *New Jersey's Jeffersonian Republicans*, p. 17; Fee, *The Transition from Aristocracy to Democracy*, p. 70.

101. *Genius of Liberty and New Brunswick Advertiser*, September 4, 1795.

102. *New Jersey Journal*, September 30, 1795.

4

NEW JERSEY FEDERALISTS
MAINTAIN THEIR DOMINANCE

After 1795, the New Jersey Federalists faced an increasingly effective opposition. Still, for six additional years, they succeeded in marshaling the state behind the Federalist cause.

The 1796 contest over the Jay Treaty, which in virulence exceeded even that of 1795.[1] found New Jersey firmly in the administration's camp. With the opening gun of the Republicans' 1796 campaign against the Jay Treaty appropriation, the New Jersey Federalists had thrown the state's weight solidly behind the administration.[2]

First, the New Jersey legislature soundly rejected the Virginia General Assembly's anti-treaty appropriation resolves.[3] Then New Jersey Federalists fostered demonstrations of pro-treaty sentiment on the part of the New Jersey citizenry so that when the treaty appropriation session of the Republican-dominated House convened, it learned that in New Jersey public meetings were occurring in favor of the treaty.[4]

The New Jersey Federalists also attempted to persuade Jerseyans opposed to the treaty to abandon their view in favor of the Federalist one. At a hostile town meeting in central New Jersey, a "famous, overbearing" New Jersey Federalist treated the gathering to a pro-treaty harangue. This same "Friend to the Constitution" later published an article calling upon the opposition to rally in favor of the treaty appropriation.[5]

Furthermore, answering the desperate cry of the House's

Federalist leadership for further support, New Jersey Federalists readily gathered petitions against the blocking of the appropriation. By April 26, 1796, four days before the appropriation passed, the New Brunswick *Guardian* expressed the conviction that most citizens had signed pro-treaty petitions addressed to the House.[6] Some had been sent by New Jersey Grand Juries.[7] Others had been forwarded by New Jersey banks and insurance companies, which had used economic pressure to gain signatures.[8] In the face of this deluge from his home state, New Jersey Congressman Thomas Henderson concluded that the collective body of Jerseyans "representing nine-tenths of the property" in the state favored the measure.[9]

During their treaty appropriation campaign, Jerseyans had singled out one member of the House of Representatives for particular attention, the reluctant Speaker, Jonathan Dayton of New Jersey. To cap off a 1,400 signature pro-treaty petition from the citizens-at-large, the state's Society of Cincinnati contacted Dayton, and he was sent a warning from his brother-in-law that the New Jersey populace

would tear any of their representatives to pieces who should vote against the treaty.[10]

Thereafter, Dayton actively worked for the treaty appropriation, which passed on April 30, 1796.

By the following July, however, anxiety over the state's forthcoming presidential polling had gripped the New Jersey leadership. Speaker Dayton's latest flirtation with Republicanism caused the highest circles of the Federalist leadership to worry that he would create a split in the New Jersey electoral vote. To forestall this, Hamilton advised Elias Boudinot to seek assiduously the support of the troublesome Dayton.[11] Although in mid-September Dayton did give assurance that to his mind "the man from Monticello" would receive no support from New Jersey,[12] his declaration did not bring an end to the Republican threat.

In late November, virtually on the eve of the presidential

balloting, frightful news reached Elias Boudinot. One of the electors chosen by the legislature recently was said to have stated that he and another New Jersey elector would vote not for Adams but for Jefferson.

The loss of two votes from New Jersey will put Mr. Adams out of the probability of being elected.

lamented Elias Boudinot.[13] But the doubtful New Jersey electors did not bolt the party. To the joy of the Federalists, New Jersey's late 1796 electoral vote was unanimous for John Adams.[14]

The same pressure which influenced two future Republicans to cast their electoral votes for Federalist John Adams in 1796[15] also influenced 1797 Congressional candidates Aaron Kitchell and Joseph Bloomfield to attempt to retain a relationship with the New Jersey Federalist party, at least until after the election. The Federalists, however, would have none of these surreptitious Republicans, pretending to be members of the dominant party in order to gain Federalist votes.

It was Anthony Walton White who publicly expelled Kitchell from the Federalist party. During election week he brandished for all to see a letter Kitchell had written, expressing democratic sentiments. These sentiments White labeled as the true feelings of Kitchell, a man elected to the previous Congress as a Federalist who, once there, had voted with the Republicans.[16] This pretended Federalist, White declared, was nothing but a "trimming, time-serving politician," a denunciation that received wide coverage in the Federalist press.[17]

Federalists conferred the Republican stigmata upon Congressional candidate Joseph Bloomfield because of sympathetic remarks he had made to a Frenchman, a guest in his home. Bloomfield's supporters protested that the Frenchman was not fluent in English and had inadvertently misquoted Bloomfield, but the protests were to no avail. Nor were Bloomfield's newspaper and broadside defenses against the "blast[ing] . . . [of his] character with Anti-Federalism."[18] Like Kitchell, who lost his

Congressional seat, Bloomfield was branded as a Republican, and he, too, went down to defeat.[19]

At the beginning of Adams' administration, the New Jersey Federalists experienced a lull in opposition, which in part may be attributed to the President's conciliatory attitude toward the Republicans.

Even the democrats pretend he is the right man for the office,

observed New Jersey Federalist Samuel Bayard. The fact that prior to the inauguration

Mr. Adams and Mr. Jefferson [had even] lodge[d] together

and the friendly tone of Adams' inaugural address went so far as to give some New Jersey Federalists hope that parties had come to an end.

However, as Samuel Bayard had predicted, this Federalist-Republican entente was but temporary.[20] With Adams' anti-French address to a special session of Congress on May 16, 1797, New Jersey Republicans and Federalists again were at loggerheads.

Vice President Jefferson, the Republicans' rallying symbol, became an object of particular enmity for the New Jersey Federalists. During the 1797 New Jersey legislative election campaign, ex-Senator Frederick Frelinghuysen made a point of vilifying the Vice-President.[21] A "True American" of Middlesex County also found Jefferson fair game for attack. Had he not

toasted the success and prosperity of the very nation [France] . . . [which was] striking daggers into the vitals of his own country![22]

As tension increased between the United States and France, support of President Adams again became the mark of a Federalist. In late 1797 Jersey partisans made Adams personally aware of their approbation on at least two occasions. One was during the President's November stop in New Brunswick on his way back to Philadelphia.

According to the *Guardian,* on this occasion Adams was received by the inhabitants of New Brunswick

> with every mark of respect and esteem, due from a grateful people, to a man whose whole life has been so distinguished in promoting the public good.

Speaking for the town, John Neilson expressed its abhorrence at the voice of faction abroad in the land, while a banquet in Adams' honor featured such toasts as "The Tower of Babel to all antifederalists."[23]

When the Federalist-dominated New Jersey legislature met, it sent a laudatory address to the President, indicating its "high respect for his personal and political character."[24]

Several months later, New Jersey's support for Adams reached a new high when Adams' popularity increased in reaction to the XYZ affair.

As a member of the United States Senate, Richard Stockton had learned of the XYZ incident in advance of the general public. As the story unfolded to privileged ears, Stockton provided an ill Senator Rutherfurd with a step-by-step report on the development of support for the administration.

First, he said, the President's announcement of the failure of the peace mission to France had brought about a "complete union" in the already Federalist-dominated Senate.[25] Then the reading of the dispatches themselves so "entirely dismayed" the Republican party in the House that

> hopes were entertained . . . the [opposition] party would become extinct.[26]

Stockton predicted the citizens at large would soon rally to the government's side, for the House had voted to publish the XYZ dispatches and the public would therefore shortly become aware of the situation.[27]

Stockton's prediction about the effect the XYZ dispatches would have on the populace certainly was born out in New Jersey's case. Within little more than a week of the XYZ disclosure, a spate of public meetings began.[28]

The first pro-Adams meeting in New Jersey following the XYZ affair disclosure appears to have been in Burlington City. Here ten prominent men were appointed to a committee charged with marshaling support for the administration. The next day seven of the Burlington City men attended a county-level meeting in Mount Holly, which passed resolutions praising Adams. Twenty-one members of this meeting were appointed to obtain signatures to the adopted resolutions, preparatory to their being sent to the capital.[29]

Many other citizens' meetings followed, conforming to the general pattern of those of Burlington. These meetings were held by citizens of the towns of Trenton, Princeton, Kingston, New Germantown, New Brunswick, Elizabeth, Newark, and Flemington and the counties of Gloucester, Cumberland, Monmouth, and Sussex.[30]

Besides the general populace of various towns and counties, addresses in support of the government also originated with other New Jersey groups. For example, two groups of central New Jersey youth sent resolutions. The young men of the vicinity of New Brunswick informed President Adams they were ready to arm,

for [their] lives [they held] cheap, when put in competition with . . . national honor and independence,[31]

and the students of the College of New Jersey "offer[ed] their feeble, though hearty concurrence" in the Adams policy.[32] The judicial officers and grand jury of Somerset County also forwarded a memorial to the President.[33] Equally strong in its support was the New Jersey Society of the Cincinnati.[34]

The militia, too, tendered its approval. One address with some 100 signatures emanated from the state militia's commander-in-chief, general officers, general staff and field officers.[35] However, because of its wording, another from a county militia unit, the First Troop of Middlesex Light Dragoons, struck a particular chord with the generation of the American Revolution. Harking back to the pledge made in the Declaration of Independence, the men of the Middlesex unit, led by General Anthony Walton White, offered the government "their lives, their fortunes and their honor."[36]

Some Jerseyans did not confine themselves to words but also expressed their patriotism in symbolic acts against the French. In most cases, the chosen activity was evincing contempt for the liberty cap.

Scorn for what Federalists now regarded as a French symbol was exhibited in all three New Jersey counties where Republicanism had gained a foothold. In Sussex County a cavalry troop, an infantry troop, and "a large number of respectable citizens" summarily pulled down the liberty cap that had been atop the flag pole since the preceding Fourth of July.[37]

In Morris County, where Republicanism had taken firmer hold, the liberty cap was not deposed so easily. It took "a considerable body of Patriotic Jerseymen" (or, to the Republicans, "a banditti of ruffians") from New Brunswick to accomplish the feat. At 11:00 A.M. on August 30, 1798, General Anthony Walton White led horsemen,

> . . . 23 in number, armed with swords, pistols and clubs [into Mendham.] With many oaths and imprecations [the group triumphantly bore away to New Brunswick] the *French cap*, emblematic of . . . allegiance to the *five headed* monster [the French Directory.][38]

In Newark, the cradle of New Jersey Republicanism, Federalists had to remove "this very bloody emblem of the French Revolution"[39] clandestinely. Under the cover of darkness

> The liberty cap was taken from the [Newark] flag-staff . . . and [from] the Emblem of Justice . . . over the Judge's seat in the Court-House.[40]

The rabid *Federalist* also participated in the campaign against the liberty cap. Since it could not remove the hated French symbol from the masthead of its rival the *Centinel of Freedom*, the *Federalist* countered that abomination by itself displaying the patriotic motto "Adams and Liberty."[41]

The Federalist external and internal defense program, passed by the Fifth Congress, was enacted with the help of New Jersey's representatives.[42] Their action won the New Jersey representatives favor at home. For over a year Jerseyans had felt a need for security measures such as those Congress passed during the spring and summer of 1798; indeed, more than a year earlier the New Jersey legislature had tried to meet this need through statewide legislation.[43]

Governor Howell had tried personally to keep out subversives from Pennsylvania by entering into a gentleman's agreement with Governor Thomas Mifflin. If Governor Mifflin would stop and "examine suspected strangers" before they attempted to cross the border into New Jersey, Howell would greatly appreciate it, he wrote.[44]

In spite of their efforts New Jersey Federalists were convinced by May, 1798, that French "spies and emissaries" were everywhere.[45] Federalists felt that only national legislation against immigrants could help. In his college copybook, William B. Paterson declared that

> In a political sense it is from the importation of foreign citizens that our country maintains the most serious injury.[46]

Joseph Hopkinson insisted that a

> . . . check . . . [must be] . . . applied to . . . [the] enormous and growing influence [of foreigners or] the time approaches when the American knee shall bend before the foot-stool of foreigners. . . .[47]

On the Fourth of July, 1798, New Jersey Federalists declared that native American Republicans were just as dangerous to the state as their Jacobin allies and therefore they called for "a speedy transportation to all . . . Frenchified Tories" as well as Jacobins.[48] New federal law prescribed this punishment only for alien agents, but other penalties were provided in the Sedition Act for such native "railers at every measure of government"[49] as New Jersey's French Tories (Republicans).

The state Federalists wasted no time in utilizing this "important and useful"[50] law to try to silence their opponents. Before the law was two months old, legal proceedings had been instituted leading up to all of the indictments for sedition that would occur in New Jersey.[51] In every instance the accused resided in Republican Newark.

The first arrests occurred as an outgrowth of the rousing reception Federalists accorded President Adams when in late July, 1798, he passed through Newark on his way to Quincy. The party faithful of the town greeted Adams with cheers and pealing bells, and then, as his coach pulled away, they accorded him a sixteen-gun canon salute. Perhaps wishfully, Brown Clark exclaimed to Luther Baldwin, as the latter reached the tavern before which Clark was standing, "There goes the President and they are firing at his a____." Even less enamored of the President than Clark, Baldwin replied that "he did not care if they fired thro' [sic] his a____."

John Burnet, Federalist postmaster of the town and the tavern's proprietor, chanced to overhear the exchange. Immediately he declared it seditious. The "respectable citizens" who subsequently gathered at the scene agreed. So did the court, which later fined and jailed the men for having uttered

. . . seditious words tending to defame the President and Government of the United States.[52]

In August of 1798 sedition charges were brought against the most ardent Republican organ in New Jersey, the Newark *Centinel of Freedom*[53] as the result of a heated Federalist-Republican quarrel dating back several months. In May Republican officers had refused to add their names to the state militia's expression of support for President Adams. A final draft of the address, sent to the President, included a reference to the Republicans' disloyalty. Noting that "a few degraded and deluded characters" had refused to support the government during the current crisis, the Federalists promised that at the earliest opportunity they would convey these French Tories within the lines of the invading enemy.[54]

In reply, the Republicans forwarded addresses both to the President and the Governor, charging that the Chief Executive was at fault, not they. It was because Adams had violated the Constitution that they had no confidence in the government.[55]

Almost beside himself with rage at their audacity, Governor Howell lashed out at the authors of these addresses, terming them

> . . . the shreds of a French faction [that operated as a] dagger in the hands of . . . [a French] assassin.

The Republicans retorted that such

> . . . an immense discharge of bile, spleen, and other acrimonious humors

as that directed against them by Howell could only have come from "the Prince of Blackguards" himself.[56]

The conferral of the epithet "Prince of Blackguards" upon the governor of the state brought an immediate response from the Federalists. The day after the objectionable article had appeared in the *Centinel of Freedom* "a number of respectable characters" from Woodbridge, Elizabeth, and Newark converged upon the publishers, demanding the identity of the defamer. When the *Centinel*'s publishers refused to disclose it, the group lodged their seditious libel charges against the publishers themselves.[57]

One foremost supporter of rigid enforcement of the Sedition Act, New Jersey Supreme Court Judge Elisha Boudinot, also pressed for the application of the Alien Act in at least one case, that of French General Victor Collot.[58] In making this fruitless attempt to have Collot deported, Boudinot worked closely with Secretary of State Timothy Pickering, the chief enforcement officer of the Alien Act.

First Collot had to be found, for he had disappeared in June of 1799, leaving Pickering with an unexecuted arrest order signed by the President. By August 7, 1799, however, Judge

Boudinot had been successful in locating the General, who was living in Republican Newark. Along with the news of his discovery the Judge sent Pickering some scraps of information he hoped would add to the case against Collot. First, he had learned that the General was living under an assumed name, and in this name he had taken out a subscription to the Republican *Aurora*. Also, Boudinot had obtained statements documenting Collot's "intriguing spirit," his criticism of Washington and Adams, and his inquisitiveness as to "the character of every frenchman in . . . the neighborhood."

When a week had elapsed during which Pickering had taken no decisive action on his information, Boudinot again contacted Pickering, notifying him that he had garnered yet additional evidence against Collot. A witness claimed Collot had declared

> . . . he would be one of the first to step forward and plunder the property of certain individuals

if a war occurred between France and the United States. Furthermore Boudinot had heard that a cache of papers Collot kept in his lodgings would yield incriminating evidence if confiscated.

Boudinot became very insistent. If Pickering would only authorize Collot's arrest, Boudinot would see that "The business would be effectually done." Indeed, had success in acting against Collot depended solely on the zeal of Elisha Boudinot, Collot would have been deported. But other, more influential factors nullified the New Jersey Federalist's efforts.[59]

Because they believed so firmly in the necessity of the Alien and Sedition Laws, the New Jersey Federalists' reaction to the Virginia and Kentucky Resolutions was a virulent one. *Treason!*, shouted the New Jersey Federalist press.[60] And soon Federalist meetings and a grand jury joined the press in denouncing the Virginia and Kentucky resolves.[61]

In the state Assembly, the Federalists gave the Virginia and Kentucky Resolutions very short shrift indeed. Immediately after the Republicans had introduced the resolutions, the Federalists called for their dismissal.[62] When the Republicans protested that a summary dismissal of the resolves would affront sister states, the Federalists snapped that "immediate dismissal would show no more contempt" for the resolves than they deserved.[63]

In such a frame of mind the Federalists defeated a Republican proposal for a second reading of the resolves. Next, they voted to dismiss first the Virginia Resolutions and then those of Kentucky, becoming the only state legislature in the north to send no reply to either set of resolves.[64]

No sooner had the Federalist legislators successfully met the Republican challenge over the Virginia and Kentucky Resolutions than another challenge appeared. Looking forward to the next presidential election and knowing that a Federalist legislature would appoint Federalist electors, New Jersey Republicans petitioned the legislature to cease appointing electors. The Federal Constitution had vested this right in the people, they said. Therefore, the legislature should pass a law providing for the popular election of presidential electors.[65]

The Republican legislators, of course, agreed, but when this petition came to the Assembly floor, they found it expedient to move that it be referred to the next legislature. Possessing only some 22 percent of the seats and lacking significant Federalist support, the Republicans wished to postpone a vote on the issue to a more opportune time. The Federalists, however, overruled the Republican motion, so the debate immediately commenced.

The Assembly's speaker William Coxe took the floor for the Federalists. He would willingly and with all seriousness reply to the petition's charge that the appointment of electors was unconstitutional, Coxe said, and he proceeded skillfully to do so. But he fervently maintained that the petition had not originated in true doubt over the constitutionality of the legislature's appointing presidential electors but in base partisanship.

Republican Assemblyman William Pennington, who rose next, ignored the partisanship charge. Moving directly to the constitutional question, he asserted that to him it was "self-evident" that the Constitution had vested the people with the power to choose presidential electors. However, he conceded that doubt could arise over whether the Constitution had designated the people or the legislature to choose electors. Those who experienced such doubt should follow "a wholesome rule of construction," which called for the people to be given the benefit of the doubt; they should vote to give the presidential franchise to the people.

The Federalist majority, unswayed, voted to dismiss the Republican petitions.[66]

However, the next legislative year the Republicans again petitioned the Assembly to authorize the popular election of presidential electors. This time, with its strength reduced by some 28 percent as a consequence of the recent election, the barely dominant Federalist party employed somewhat different tactics in responding to the Republican challenge. Aware that a significant delay of action on the petitions would make it too late to pass a law in time for the 1800 election, the Federalists moved for a year's postponement. They were not successful.

This defeat brought the Federalist leadership up short. They realized that with a majority of only one no Federalist must be allowed to defect to the Republican position. By the next vote that party's leadership had enforced strict party discipline. As a result, Federalist Joseph Stillwell was elected chairman when the Assembly resolved itself into a committee of the whole for the purpose of considering the petitions.[67]

William Coxe again acted as the major Federalist debater. Although by no means ignoring the constitutional question, this time he bore down much harder on the partisanship charge. At the very outset he labeled Republican tactics as those of "veterans in political warfare." Their arguments were emotional, not intellectual, he said; the Republicans themselves did not believe that it was unconstitutional for the legislature to appoint electors; the petitioners' stance was grounded completely in "ideas of party." In short,

. . . party prejudice [and nothing else was] at the bottom of these petitions, Coxe declared.

During the crucial vote on the petitions' request, not even one Federalist Assemblyman defected from his party's position. Strict Federalist party discipline safeguarded the legislature's power to allocate New Jersey's presidential votes.[68]

NOTES

1. Beckwith, "Mahlon Dickerson of New Jersey," p. 84; Sher, "Party Battles in Middlesex County," p. 21; Fee, *The Transition from Aristocracy to Democracy*, p. 16; Noble E. Cunningham, *The Jeffersonian-Republicans: The Formation of Party Organization, 1789–1801* (Chapel Hill, North Carolina: The University of North Carolina Press, 1957), p. 45.

2. Jerald Combs, *The Jay Treaty* (Berkeley: University of California Press, 1970), p. 172.

3. Stephen Kurtz, *The Presidency of John Adams: The Collapse of Federalism, 1795–1800* (Philadelphia: University of Pennsylvania Press, 1957), p. 28.

4. *Woods' Newark Gazette and New Jersey Advertiser*, December 16, 1795; Fee, *The Transition from Aristocracy to Democracy*, p. 67; *New Jersey State Gazette*, December 29, 1795; *New Jersey Journal*, December 16, 1795.

5. *Genius of Liberty and New Brunswick Advertiser*, December 14, 1795.

6. *Guardian*, April 26, 1796.

7. *Woods' Newark Gazette and New Jersey Advertiser*, April 13, 1796; Fee, *The Transition from Aristocracy to Democracy*, p. 68.

8. Kurtz, *The Presidency of John Adams*, p. 57.

9. Fee, *The Transition from Aristocracy to Democracy*, p. 69; *Annals of Congress*, vol. V, 1170.

10. Kurtz, *The Presidency of John Adams*, pp. 69–70; Jonathan Dayton to Ebenezer Elmer, March 15, 1796, Dayton Papers, New York Historical Society.

11. Kurtz, *The Presidency of John Adams*, p. 158.

12. Ibid., p. 159.

13. Elias Boudinot to Elisha Boudinot, November 28, 1796, Boudinot Papers, Princeton University.

14. ". . . all hands to quarters . . . leave the rigging pole to John Adams," exclaimed an elated Governor Howell when the President was elected by three votes. Richard Howell to Jonathan Dayton, December 22, 1796, Gratz Collection, Historical Society of Pennsylvania.

15. According to 1796 presidential elector Aaron Ogden, it was New Jersey's ". . . tried attachment to . . . the federal party [that had] insure[d] the vote of

every elector." Aaron Ogden to Jonathan Dayton, December 10, 1796, Park Collection, Morristown National Historical Park, Morristown, New Jersey; Prince, *New Jersey's Jeffersonian Republicans*, p. 18.

16. Manning Dauer, *The Adams Federalists* (Baltimore: The John Hopkins University Press, 1953), p. 291; Prince, *New Jersey's Jeffersonian Republicans*, p. 22.

17. *Woods' Newark Gazette and New Jersey Advertiser*, January 11, 1797; *State Gazette and New Jersey Advertiser*, January 10, 1797; *Guardian*, January 3, 1797.

18. *Guardian*, January 3, 10, 1797; Joseph Bloomfield, *To the Public*, Burlington, New Jersey, December, 1796.

19. Because of his Republican votes in the Congress Kitchell believed that the New Jersey Federalists had marked him to be ". . . executed the . . . [next] time [he was] a candidate." *Centinel of Freedom*, July 12, 1796; Prince, *New Jersey's Jeffersonian Republicans*, p. 22.

20. Samuel Bayard to Elias Boudinot, April 22, 1797, Boudinot Papers, Princeton University; William Paterson to James Iredell, March 7, 1797 in Kurtz, *The Presidency of John Adams*, p. 222.

21. *New Jersey Journal*, August 16, November 8, 1797; *Guardian*, September 26, 1797.

22. *Guardian*, September 26, 1797.

23. Ibid., November 14, 1797; Sher, "Party Battles in Middlesex County," p. 53.

24. Fee, *The Transition from Aristocracy to Democracy*, p. 77; *Votes and Proceedings of the General Assembly*, 22nd Session, 1st Sitting, p. 68.

25. "Letters from Richard Stockton to John Rutherfurd," *Proceedings of the New Jersey Historical Society*, Second Series III (1873, no. 3):186.

26. Ibid., p. 189.

27. Ibid., p. 188.

28. Ibid., p. 180; *Annals of Congress*, vol. VII, pp. 545, 551, 552, 556, 558–60, vol. VIII, p. 1152. Adams' bellicose replies to the New Jersey addresses, one of which even the arch-Federalist Alexander Hamilton termed "intemperate," only served to increase anti-French feeling in the state as did Speaker Dayton's May 10 announcement that the French Army was about to invade the United States. Dauer, *The Adams Federalists*, p. 150; *Annals of Congress*, vol. VIII, p. 1679; Alexander De Conde, *The Quasi-War: The Politics and Diplomacy of the Undeclared War with France, 1797–1801* (New York: Charles Schribner's Sons, 1966), p. 84.

29. *State Gazette and New Jersey Advertiser*, May 1, 1798; Pasler and Pasler, "The Federalist Party in Burlington County, New Jersey," p. 78.

30. *State Gazette and New Jersey Advertiser*, April 24, 28, May 1, 8, 15, 29, July 24, 1798; *New Jersey Journal*, May 1, 22, 1798; *Centinel of Freedom*, May 8, 1798; *Guardian*, May 15, 22, July 10, 1798; *Newark Gazette*, July 17, 1798; *Annals of Congress*, vol. VII, pp. 545, 551, 552, 556, 558–60; vol. VIII, p. 1152;

90   THE NEW JERSEY FEDERALISTS

Sher, "Party Battles in Middlesex County," pp. 48–50.
  31. Sher, "Party Battles in Middlesex County," p. 50; *Guardian*, June 5, 1798.
  32. Kurtz, *The Presidency of John Adams*, pp. 299–300; Fee, *The Transition from Aristocracy to Democracy*, p. 80; *State Gazette and New Jersey Advertiser*, May 22, 1798; *Guardian*, May 29, 1798.
  33. Fee, *The Transition from Aristocracy to Democracy*, p. 81; *State Gazette and New Jersey Advertiser*, September 25, 1798.
  34. *New Jersey Journal*, September 10, 1798.
  35. Fee, *The Transition from Aristocracy to Democracy*, p. 80; *State Gazette and New Jersey Advertiser*, May 22, 1798; *New Jersey Journal*, May 5, 1798; *Newark Gazette*, June 12, 1798.
  36. *Guardian*, May 22, 1798; Sher, "Party Battles in Middlesex County," p. 49.
  37. Fee, *The Transition from Aristocracy to Democracy*, p. 80. *State Gazette and New Jersey Advertiser*, June 12, 1798.
  38. *Federalist*, August 20, 27, 1798; *New Jersey Journal*, September 4, 1798; *Guardian*, September 4, October 23, 1798.
  39. *Newark Gazette*, May 1, 1798.
  40. *Centinel of Freedom*, April 17, 1798; *Newark Gazette*, May 1, 1798.
  41. *Federalist*, July, 1798; Sabine, "Antecedents of the Newark Public Library," p. 138.
  42. Dauer, *The Adams Federalists*, p. 316. New Jersey's Federalist representatives to the fifth House of Representatives evinced none of the deviation from the regular party stance that those to the fourth had. Ibid., pp. 297, 316. This change occurred partly as a result of a change in personnel. Neither of the two representatives whose voting pattern in the fourth Congress had deviated from the regular party position was reelected. Both Aaron Kitchell, the Federalist who had voted as a Republican in the fourth Congress, and Thomas Henderson, the Federalist who had voted as a moderate, went down to defeat in the fifth Congressional election, held in January, 1797.
  43. Bloomfield, *Laws of the State of New Jersey*, pp. 266–67, 297.
  44. Richard Howell to Governor Thomas Mifflin, August 20, 1797, Ferdinand Dreer Collection, Historical Society of Pennsylvania.
  45. *Guardian*, May 15, 1798.
  46. William B. Paterson, "Has Immigration of Foreigners Promoted the General Interest of the United States?" c. 1798, Princeton College Copybook, William B. Paterson Papers, Princeton University.
  47. John Miller, *Crisis in Freedom: The Alien and Setition Acts* (Boston: Little, Brown and Company, 1951), p. 192.
  48. *Guardian*, July 10, 1798.
  49. Ibid., May 15, 22, 1798.
  50. *Federalist*, January 14, 1799.
  51. In 1798–99 only Massachusetts equalled New Jersey in the number of indictments made under the Sedition law. James Smith, *Freedom's Fetters* (New York: Cornell University Press, 1956), p. 187.

52. *Centinel of Freedom*, August 14, 1798; November 6, 1799; *Aurora*, April 16, 1799; Smith, *Freedom's Fetters*, pp. 270–71; Miller, *Crisis in Freedom*, pp. 112–13; Elmer, *The Constitution and Government of the Province and State of New Jersey*, p. 98; Prince, *New Jersey's Jeffersonian Republicans*, p. 39.

53. *State Gazette and New Jersey Advertiser*, August 27, 1798; Prince, *New Jersey's Jeffersonian Republicans*, p. 38.

54. *Newark Gazette*, June 12, 1798; *Centinel of Freedom*, May 25, 1798; Dauer, *The Adams Federalists*, pp. 144–45.

55. Fee, *The Transition from Aristocracy to Democracy*, p. 84; *New Jersey Journal*, June 12, 1798.

56. *Centinel of Freedom*, August 14, 1798; Aaron Ogden to Jonathan Dayton, August 29, 1798, Dayton Manuscripts, New Jersey Historical Society.

57. *State Gazette and New Jersey Advertiser*, August 27, 1798; Prince, *New Jersey's Jeffersonian Republicans*, p. 38.

58. Smith, *Freedom's Fetters*, p. 168.

59. As Boudinot himself grudgingly acknowledged, it appeared more and more likely that the United States would return to her *"dear Sister's* [France's] *warm embraces"* as indeed she did, a development which rendered Collot's removal unnecessary. Smith, *Freedom's Fetters*, pp. 166–69, 175; Miller, *Crisis in Freedom*, pp. 189–90.

60. *Newark Gazette*, January 29, 1799.

61. Ibid., April 16, 1799.

62. *Votes and Proceedings of the General Assembly of the State of New Jersey*, 23rd Session, 2nd Sitting, p. 10; Fee, *The Transition from Aristocracy to Democracy*, p. 87; Frank M. Anderson, "Contemporary Opinion of the Virginia and Kentucky Resolutions," *American Historical Review* V (1899–1900): 52.

63. Prince, *New Jersey's Jeffersonian Republicans*, p. 35; Fee, *The Transition from Aristocracy to Democracy*, p. 87; *Federalist*, January 21, 1799.

64. *New Jersey Journal*, January 29, 1799; *Newark Gazette*, January 22, 29, 1799; Fee, *The Transition from Aristocracy to Democracy*, p. 88.

65. *New Jersey Journal*, January 29, 1799.

66. *Newark Gazette*, February 19, 1799; McCormick, *The History of Voting in New Jersey*, p. 109; Pole, "Jeffersonian Democracy and the Federalist Dilemma in New Jersey," pp. 276–77.

67. The previous legislature had seated Republican Henry Southard as chairman.

68. With a majority of only one, a single Federalist vote for the opposition's view would have meant defeat for the party. *Newark Gazette*, December 3, 1799; McCormick, *The History of Voting in New Jersey*, p. 109; Pole, "Jeffersonian Democracy and the Federalist Dilemma in New Jersey," pp. 277–79.

5

THE DECLINE OF THE NEW JERSEY FEDERALIST PARTY

After 1797 the power of the New Jersey Federalist party began to diminish.[1] The increasingly vital opposition that Federalists encountered after this date was not the sole cause of their difficulty. Rather, splits in the Federalist party's own ranks did much to foster the party's decline.

By 1798 Federalist disunity was in evidence on the floor of the New Jersey legislature, where party members fought each other over key state issues, forming alliances that shifted according to the particular issue at hand. First, there was dissension over the issue of slavery. On this question the Federalists from the strong Quaker areas of West Jersey were allied against the Federalists from East Jersey, the major slaveholding area of the state.[2] Two other reform issues also divided the New Jersey Federalists in the last years of the eighteenth century, although in less clear-cut fashion. These were the movements for revision of the state constitution and for the enactment of debtor relief laws.[3]

However, it was Federalist division over the Republican-sponsored district election bill which took the most immediate toll upon Federalist fortunes at the polls. The split between northern and southern Federalists on this occasion can be seen as the root cause of the Federalist party's loss of the majority of the sixth Congressional delegation, elected in October, 1798.[4]

Despite northern Federalists' plea that the district election bill be defeated, the southern Federalists helped to pass Republican leader Aaron Kitchell's measure. Indeed, the largest bloc of votes for the measure came from Federalist representatives of the southern counties.[5]

While northern Federalists saw in the passage of Kitchell's gerrymander the Congressional dethronement of the Federalists, southern Federalists saw in it a rare opportunity to gain direct Congressional representation for their area of the state. To the southerners' minds, only drastic action on their part would end northern Federalists' long-standing monopolization of Congressional seats, which at-large elections for Congress had made possible.[6]

Thus, the southern Federalists decided to seize their opportunity, and they did gain direct Congressional representation in 1798 as a result. But, as the northern Federalists had feared, the southerners' gain proved to be the party's loss. In October of 1798, the New Jersey Federalist party lost three of the five House seats to the Republicans.[7]

The Republican-sponsored gerrymander, directly responsible for the loss of two of these seats, had placed populous Republican Essex and Morris counties, contiguous geographically, in two separate districts. Essex County was bracketed with Federalist Bergen and Middlesex to form the Eastern District; Morris was paired with Sussex to form the Northern District.[8]

The Federalists lost both of these districts, the Eastern as well as the Northern. As might have been expected, the abundant Republican votes delivered by Essex in the Eastern District and Morris in the Northern District were sufficient to overcome the Federalist votes in both instances, even when, in the case of Essex, one Republican county was bracketed with two Federalist counties.[9]

Unlike the first two districts, the third Congressional district was not lost by the Federalists as a direct result of the north-south split, which was responsible for the passage of the gerrymander. The third district was lost primarily because of a local schism in the Federalist party.

In the Western District two Federalist nominees ran against each other, for Federalists in this region had allowed a breach in the party to affect the nomination process. Each wing of the party had named its own candidate. As a result, Western District Federalists were forced to split their party's vote, giving victory to the Republican candidate.[10]

In the late 1790s, the New Jersey Federalists' division over issues was not limited to state matters. By 1798 they also were divided over foreign policy.

Such party leaders as Governor Richard Howell, Jonathan Dayton, and Frederick Frelinghuysen wished for war.[11] Others, like Andrew Kirkpatrick, Richard Stockton, and Elias Boudinot, did not.[12] A number of southern New Jersey Federalists concurred with Adams in emphasizing the importance of the navy; many northern New Jersey Federalists placed their hopes in the army.[13]

Among the state's most active navy supporters were the Burlington County Federalists who met on July 21, 1798, and formulated a plan to help strengthen the navy by purchasing a warship for it.[14] Their venture was to be financed through a subscription.

Committees were chosen to collect funds in each township in the county. The meeting directed secretary William Griffith to publicize its proceedings throughout the state, hoping that news of its undertaking would inspire others to take like action. In anticipation of such a happy development, the Burlington County meeting named a committee with the responsibility of coordinating its activities with those of any other similarly empowered committees formed in the future.[15]

The militant Federalists of New Jersey were among those who sought and obtained army commissions.[16] Jonathan Dayton and Anthony Walton White both became brigadier generals.[17] Jonathan Rhea received the rank of colonel.[18] Aaron Ogden, named a lieutenant colonel, served as second in command of the New Jersey Eleventh Infantry Regiment, led by Governor Howell.[19]

Other militant New Jersey Federalists secured contracts to

supply the army. General Jonathan Dayton's father Elias Dayton was such a one. In the elder Dayton's case, the tendered contract was for the provision of rations.[20]

These militant Federalists of New Jersey were greatly pleased by the October, 1798, tour of former minister to France C. C. Pinckney which took him to three towns in northern New Jersey. His statement at the capital,

> ... [if] we would have Peace with France it must be obtained not by negociation, [sic] but by the sword,[21]

suited their convictions exactly.

But in February of 1799 the Hamiltonian Federalists in New Jersey received a severe blow. President Adams had named a peace envoy to the French republic. Knowing that the act probably would not have been accomplished had Adams received and taken the advice of his predominantly high Federalist cabinet, Elisha Boudinot, an ardent Hamiltonian, protested that Adams had

> ... done the thing wholly without the advice or knowledge of his counsel.[22]

When the peace envoys finally set sail on November 3, 1799, the state's extreme Federalists evinced deep disappointment and even embitterment.[23]

Perhaps only a crisis could have prompted the factionalized New Jersey Federalists to come together again in common cause. But a crisis is just what the Federalists felt they faced in 1800. To their minds, the very existence of the nation depended upon the outcome of the elections of 1800.[24] For these elections the New Jersey Federalists unified to the extent that they were able to put forth their most vigorous electoral efforts to date.[25] From the prenomination stage through the elections themselves the Federalists made unusual exertions, even to the point of emulating Republican techniques.

Prior to the first of the two popular elections of 1800, October's state legislative election, the New Jersey Federalists took steps toward becoming public-oriented. One way such a development revealed itself was in the Federalists' choice of a leading party organ in July, 1800.

It was the Trenton *Federalist,* a newspaper "edited in a popular spirit,"[26] that the Federalists adopted as their state organ at this time.[27] The *Federalist's* motto,

> The Public Will Shall Be Our Invariable Guide—the Public Good Our Friend,

clearly indicated the paper's emulation of the Republican technique of appealing to the public.[28] Furthermore, immediately upon its founding in 1798, the *Federalist* had shown considerable interest in the public viewpoint in its first-issue announcement that

> . . . a letter box [had been placed] at the window for the reception of communications.[29]

A second way the Federalists demonstrated a growing public orientation in 1800 was by making efforts to demonstrate that the party's nominations did not emanate from closed caucuses. For the state legislative election these efforts apparently were confined to three southern counties—Burlington, Gloucester, and Salem—the probable leaders in this movement.[30]

The proceedings of these counties' nomination meetings carefully noted that the members of the meetings had assembled in response to advance notice, given so that all might attend. From among those attending, each meeting elected a nominating committee, which, according to Burlington and Gloucester, contained representatives of every township. Each committee then retired for some time before presenting the meeting with a list of recommended nominees for the legislature and for county posts. Finally, the body of each meeting voted to accept its committee's recommendations.

In Burlington's case, every member of the meeting had been allowed a direct influence upon the choice of the nominees. Secretly, each member of the meeting first had made his own nominations. Then, the nominating committee made its selections from among the names provided by the members of the meeting.[31]

The address produced by the Burlington County meeting showed yet another Federalist attempt to steal the Republicans' thunder. Culminating the New Jersey Federalists' long-standing claim to being republicans no less than their opposition, the Burlingtonians made the party's claim graphic by referring to its members as Federal Republicans. Three months later the state party followed suit.[32]

At the same time the Federalists of 1800 were working to improve their own organization by such additional moves as attempting to narrow the field to party nominees and urging ticket voting,[33] they also were laboring to stymie the Republicans' organizational efforts. It was in Bergen County that the Federalists experienced the greatest success in the latter category.[34] As a result of Federalists efforts here, Bergen's Republican machinery disintegrated three weeks before the October election, leaving the Republicans without a viable opposition ticket. Under Federalist pressure all but one of the county's Republican candidates either had dropped out of the race entirely or had decided to run on the Federalist ticket.[35]

There was at least one electioneering technique in which the New Jersey Federalists of 1800 led the Republicans. That was in sending party spokesmen around the state.[36] After the elections, the Republicans paid tribute to the efficacy of this method of electioneering when they named the major circuit-riding Federalists, L. H. Stockton and William Griffith, as the two Federalists who had most damaged the Republicans' cause in 1800.[37]

Besides speaking, the Federalist circuit riders distributed political pieces during their traverse of the state.[38] Many Federalist polemics, especially those placed in wide distribution, were anti-Jefferson propaganda.[39] In particular, Jefferson was vilified for his irreligion.[40]

At this juncture, when the New Jersey Federalist party baldly stated the issue of the 1800 legislative-presidential election thusly,

[Should one] continue allegiance to God and a religious President or impiously declare for Jefferson and No God?[41]

the clergy finally began to give the New Jersey Federalists the
significant electoral aid for which they long had called.[42] Such
partisan actions of the clergy as speaking and writing in behalf
of the Federalists[43] resulted in the Republican charge that the
Federalist party was clergy-ridden.[44]

The Republicans also charged in 1800 that, like the clergy,
judges too were

incorporated with the Government [party] for political purposes.[45]

Most New Jersey judges were indeed Federalists and a number
of them did not hesitate to so indicate from the very bench
itself.[46] The sometimes published grand jury charge was the
major public medium Federalist judges used to express their
political opinions.[47] Federalist Judge Isaac Smith, for one,
helped his party emphasize the deism issue by his charge before
the grand jury of Gloucester County.[48]

As with some grand jury charges that year, the Fourth of July
celebration of 1800 also was used to further electoral efforts.[49]
With Federalists and Republicans generally meeting separately
since 1798, the commemoration of Independence Day had become more a political occasion than a patriotic one. Therefore,
for the organizers of the 1800 event, the partisan orations, some
given by Federalist clergymen, as well as the partisan toasts and
songs, constituted the substantive part of the proceedings.[50]

In the legislative campaign of 1800 the Federalists also re-
sorted to the device of the ethnic appeal. Addressing themselves to the large Dutch population of Somerset County, the
Federalists brandished their ticket, which was 100 percent
Dutch. Voting for the Republican ticket, the Federalists
pointed out,

. . . would exclude the Dutch interest from all share in the
legislature,

for the opposition's ticket did not contain the name of a single Dutchman.[51]

Federalist electoral efforts in 1800 continued through the polling itself. No less than the Republicans, the Federalists on this occasion exhibited behavior ranging from political astuteness to chicanery.[52] First, the Federalists provided printed ballots for the convenience of all voters, which also served to aid illiterates in voting for the party.[53] Then, to the consternation of the far from innocent Republicans, the Federalists accepted the votes of women and aliens, two groups whose possession of the franchise was debatable.[54] Finally, stepping completely over the line of propriety, the Federalists dispensed free food and liquor to the voters.[55] In Elizabeth the Federalists even nullified the secret ballot in an attempt to retain the votes of wavering members of the electorate. Jonathan Dayton had surmised that faltering voters, seeing that the back of the Federalist ballot was ruled in red, would know that the Federalist ballot box watchers could tell if they bolted the party. Thus, he believed, they would be less likely to vote Republican than they would under conditions of secrecy.[56]

To the Federalists' delight the results of the October, 1800, election gave them a margin of more than three to one in the state legislature.[57] In many counties Federalist legislators assumed seats that had been held by Republicans in the previous session.[58]

Then, at joint meeting, encountering no opposition from the demoralized Republicans, the Federalists unanimously elected their candidates for governor, secretary of state, and speaker of the assembly.[59] Following this, the Federalists chose electors who subsequently cast all of New Jersey's electoral votes for President Adams.[60] Having thus exhibited a predominance absent in the recent past, it is no wonder that the party joyfully proclaimed, "Federalism . . . has completely triumphed in New Jersey."[61]

Only days later the euphoric Federalists began to prepare for December's Congressional election. In anticipation of the second popular election of 1800, the New Jersey Federalists took the additional and, for them, unprecedented step of creating formal, state-wide machinery.

The Federalist state meeting in 1800 even preceded that of the Republicans by about three weeks. However, the ticket that emerged from this November 13 meeting at the State House actually was a product of an earlier informal closed caucus held in Trenton.[62] In reality, the "open" meeting merely endorsed the ticket; it did not select it.

However, as in the case of some of the earlier county meetings, which had nominated legislative candidates, the planners were anxious that the state meeting not appear to be closed. Therefore they strove to see that each county was represented, and not solely by lawyers and legislators,[63] whom the Republicans continually claimed ruled the party to the detriment of the common people.

The exact composition of the November 13 state Federalist meeting never was fully revealed. But, according to the Federalists, every county and moreover the entire Federalist interest was represented.[64]

Still, it is probable that state legislators dominated the meeting. By the Federalists' own admission, nearly every Federalist then holding a state legislative seat attended.[65] When it came to choosing one individual from each county to head that county's campaign, a legislator was chosen whenever possible. Nonlegislators were appointed to head the campaign in only three out of the thirteen counties—Essex, Sussex, and Morris—none of which possessed any Federalist legislators.[66]

In its address, the state meeting urged the Federalists of New Jersey to unify in imitation of the Republicans.[67] Moreover, the meeting's proceedings called upon the several counties to hold meetings, endorse the ticket, and work for its election, an appeal which did not go unheeded.[68]

From the New Jersey Federalists' behavior it is evident that their machinery was "operated from the top."[69] Far from functioning on the initiative of the grassroots, the state party made the decisions and passed down instructions to be carried out by the counties.[70]

The state meeting failed to mention townships not solely because it was the counties which were to dictate to the townships but also because, traditionally, the New Jersey Federalists were less concerned with the township level as opposed to the county one. As Pole has stated, for the Federalists the county was primary, the township secondary.[71]

Yet inactivity at the township level was not the result. According to state Republican leader Joseph Bloomfield, during the Congressional campaign of 1800 Federalists possessed scores of committeemen in every township.[72]

Indeed, until November 26, 1800, the New Jersey Federalists publicly entertained hope that Adams would be reelected,[73] and their Congressional campaign profited from this hope and the momentum the state party had gained from its recent series of local victories.[74] But shortly thereafter the Federalists' high hopes turned to anxiety.[75] The outcome of the presidential election now hung on South Carolina's doubtful vote.

Then, on December 3, 1800, that state gave the election to the Republicans. Thereafter, although the New Jersey Federalists continued their electoral efforts,[76] they could not but be handicapped by the revelation that the Republicans had won the presidency.

The New Jersey Republicans, on the other hand, used their victory to great advantage in the weeks remaining before the December 23–24 Congressional election.[77] It is certain that the Republicans' presidential triumph was most influential in helping the New Jersey party narrowly gain the first all-Republican Congressional delegation.[78]

Even at its peak in 1800 the New Jersey Federalist organization had been inferior to the Republican one.[79] Now, in 1801, the gap between the efficacy of the Federalist and Republican organizations in the state widened considerably, for the Federalists' formal statewide machinery disintegrated after the election of 1800.[80]

However, in some areas, primarily in the southern and central portions of the state, New Jersey Federalists did exhibit county and township level machinery in 1801.[81] In fact, so active were southern and central New Jersey Federalists during the legislative campaign of 1801 that Joseph Bloomfield depicted them as "men determined to win at any cost."[82]

As in 1800, the Federalists of some central and southern New Jersey counties held "public" nomination meetings, a fact the *Federalist* took care to publicize, particularly after the fact.[83] Also, the Federalist party organs, located in central New Jersey, issued pleas for party loyalty.[84]

Independent Federalist candidates were publicly exhorted to resign, as they never had been before, to avoid dividing the Federalist vote.[85] Noting regretfully that a number of Federalists were not overly "fond of trouble," the principal Federalist organ outlined still a third method of resigning for those independent candidates who found the first two it had given to be "too troublesome."[86]

The "friends of the late wise and virtuous administration"[87] were urged to vote the full Federalist ticket in the forthcoming state legislative election.[88] Particularly in Burlington County, Federalists in 1801 were warned against voting for "wolves in sheeps' clothing," former Federalists who now were running as Republicans.[89]

In one of their calls for unity in 1801 the Federalists included a remark designed to appeal particularly to their long-time faithful supporters, the Dutch.

It is the motto of the United Provinces of Holland, that unity creates strength,

the Federalist press noted.[90]

Other Federalist appeals to the large Dutch population, made in 1801, were far less subtle. First the Federalists pointed out that the Republicans' friends, the French, had defiled their homeland. Then they printed an address to the Dutch in their native tongue, which the Dutch still used in New Jersey.[91]

Most unusual of all, in 1801 the Federalists made a concerted public attempt to woo the "mechanics" of the state, probably for the first time. The so-called Republicans were not the mechanics' true friends, the Federalists informed them. In spite of their "equalizing professions," the Republican leaders, the Federalists alleged, had definitively revealed themselves to be aristocrats in disguise the previous Fourth of July, when they had refused to allow the mechanics to be seated at their table. As a result of that incident, the Federalists declared, it should be clear to all mechanics that the Republicans merely had used them to gain power, a fact the Federalists urged the artisans to remember and act upon during the forthcoming election.[92]

But while the Federalists were active in Central and South Jersey in 1801, so were the Republicans. As in 1800 the Republicans again regarded these traditionally Federalist counties as the key to Republican success in the state.[93] Unsuccessful in their vigorous attempt of October, 1800, the Republicans only redoubled their efforts in 1801.

Among the many additional steps the Republicans took to win the Federalist areas of the state in 1801 was the founding of the Trenton *True American*, whose mission it was to help Republicanize Central and South Jersey.[94] It succeeded.

For the first time, the New Jersey Federalists lost the southern counties of Cumberland and Salem and the central county of Monmouth. Also, the formerly mixed county of Hunterdon went Republican.

These first-time losses for the Federalists coupled with their usual defeat in the Republican counties of Essex, Morris, and Sussex brought them down. In 1801, the Federalist interest was reduced to a minority party, a development which signaled the end of the Federalist era in New Jersey.[95] Among the myriad reasons for the New Jersey Federalists' defeat two were paramount: the state party's support of the national administration's unpopular policies, connected with the Quasi-War, and the waning of the age of deference.

NOTES

1. Sher, "Party Battles in Middlesex County," p. 41.
2. *State Gazette and New Jersey Advertiser*, March 20, 1798; *Minutes of the Legislative Council*, 24th Session, 1st Sitting (November 11, 1799, November

13, 1799), pp. 20–30; Arthur Zilversmit, *The First Emancipation: The Abolition of Slavery in the North* (Chicago: University of Chicago Press, 1967), pp. 175, 192–99; MS. Minutes of the New Jersey Abolition Society, Quaker Collection, Haverford College.

3. *Centinel of Freedom*, February 13, March 20, 27, 1798; *Federalist*, November 19, 1798; March 25, 1799. Despite their party's claim to being the champion of the common man, leading Republican legislators voted against debtor relief laws. Henry Southard even declared that the surest way to secure payment for a debt was to seize the person. *New Jersey Journal*, January 30, 1798; Pole, "Jeffersonian Democracy and the Federalist Dilemma in New Jersey," p. 290; Pole "The Reform of Suffrage and Representation in New Jersey," p. 203.

4. *Newark Gazette and New Jersey Advertiser*, November 6, 1798; *Guardian*, November 6, 1798.

5. *Minutes of the Legislative Council*, 22nd Session, 2nd Sitting, pp. 41, 51–53; *Votes and Proceedings of the General Assembly*, 22nd Session, 2nd Sitting, pp. 45–46.

6. Sher, "Party Battles in Middlesex County," p. 56; Fee, *The Transition from Aristocracy to Democracy*, p. 96. Truly, the Federalist candidates for the at-large or general Congressional elections, held from 1789 to 1796, had included only one southern New Jersey Federalist. The state's northern Federalists were not unaware of the southerners' discontent on this score. Recently the northern legislators had agreed to support the appointment of a southerner as United States senator. Aaron Ogden to Jonathan Dayton, January 25, 1799, Ely Collection, New Jersey Historical Society. But, obviously, this did not satisfy the southerners.

7. *Federalist*, November 19, 1798.

8. *Minutes of the Legislative Council of the State of New Jersey*, 22nd Session, 2nd Sitting, p. 41.

9. *Newark Gazette and New Jersey Advertiser*, October 16, 1798.

10. *Federalist*, November 19, 1798; *Guardian*, October 23, 1798.

11. Frederick Frelinghuysen to Jonathan Dayton, April 1, 1799, Gratz Collection, Historical Society of Pennsylvania; Aaron Ogden to Jonathan Dayton, January 25, 1799, Ely Collection, New Jersey Historical Society; Richard Howell to Timothy Pickering, July 13, December 4, 1798, Massachusetts Historical Society; Kurtz, *The Presidency of John Adams*, p. 387.

12. "Letters from Richard Stockton to John Rutherfurd," pp. 181–83, 85, 87; Elias Boudinot to Mrs. Boudinot, June 21, 1798, Stimson-Boudinot Collection, Princeton University Library. In fact, in October of 1798 President Adams included Richard Stockton on his list of four men from among whom he futilely suggested to his cabinet that a peace envoy to France be selected. New Jersey's William Paterson also was on Adams' list. John Adams to Timothy Pickering, October 20, 1798 in Charles Francis Adams, *The Works of John Adams, Second President of the United States with a Life of the Author*, vol. VIII (Boston: Little, Brown and Company, 1854), p. 609; Kurtz, *The Presidency of John Adams*, pp. 341–42.

13. *Federalist*, April 22, 1799; De Conde, *The Quasi-War*, p. 112.

14. It was off nearby Egg Harbor in South Jersey that the new navy had taken its first prize about three weeks earlier. With only a "small . . . [converted] merchant packet," the Americans managed to capture a larger French vessel. De Conde, *The Quasi-War*, p. 127.

15. *Federalist*, July 23, 1799; *Newark Gazette and New Jersey Advertiser*, July 31, 1798.

16. One New Jersey Republican referred to these militant state Federalists as the "fiery" ones. Mary Jamieson, ed., *The Letters of Moore Furman* (n.p.: Daughters of the American Revolution, 1912), p. 114.

17. *Federalist*, August 27, 1798; Aaron Ogden to Jonathan Dayton, August 29, 1798, Jonathan Dayton Papers, New Jersey Historical Society. To General Washington's mind, too many of the army's brigadier generalships had been conferred upon Jerseyans. Fitzpatrick, *The Writings of George Washington*, vol. XXXVI. pp. 442–43.

18. Jonathan Dayton to Richard Howell, April 10, 1799, Anthony Walton White Papers, Rutgers University Library.

19. Thayer, *As We Were: The Story of Old Elizabethtown*, p. 198. It was Aaron Ogden who spearheaded a fruitless movement to develop a 2,000-man New Jersey Legion of Volunteers, designed as an augumentary force. Aaron Ogden to Jonathan Dayton, July 9, 1798, Jonathan Dayton Papers, Rutgers University Library; Richard Howell to Timothy Pickering, December 4, 1798, Timothy Pickering Papers, Massachusetts Historical Society.

20. James McHenry to Elias Dayton, September 13, 1799, Jonathan Dayton Papers, New Jersey Historical Society; Aaron Ogden Papers, Morristown National Historical Park.

21. De Conde, *The Quasi-War*, p. 164; Marvin Zahniser, *Charles Cotesworth Pinckney* (Chapel Hill: University of North Carolina Press, 1967), p. 198; *Newark Gazette and New Jersey Advertiser*, October 16, November 6, 1798; *Federalist*, November 5, 1798; *Porcupine's Gazette*, October 31, 1798; *State Gazette Extra*, October 30, 1798, Historical Society of Pennsylvania; *Gazette of the United States*, November 3, 1798.

22. Mrs. Boudinot to Elisha Boudinot, February 26, 1799, Princeton University Library.

23. Anthony Walton White Papers, Rutgers University Library; Kurtz, *The Presidency of John Adams*, p. 334; Miller, *The Federalist Era*, p. 245; De Conde, *The Quasi-War*, p. 187. To effect the departure of the stalled peace mission, President Adams had come to Trenton, New Jersey, on October 10, 1799, for that town was once again the nation's temporary capital because of an outbreak of yellow fever in Philadelphia. Hamilton, who had left troops that were stationed in Newark, as well as Secretaries Pickering, Wolcott, and McHenry, tried assiduously to prevent the peace envoys from setting sail, but Adams' wish prevailed. De Conde, *The Quasi-War*, pp. 219, 346; Mitchell, "Alexander Hamilton in New Jersey," p. 111; Kurtz, *The Presidency of John Adams*, pp.

106 THE NEW JERSEY FEDERALISTS

388–89; Dauer, *The Adams Federalists*, p. 240; *New Jersey State Gazette*, October 15, 1799.

24. *Federalist*, September 30, 1800; *Newark Gazette and New Jersey Advertiser*, September 16, 1800; Marshall Smelser, "Jacobin Phrenzy: The Menace of Monarchy, Plutocracy, and Anglophobia," *Review of Politics* XXI (1959): p. 239; John R. Howe, "Republican Thought and the Political Violence of the 1790's," *American Quarterly* XIX (1967, no. 2); p. 149.

25. L. H. Stockton to Elisha Boudinot, August 19, 1800, Stockton Papers, Princeton University Library; Jamieson, *The Letters of Moore Furman*, p. 118; Prince, *New Jersey's Jeffersonian Republicans*, p. 57; *Philadelphia Gazette*, October 24, 30, 1800; Jonathan Dayton to Aaron Ogden, December 16, 1800, Historical Society of Pennsylvania. Efforts were made to choose as nominees for legislative posts those individuals who were "most likely to unite the Federalist interest." *Federalist*, September 30, 1800. Regarding the presidential contest, even Hamiltonian Jonathan Dayton conceded that "the great object of uniting Adams and Pinckney universally in the same ticket . . . [was] the only means of [Federalist] success." Therefore, he said that like other "good Federalists" in the state he heartily disapproved of Hamilton's efforts to the contrary. Jonathan Dayton to Aaron Ogden, November 28, 1800, Rutgers University Library.

26. Fischer, *The Revolution of American Conservatism*, p. 330.

27. By May of 1800 leading Republican organizer Aaron Kitchell had conceded that the most popularly oriented of the Federalist papers, the Trenton *Federalist*, was the one that best reflected "the temper of the [Federalist] party." Ebenezer Elmer to Col. [David] Moore, May 12, 1800, Historical Society of Pennsylvania. (This letter constitutes, in part, a copy of Kitchell's earlier letter to Elmer.) Three months later the Trenton *Federalist*'s rivalry with the much older Federalist *New Jersey State Gazette* ended when the latter paper collapsed. *New York Times*, September 4, 1932. Besides the *Federalist*, the New Jersey party possessed two other party organs in 1800, the *Newark Gazette* and the New Brunswick *Guardian*. The party also used Philadelphia papers, which circulated in South Jersey, an area of the state which lacked local newspapers. *Federalist*, September 30, 1800.

28. *Federalist*, July 9, 1798. In fact the *Federalist*'s device was a virtual paraphrase of a motto previously displayed by that most avid of New Jersey Republican newspapers, the *Centinel of Freedom*. On the Republican paper's masthead the motto had read, "The Public Will Our Guide—The Public Good our End." *Centinel of Freedom*, May 3, 1797.

29. "The Founding of the State Gazette," *Trenton Times*, October 16, 1932.

30. The similarity in the way these three nominating meetings were conducted also furnishes indirect evidence of Federalist coordination above the single county level. For other evidence on this point see L. H. Stockton to Elisha Boudinot, August 19, 1800, Stockton Papers, Princeton University Library. There is no significant evidence, however, of formal, statewide Federalist machinery such as the Republicans possessed for the election of October, 1800.

Cunningham, *The Jeffersonian-Republicans . . . 1789–1801*, p. 158.

31. *Federalist*, September 30, 1800; *Newark Gazette and New Jersey Advertiser*, September 16, 1800; Francis B. Lee, *New Jersey as a Colony and as a State*, vol. III (New York, 1902), p. 41; *Address to the Federal-Republicans of Burlington County . . . by a Committee Appointed at the Court House on August 30, 1800* (Trenton: Sherman, Mershon, and Thomas, 1800).

32. *Address to the Federal-Republicans of Burlington County . . . by a Committee Appointed at the Court House on August 30, 1800; Address to the Federal-Republicans of the State of New Jersey. . . .* (Trenton: Sherman, Mershon, and Thomas, November 13, 1800). The Federalist slate of presidential electors also bore the heading "Federal-Republican." *Philadelphia Gazette*, November 1, 1800.

33. *Federalist*, November 25, 1800; *Address to the Federal-Republicans of Burlington County. . . .*, p. 8; *Federalist*, September 30, 1800; Cunningham, *The Jeffersonian-Republicans . . . 1789–1801*, p. 254; *Address to the Federal-Republicans of New Jersey. . . .*, p. 17.

34. In Burlington County, however, the Federalists did succeed in frustrating the Republicans' desire to form a democratic association. Joseph Bloomfield to Ebenezer Elmer, April 20, 1800, Elmer Papers, Rutgers University Library. And in Gloucester County the Federalists were so persistent in their efforts to infiltrate the Republican organization that the opposition had to adjourn their county meeting to the cramped quarters of a private home in order to rid themselves of the Federalists, who had appeared at the meeting convened at the town's schoolhouse. Cunningham, *The Jeffersonian-Republicans . . . 1789–1801*, p. 157; *Gloucester County: Jersey . . . Address to the Inhabitants of Gloucester. . . .*, [1800], Historical Society of Pennsylvania.

35. *Centinel of Freedom*, September 30, October 7, 1800.

36. *Aurora*, October 8, 1800; Prince, *New Jersey's Jeffersonian Republicans*, p. 58.

36. Joseph Bloomfield to Dear Doctor [Ebenezer Elmer], January 25, 1802, Gratz Collection, Historical Society of Pennsylvania.

38. Federalists also used the mails to send some material to leaders in other counties for distribution there. Locally, county meetings handled the distribution of certain handbills and pamphlets. L. H. Stockton to Elisha Boudinot, August 19, 1800, Stockton Papers, Princeton University Library.

39. The New Jersey legislative campaign was run primarily on the presidential question, for the new legislators would choose the presidential electors.

40. Elmer, *The Constitution and Government of the Province and State of New Jersey*, p. 130.

41. *Newark Gazette and New Jersey Advertiser*, September 22, December 9, 1800; Chambers, *Political Parties in a New Nation*, p. 153.

42. *Aurora*, October 14, 1800; Fee, *The Transition from Aristocracy to Democracy*, p. 112; Gary B. Nash, "The American Clergy and the French Revolution," *William and Mary Quarterly*, Third Series XXII (July, 1965);

407–9. Earlier, New Jersey Federalists had received a measure of clerical support against the Republicans. See, for example, [Rev.] Uzal Ogden, *The Deist Unmasked* (Newark, New Jersey, November, 1795); [Rev.] Holloway Hunt, *Discourse on the Necessity of Unity in America* (Newton, New Jersey: Hopkins and Smith, July, 1798), Papers of Rev. Solomon Froeligh, Rutgers University Library; [Rev.] Uzal Ogden, *The Antidote to Deism* (Newark, New Jersey, 1798); and the Rev. T. Grant's Fourth of July oration in the *Philadelphia Gazette*, October 19, 1799, which reads in part, "O' Adams; wise, dignified, firm, enlightened statesman and patriot, thy country's pride and salvation. . . ." But up to 1800 the New Jersey Federalists complained that the clerical support they had received was insufficient. Fee, *The Transition from Aristocracy to Democracy*, p. 112; Boudinot, *The Life, Public Service, Addresses and Letters of Elias Boudinot*, II; 119.

43. Of all the polemics written by New Jersey Federalist clergymen the following one probably most irritated the Republicans: William Linn, *Serious Considerations on the Election of a President*. . . . (Trenton: Sherman, Mershon, and Thomas, 1800). Republican leader Joseph Bloomfield referred to it as "Parson Linn's poisonous pamphlet." Joseph Bloomfield to Dear Doctor [Ebenezer Elmer], January 25, 1802, Gratz Collection, Historical Society of Pennsylvania.

44. *Address to the Federal-Republicans of New Jersey.* . . ., p. 10; *Aurora*, October 14, 1800.

45. *Aurora*, October 14, 1800.

46. Rosenberg, "William Paterson: New Jersey's Nation-Maker," pp. 29, 31–32.

47. *Aurora*, January 21, 1797; *Federalist*, January 30, 1798; *State Gazette*, February 13, 1798; *Guardian*, April 16, 1799. One Federalist state judge himself admitted that grand jury charges of the day often did not fulfill their original function of explaining to the jury the nature of its duty. Rather, he said, frequently they "assumed the form of [a political] address." *New Jersey State Gazette*, February 10, 1800.

48. *Philadelphia Gazette*, October 14, 1800.

49. Pasler, "The Federalist Party in Burlington County, New Jersey," M. A. thesis, p. 78; *State Gazette*, July 10, 1798; *Centinel of Freedom*, July 8, 1798; *Newark Gazette and New Jersey Advertiser*, June 12, 1798; *Guardian*, July 10, 1798; *Federalist*, August 6, 1798; Urquhart, *A History of the City of Newark, New Jersey*, I, 472–73; *Philadelphia Gazette*, October 19, 1799; Sher, "Party Battles in Middlesex County," p. 50.

50. At the Burlington celebration the Rev. Dr. C. H. Wharton gave an anti-Jeffersonian speech and in Flemington the song "Adams and Liberty" was sung. *Federalist*, July 15, 1800; *Newark Gazette and New Jersey Advertiser*, June 24, 1800. (The latter newspaper announced in advance the plans made for the forthcoming celebration.) "Hail Columbia," a song written by sometime Jerseyan Joseph Hopkinson, was a particular favorite of Newark Federalists. Urquhart, *A History of . . . Newark, New Jersey*, I; 472–73; George Douglas How-

ard Cole, ed., *Letters from William Corbett to Edward Thornton, 1797–1800* (New York: Oxford University Press, 1959), p. 65. For additional information on Fourth of July orations given in New Jersey see the collections of these at Rutgers University Library (a total of 350 may be found at Rutgers), New Jersey Historical Society and New-York Historical Society, as well as Frederick Lawton, "Fourth of July Orations," *The Journal of the Rutgers University Library* XVII (June, 1954):63. There is no record of Federalists using fireworks at the Fourth of July celebration of 1800. However, they did sometimes use them for political purposes. Once, in 1799, the Federalists employed fireworks to spell out "J.A. and G.W.," graphically linking the campaigning President with the venerable George Washington. *New Jersey State Gazette*, October 15, 1799.

51. *Federalist*, September 30, 1800.

52. Pole, "Jeffersonian Democracy and the Federalist Dilemma in New Jersey," pp. 291–92.

53. McCormick, *The History of Voting in New Jersey*, p. 104.

54. Pole, "The Reform of Suffrage and Representation in New Jersey," Ph.D. diss., p. 213; Pasler, "The Federalist Party in Burlington County, New Jersey," M. A. thesis, pp. 21–23; *Centinel of Freedom*, December 9, 1800; William Whitehead, "The Origin, Practice, and Prohibition of Female Suffrage in New Jersey," *Proceedings of the New Jersey Historical Society* VIII (January, 1858): 103; Mary Philbrook, "Women's Suffrage in New Jersey Prior to 1807," *Proceedings of the New Jersey Historical Society* LVII (April, 1939): 93; *Philadelphia Gazette*, October 20, 1800; *Federalist*, October 28, 1800. Women and aliens continued to vote in New Jersey until 1807, when by law they were explicitly disenfranchised. *New Jersey Laws*, 32nd Session, 1st Sitting (November 6, 1807); Williamson, *American Suffrage*, p. 181. According to at least one scholar, "the earliest and most important instance of voting by women in the United States" occurred in New Jersey in 1797. At that time the Republicans had termed the phenomenon a Federalist one, a charge they repeated in subsequent years. Edward Raymond Turner, "Women's Suffrage in New Jersey, 1790–1807," *Smith College Studies in History* I (July, 1916): 186; *Aurora*, October 20, 27, 1797; *Centinel of Freedom*, October 18, 1797; February 17, 1807.

55. Pasler, "The Federalist Party in Burlington County, New Jersey," M. A. thesis, pp. 94–96, 104–7; *Federalist*, October 26, 1800.

56. Jonathan Dayton to Aaron Ogden, December 16, 1800, Gratz Collection, Historical Society of Pennsylvania.

57. The Republicans had hoped to have much greater success than they did in the legislative election of 1800. Joseph Bloomfield to Ebenezer Elmer, April 20, 1800, Rutgers University Library; Jamieson, *The Letters of Moore Furman*, p. 15.

58. "Roster of the Twenty-fourth New Jersey State Legislature," *Minutes of the Joint Meeting*, 24th Session, 1st Sitting (October 30, 1799); "Roster of the Twenty-fifth New Jersey State Legislature," *Minutes of the Joint Meeting*, 25th Session, 1st Sitting (October 31, 1800).

59. *Philadelphia Gazette,* November 1, 1800; *Guardian,* November 5, 1800.

60. *Philadelphia Gazette,* November 1, 1800.

61. *Guardian,* November 5, 1800.

62. Richard Stockton to Aaron Ogden, November 6, 1800, Princeton University Library. This was equally true in the case of the Republicans' Congressional "nominating" convention of December 2, 1800, which actually only sanctioned a previously-chosen ticket. Prince, *New Jersey's Jeffersonian Republicans,* pp. 62–63. Without acknowledging that they had proceeded in much the same fashion, the Federalists publicly refuted the Republicans' claim that Republican "delegates . . . from ten counties" had selected their Congressional ticket. The Federalists also reprimanded the Republicans for stating that their chosen candidates were farmers, "like the great body of voters in New Jersey. John Condict and Ebenezer Elmer are, by all accounts, what are usually called Doctors in the country—As to Jemmy Mott, it will be hard to prove that he has seen a plow in many a day—This Mr. Helms, as you modestly call him, is . . . a General; and as to Henry Southard, he has long since abandoned the peaceable profession of a farmer for the trade of Jacobinism." *Guardian,* December 17, 1800. But, although the Republicans at this time did not have either democratic organization or farmer candidates any more than the Federalists, the Republicans were wise enough to pretend they did at every turn. Prince, *New Jersey's Jeffersonian Republicans,* p. 72. While the Republicans allowed each county to select delegates to their state meeting by popular choice and called their candidates farmers, in response to their realization that most New Jersey voters were self-sufficient farmers, the Federalists never revealed how the persons who attended their state meeting had been selected and questioned the making of a special appeal to the largest group of New Jersey voters. Said the Federalists, "Who told you [Republicans] . . . that all the voters in New Jersey were farmers—What; are there no tradesmen—no mechanics—no merchants—no men of private fortunes?" *Guardian,* December 17, 1800.

63. Richard Stockton to Aaron Ogden, November 6, 1800, Richard Stockton Additional Papers, Princeton University Library.

64. *Federalist,* November 25, 1800.

65. *Newark Gazette and New Jersey Advertiser,* December 16, 1800.

66. "Roster of the Twenty-fifth New Jersey State Legislature," *Minutes of the Joint Meeting,* 25th Session, 1st Sitting (October 31, 1800); *Federalist,* November 25, 1800.

67. *Address to the Federal-Republicans of New Jersey . . .,* p. 16.

68. *Federalist,* November 18, December 2, 16, 1800; *Newark Gazette and New Jersey Advertiser,* December 16, 1800.

69. For a like conclusion regarding Massachusetts, see Banner, *To the Hartford Convention,* p. 248.

70. Pole, "Jeffersonian Democracy and the Federalist Dilemma in New Jersey," pp. 264–65.

71. Ibid., p. 266.

72. Joseph Bloomfield to Ebenezer Elmer, December 28, 1800, Joseph Bloomfield Papers, New Jersey Historical Society.

73. *Guardian*, November 26, 1800.

74. At this time Federalist optimism about the forthcoming Congressional election contrasted sharply with Republican pessimism. On November 25, 1800, one leading New Jersey Republican expressed the opinion that the Republicans surely would lose the Congressional election. Jamieson, *Letters of Moore Furman*, p. 116.

75. Jonathan Dayton to Aaron Ogden, November 28, 1800, Jonathan Dayton Papers, Rutgers University Library.

76. Jonathan Dayton to Aaron Ogden, December 16, 1800, Historical Society of Pennsylvania.

77. *Address of the Republican Committee of the County of Gloucester, New Jersey*, December 15, 1800, Library of Congress.

78. Cunningham, *The Jeffersonian-Republicans . . . 1789–1801*, pp. 246–47; Prince, *New Jersey's Jeffersonian Republicans*, p. 61; *Guardian*, January 8, 1801. "The margin of Republican victory was narrow—by fewer than 800 votes out of a total of more than 25,000." Robert M. Rodgers, "Some Phases of New Jersey History in the Jeffersonian Period," M. A. thesis, University of Chicago, 1931, p. 7.

79. Yet, while it did not compare favorably with the Republicans', the New Jersey Federalist organization of 1800 was one of the most advanced Federalist organizations in the nation. Fischer, *The Revolution of American Conservatism*, pp. 52–53.

80. McCormick, *The Second American Party System*, p. 127.

81. *Guardian*, September 17, 24, October 1, 18, 1801; *Federalist*, July 28, August 13, 18, 25, September 1, 15, 22, 1801; Pasler, "The Federalist Party in Burlington County, New Jersey," M.A. thesis, pp. 123–24, 128; Joseph Bloomfield to Ebenezer Elmer, August 25, 1801, Ely Collection, New Jersey Historical Society.

82. Fee, *The Transition from Aristocracy to Democracy*, p. 123; Joseph Bloomfield to Ebenezer Elmer, August 25, 1801, Ely Collection, Historical Society of Pennsylvania.

83. *Federalist*, July 28, August 13, 18, September 29, 1801; Pasler, "The Federalist Party in Burlington County, New Jersey," M. A. thesis, p. 123.

84. *Guardian*, September 24, 1801.

85. Scattering of the party's vote because of the existence of independent candidates was a long-standing problem for the Federalists. The first year the Republicans ran a Congressional ticket, there were five independent Republican candidates in the race but thirty-one Federalist ones. And the fledgling Republicans gave their independents only 20 percent of the Republican vote while the Federalists gave their independents 30 percent of the Federalist vote. *State Gazette and New Jersey Advertiser*, December 27, 1796, January 28, 1797.

86. *Federalist*, September 29, 1801.

112   THE NEW JERSEY FEDERALISTS

87. *Federalist,* April 7, 1801.

88. *Federalist,* October 13, 1801. Federalists could not but express consternation at the high degree of party loyalty demonstrated by the Republicans. *Federalist,* September 1, 1801.

89. *Federalist,* September 29, October 13, 1801.

90. *Guardian,* September 24, 1801.

91. Ibid., September 24, October 8, 1801; American Council of Learned Studies, *Surnames in the United States Census of 1790,* p. 372; Hanson, "The Interior Architecture and Household Furnishings of Bergen County, New Jersey, 1800–1810," M. A. thesis, p. 19.

92. *Federalist,* October 6, 1801.

93. Ebenezer Elmer to Col. [David] Moore, May 12, 1800, Gratz Collection, Historical Society of Pennsylvania.

94. Joseph Bloomfield to Ebenezer Elmer, Dec. 28, 1800, Joseph Bloomfield Papers, New Jersey Historical Society; Joseph Sickler, *The History of Salem County, New Jersey* (Salem: Sunbeam Publishing Company, 1937), p. 185.

95. Federalist loss of New Jersey in 1801 had been predicted by William Griffith a few days before the election. William Griffith to Elisha Boudinot, October 10, 1801, Princeton University Library. Except for one year, 1812–1813, the New Jersey Federalists never again would dominate the state.

6

NEW JERSEY FEDERALISTS
AS THE OPPOSITION

After October, 1801, the New Jersey Federalists gained dominance of the state only once, during the year 1812–1813. The history of the New Jersey party from 1801 onward, then, generally is not one of success in the absolute sense. In fact, on the statewide level, it primarily is a story of failure.

Still, if a story of failure, it is the story of a highly significant failure. For in defeat the New Jersey Federalist party proved to be a worthy opponent,[1] one which, even after being reduced to the county level in 1816, doggedly hung on until the last vestiges of the first party system had disappeared.

Soon after becoming the minority, the New Jersey Federalist leaders dug in their heels and thereafter generally fought the good fight, although year after year they repeatedly failed to win the state.[2] To the party faithful, defectors were the objects of scorn, equally in the early years as in the later ones.[3] Such men were unprincipled office-seekers, the consistent Federalists declared, a charge they buttressed periodically with a list of defectors together with the high offices the deserters received after their political conversion.[4]

In their intensive, albeit uneven, drive to regain dominance the minority Federalists always depended upon the "freedom of suffrage" to reestablish them in power.[5] And, to obtain the people's suffrage, the New Jersey Federalists freely entered the political fray.[6]

113

The primary public outlet for political invective was the partisan press, and here the Federalist printers of New Jersey usually gave as good as they received. All of the Federalists continuously engaged their rival editors and participated with them in the duels in print that often descended to the level of name-calling.

To the Trenton *Federalist* the Trenton *True American* always was the "Gibbet of Infamy" and its editor the "Gibbetman."[7] Also, typically, the Federalist *Newark Gazette* of November 22, 1803, refers to the Republican Newark *Centinel of Freedom* as providing

> . . .weekly effusions of ignorance, stupidity and rancorous malevolence.[8]

In the same vein, the Federalist New Brunswick *Guardian* scored the "malicious falsehoods" of that "sickly, puny" newspaper, the Republican New Brunswick *Fredonian*.[9]

Federalist political quarrels, begun in print and verbally, sometimes went so far as to result in Federalist-instigated physical violence.[10] For example, a few months after the Federalists had lost the state, two young Burlingtonian Federalists, William Coxe, Jr. and William Pearson, assaulted their long-time Republican foe Ebenezer Tucker.[11] Later, young Federalist Garret D. Wall publicly whipped James J. Wilson, the troublesome editor of the most powerful Republican organ in the state.[12]

During the period of their minority, New Jersey Federalists' electoral efforts normally did elicit substantial support at the polls, enough in fact to challenge the Republicans' hold on the legislature four times in the first dozen years of the Federalist party's minority and three times in the second dozen years. In 1801, their first year as the minority party, the Federalists won 42 percent of the legislature; in 1802 50 percent; in 1806 49 percent; and in 1808 44 percent.

Even in other minority years when Federalist numbers in the legislature were not so great, the party's strength rarely descended to the point of negligibility. For nine of the sixteen

minority years not accounted for by the peak years mentioned
above, Federalists constituted between 35 percent and 40 percent of the New Jersey legislature. In only six of the party's some
twenty-four years as the minority, four of them during the Era
of Good Feelings, did the Federalists comprise as little as 29–30
percent of the legislature, and in only one year, 1820, did the
Federalists fall as low as 23 percent.

New Jersey Federalism's minority strength in the state legislature was based upon the existence of several county strongholds, which generally continued to support the party after
1801. Five counties out of the thirteen, Bergen in northern
New Jersey; Middlesex and Somerset in the central section; and
Burlington and Cape May in the south constituted dependable
Federalist counties throughout most of the Republican era.
Also, a sixth county, Gloucester, in South Jersey, was either fully
or partially Federalist for nineteen of the New Jersey Republican era's twenty-four years.

In some of their five counties Federalist victories resulted
from their having bested a strong Republican machine. This
was particularly true in Burlington and Middlesex counties. In
other counties, such as Somerset and Cape May, Federalist victories came without their ever having faced permanent Republican machines.[13]

A study of the Federalist counties for the purpose of discovering common causes for their support of the minority party
yields only two clear-cut characteristics shared by all of them.[14]
First, all of these counties contained in important numbers one
of two groups, noted for allegiance to the Federalist party in
New Jersey. In Bergen, Middlesex, and Somerset counties, this
group was the Dutch. In Gloucester, Burlington, and Cape May
counties, it was the Quakers.

The second characteristic common to all of the Federalist
counties was their tendency to grow slowly in population.[15]
Cape May County was the model in this regard, and by the
same token, this county also constituted the most Federalist one
in the state. Cape May alone never wavered during the Era of
Good Feelings, even when that "Gibralter of Federalism,"

Burlington County, briefly allowed partial Republican delegations to be sent to the legislature.[16]

Federalist electoral efforts in those counties which constituted the party's strongholds were, of course, notable, for they resulted in repeated success at the polls. But the minority Federalists did not confine their exertions solely to the safe counties. Generally, during their first dozen years as the minority, the Federalists provided contests, at least for the annual state legislative elections, in all of the Republican counties except Morris and Essex, where Federalists efforts normally were feeble and intermittent.[17]

In two of the counties where Republicanism drew consistent electoral support, Federalists gave the opposition particularly warm contests. These were the counties of Hunterdon and Monmouth, which along with Gloucester, the state's most independent county, the *Federalist* termed as being "often on the poize [sic]."[18]

Practicing the art of the possible, Federalists often set out to win the state by tipping the balance in the close counties. Reasoning that all of the others were rather decidely for one of the parties, the Federalists centered their strategy for regaining dominance on reversing the politics of the barely Republican counties of Hunterdon and Monmouth and on making Gloucester consistently Federalist.[19]

Praiseworthy though their minority efforts soon came to be, the New Jersey Federalists' assumption of the mantle of a vigorous minority force did not occur as an instantaneous reaction to being out of power. Initially, some fear was expressed for the welfare of the country under the Republicans.[20] Also, there were some temporary disengagements from public life. United States Senator Schureman resigned his seat in Congress, and Lucius H. Stockton not only resigned as United States Attorney for New Jersey but in February, 1801, he also requested President Adams to withdraw his name from nomination as Secretary of War.[21]

Still, in New Jersey, Federalist gloom over the loss of the government did not plunge to the depths it did elsewhere.[22]

Even though he chose to retire, Senator Schureman was not overly apprehensive about the future. To Schureman, "heated imagination" was the major source of the dire predictions enunciated by some of his colleagues. Even at first, New Jersey Federalist disengagement was not general. When a few New Jersey Federalists surrendered their appointive posts between January and March, 1801, others readily accepted appointment to them by the still Federalist national and state governments and, in general, held them as long as possible.[23]

Furthermore, Federalist negativism in New Jersey was quite short-lived. Upon the loss of the state in October, 1801, New Jersey party leader William Griffith confessed that in the "metaphysical sense [he was] not alive," but a scant six months later he could opine that "federal politics [were] on the rise."[24]

However, the transition in Lucius H. Stockton's attitude, noted by the Republicans three months after the Federalists had lost the state, was even more revealing. This gentleman who had resigned in revulsion at the prospect of holding office under the "accursed" Republicans and earlier had stated that he would "rather be seen with sheep stealers than Democrats" was now acting the part of a "Jesuitical, Sly, Sycophant," professing great moderation, toasting the President's health and being "very attentive" to leading Republicans.[25] Clearly, in New Jersey, the newly out-of-power Federalists were revamping themselves and their party and rapidly assuming heretofore disdained tactics.

Both William Griffith and Lucius H. Stockton were young Federalists, but they were not the only New Jersey Federalist leaders who were active after 1801.[26] In New Jersey, many of the older party leaders, rather than retiring, joined the young Federalists in the creation of new-style Federalism.[27]

Together they thought it important that the New Jersey Federalists form the strongest opposition possible. And year after year they articulated to the voters the value of maintaining Federalist strength. The following is typical of their apologetic statements:

[a] respectable federal minority . . . operates as a check upon the wild schemes . . . of the democrats. . . .[28]

In line with national Federalist party leader Alexander Hamilton's belief,

it is to the press [that] we [the Federalists] must look for the means of our political regeneration,[29]

the improvement of the New Jersey Federalist party's propaganda techniques played an important part in its minority efforts. By early 1802 New Jersey Federalists were exhibiting concern that their handling of propaganda left something to be desired and suggesting ways in which it ought to be improved.

An "Old Whig" asserted that wider distribution of Federalist newspapers must be effected, especially to farmers, for the recent political defection of many of them was caused by their failure to receive Federalist newspapers. Generally not subscribers to any newspaper, this segment of the population had been exposed only to Republican views because only the opposition had seen fit to strew about the countryside free copies of their papers.[30]

Older Federalist Richard Stockton also wished for improvement in the Federalist handling of propaganda. His particular concern involved the less astute part of the population. For them, present newspaper coverage of certain types, such as the publication of lengthy debates, was not suitable, he said. Rather, such information should be presented for this portion of the population in the form of "brief, energetic" statements and via handbills.[31]

In the revitalization of their newspaper propaganda, the New Jersey Federalists first turned to the improvement of their existing newspapers. Major emphasis was placed upon the state party organ, the *Federalist*.[32]

Starting in 1802 changes began to appear in the Trenton *Federalist*. First, a new policy of publishing series of editorial essays went into effect. Later, the *Federalist* began to feature relatively regular columnists such as "Aristides" in 1804.[33] And finally some effort was made to increase the visual impact of the paper through better layout techniques and an occasional cartoon.[34]

The *Federalist*'s first series of editorials, entitled "To the People of New Jersey," was in twenty parts, beginning in January, 1802, and ending a few days before the legislative election of the following October.[35] The other two Federalist newspapers in the state reprinted the first of the *Federalist*'s essay series as well as later essays.[36]

But, just as the *Guardian* and the *Newark Gazette* followed the lead of the *Federalist*, to an extent the *Federalist*, at least at first, regarded the *New York Evening Post* as its model. A month after the *Post*'s inception in September of 1801, William Griffith had stated that Alexander Hamilton's paper would become the standard for the *Federalist*. Especially early in 1802 the *Federalist* did contain editorial reprints from the *Post*,[37] later called by the *New Jersey Journal* "that leading Hound of the Federal Pack."[38]

However, by the end of that year, there was some evidence that for sheer virulence the *Federalist* had outstripped its model. In October, 1802, the *Federalist* requested the *Post* to reprint its three concluding "To the People" essays, and the *Post* agreed to do so only with great reluctance. Then, when the essays appeared, the *Post* was not content merely to preface them with a heading giving their source. Instead, the editor reiterated their origin in a full-scale introduction, explaining that there was

> much [in the following] that would, if false, render an editor susceptible to libel charges

and that he had printed the material at the request of his New Jersey friends only after receiving assurances that as the responsible parties the New Jersey Federalists possessed concrete proof to support their charges against the Republicans.[39]

After the initial effort to revitalize their old newspapers was under way, the New Jersey Federalists started to establish additional newspapers. Their endeavors along this line began in 1803 and continued intermittently through 1814. In all, five newspapers were established, each lasting on the average of a year.[40]

Obviously, the Federalists hoped that by establishing a partisan press in the area the party would be strengthened locally,[41] for without exception the Federalists chose to locate their new prints in the northern part of the state where Federalism was weakest. Most often the Federalists invaded or closely approached the bastion of New Jersey Republicanism itself, Essex County. Of their five new journals, three, the *Federal Republican*, the *New Jersey Telescope*, and the *Essex Patriot*, had their offices in Essex County while a fourth, the *Impartial Register*, was published nearby, in adjacent Bergen County.

The New Jersey Federalists' timing in establishing their newer journals after 1801 indicates that they tried to utilize them in one of two major ways. The first was to enhance a recent Federalist upswing in other parts of the state. For this purpose, Federalist newspapers were established following the party's most successful legislative elections during its minority period. For example, in January, 1803, the Federalists established the *Federal Republican* three months after they had captured 50 percent of the legislature; in November, 1808, the Federalists established the *New Jersey Telescope* a month after having won 44 percent of the legislative seats; and in December, 1812, they established the *Essex Patriot* two months after having regained political control of the state.

The second major way in which the Federalists tried to utilize their new journals was to help the party recover from a recent decline at the polls. Two of the five short-lived Federalist newspapers were established to this end. The *Impartial Register* was initiated in 1804 following a 13 percent drop in Federalist legislative strength over the previous year. And the *Spirit of Washington* was established in 1814, again following a 13 percent drop in Federalist legislative membership.[42]

It was via the *Federalist* that the New Jersey party formally signaled its acceptance of the minority party mantle in the state. Following the practice of its Republican predecessor in the minority role, the *Federalist* announced its party would function as a severe critic of the administration.[43]

The New Jersey Federalists were true to their word. Republican policies—whether national or local, domestic or foreign— all received their share of New Jersey Federalist castigation. As a result, by 1803 the New Jersey Republicans became exasperated by Federalist censure of their policies, national ones in this case, and declared:

> Were an angel from heaven, or even the savior himself to descend and take upon him the name of our chief magistrate . . . he would have a second time a crown of thorns planted upon his head, and be mocked and spit upon by the false professors of . . . good order [the Federalists].[44]

Even more notable than the fact that the New Jersey Federalists became active opponents of the administration was the rhetoric they assumed in doing so. From that rhetoric it is clear that the New Jersey Federalists were attempting to "save Federalism [by] embrac[ing] democracy,"[45] for in holding up the Republican policies to censure, the Federalists almost invariably portrayed themselves as the protectors of the people, acting because they feared injury to the people, their interests, and their rights.[46]

When inveighing against proscription, as they did both long and loudly, the New Jersey Federalists' basic argument was that the people were being deprived of competent, experienced officials who could render them good service. In their stead, the Repbulicans were appointing totally unfit men to the detriment of the people.[47]

No Republican appointees came in for more attack by the New Jersey Federalists on the grounds of incompetency than judicial ones. In 1804 a Federalist went so far as to express doubt about whether Republican appointees as justices of the peace could read or write and to demand that they be given literacy tests.[48] Even Republican appointees to the State Supreme Court possessed little legal knowledge and experience, the New

Jersey Federalists charged, all of which boded ill for the general populace because, primarily, it was

> a correct administration of justice . . . [that] secure[d] equality. . . .[49]

Many acts of the Republicans were protested by the New Jersey Federalists on the grounds that the people's constitution was being violated.[50] As early as 1802 the New Jersey Federalists declared that the Republicans, those "worst of tyrants, . . . have destroyed the Constitution."[51]

The repeal of the Judiciary Act, against which New Jersey's Federalist Senators had battled mightily, was cited as a prime instance of the Republicans' violation of the Constitution.[52] Later, according to the New Jersey Federalists, Republican impeachment proceedings against Federalist judges again showed that the American system of checks and balances, designed to protect the people, was being nullified. Republicans clearly were subordinating the judiciary to the legislature.[53]

The New Jersey Federalists' protest against the Louisiana Purchase also included the Constitutional violation charge, but in addition a strong stand was made against it on the grounds that the Purchase was a sore waste of the people's money.[54] According to the New Jersey Federalists, the purchase of Louisiana

> [added] Fifteen Million Two Hundred and Fifty Thousand Dollars [to the public debt] and taxed every family in New Jersey at least *twenty dollars* and all this . . . to buy a wilderness inhabited by Savages and wholly useless to New Jersey.[55]

Speaking further to the economic issue, the New Jersey Federalists charged that Republicans were very far from being the "champions of economy," as they portrayed themselves.[56] On the contrary, to the New Jersey Federalists,

> Republican economy . . . [was] much like Republican Sense and Virtue—No where to be found but in lying and empty professions.[57]

Had the Republicans not refused to allow a Federalist to print the minutes of the Assembly for $18.00 per sheet and instead accepted a Republican bid at $26.00 a sheet and also failed to invest the New Jersey treasury for interest, choosing instead to store it in the Treasurer's home, from which, incidentally, it had been stolen?[58]

If further evidence of the falseness of Republican economy were needed, the Federalists gave the example of the so-called tax relief instituted by the Republicans. It actually operated against the people as a whole they said, for "taxes had been taken from the rich and left on the poor."[59]

Another Republican measure which operated against every Jerseyan was the creation of six state banks governed by the New Jersey legislature. From them would emanate "another paper money deluge," the Federalists charged, and all would suffer from the inflation the new banks caused.[60]

Serious alarm for the welfare of the people was expressed by the Federalists over still other Republican acts. The people's right of freedom of expression was being denied, the Federalists pointed out on such occasions as when New Jersey Federalist editors were being prosecuted by the Republicans.[61] Also, stated the New Jersey Federalists, the Republican state government failed to guarantee the people's safety, a charge they made when the Republicans committed such acts as allowing the Legislative Council to overrule a Federalist court's punishment, meted out to a Federalist sheriff's assailant.[62]

Perhaps most basic of all, the Federalists charged that the people's freedom to choose their representatives had been taken away from them by the Republican party machine, that "tyrant of the people."[63] As a result, said the Federalists with some justification, since the beginning of the Republican era, not the people but the Republican caucus had been governing elections in New Jersey. It was the undemocratic Republican caucus, not the whole people, that chose the party's nominees and thereupon decided for whom the majority Republicans would vote.[64]

In addition to their adoption of a new rhetoric after 1801,

New Jersey Federalists revealed their flexibility in other ways. For example, the minority Federalists utilized not one but several different tactics in attempting to make gains. When it suited their purposes the New Jersey Federalists could be adamant in dealing with the Republicans, as they were during most of the joint meetings up to the Era of Good Feelings. Repeatedly the Federalists insisted, usually with no more than partial success, that the Republicans extend to them in equal amounts the same legislative courtesy they accorded fellow Republicans. Federalist counties must be allowed to make all of the nominations for appointive office in their counties. Republicans from other counties had no right to interfere with the appointments in Federalist counties, and they must cease doing so.[65]

At other times, the Federalists showed a willingness to bargain with the Republicans to achieve their ends.[66] In 1802–1803, when the Federalists tied the Republicans in the legislature and no major appointments could be made by the joint meeting since both Federalists and Republicans voted strictly with their party, it was the Federalists who went to the Republicans with the following proposal. The Federalists would give their votes to the Republicans' candidate for either United States Senator or Governor, if the Republicans would vote for the Federalists' choice in the other case.[67] Again, in 1814, when two Republicans were running for the United States senatorial appointment, the Federalists offered their support first to one side and then to another in an attempt to drive the best bargain for office.[68]

Probably the tactic of the minority Federalists most feared by the Republicans was the attempt to divide the Republicans and profit thereby.[69] Indeed, the Federalists were ever on the alert to the occurrence of Republican divisions, which they might exploit.[70]

At the merest hint of a Republican intraparty quarrel the New Jersey Federalists swung into action, even doing their best to exacerbate small matters into causes for major Republican divisions. When James J. Wilson was reported to have made some unkind remarks about his fellow Republican Governor Bloomfield, the Federalists immediately took Bloomfield's side. Their state party organ detailed the injury to Bloomfield in inflammatory terms and professed astonishment at Wilson's being so callous as to offend a man who had been a "friend and father to him."[71]

Furthermore, the *Federalist* tried to drive a wedge between two Republican organs in the state. The upstart *True American*, the *Federalist* pointed out, had received printing contracts for years, while

> the poor Centinel the oldest democratic paper in the state [had been] living on bread and water,

and by all indications would be forced to continue to do so.[72]

Finally, the Federalists tried to create a split between the generations of Republicans. In 1807, when Ebenezer Elmer was soundly defeated for appointive office by a much younger man, the *Federalist* explained that, as was typical of the Republicans, they had "thrown by" a man who had seen "revolutionary service" for the *"new men* of their party," even though the new choice might be but twenty-three years of age and had joined the party only in time to share in the spoils.[73]

Of their first dozen years as the minority party it was during the years 1804–1807 that the New Jersey Federalists reaped the greatest gains because of Republican division. The earliest Federalist inroads came in the joint meeting. In 1804 Governor Bloomfield complained that because the Republicans had been divided the Federalists were able to elect their candidates for the judiciary.[74]

Next, Federalists began to benefit at the polls. In 1805 the Federalists elected one legislator from Gloucester County, which had been Republican since 1803. The next year Federalists not only increased their hold on Gloucester by gaining three of that county's four seats but they won a total of three seats in the Republican strongholds of Sussex and Cumberland counties.[75] Together with their usual victories in the Federalist counties, these successes in staunch Republican counties brought the Federalists to within a hairsbreadth of controlling the 1806–1807 state legislature.[76]

Although the relationship stopped far short of constituting an organized "Quid" faction,[77] there was some evidence of a very loose alliance between some New Jersey Federalists and moderate Republicans in the years 1803–1807.[78] As the *True American* observed,

> Vile as Federalists consider Republicans, they can yet *condescend* to make use of them when they think it will subserve their purposes.[79]

Between 1803 and 1807 there were several cases of Federalists and Republicans running together on the same ticket. In late 1803 Salem County Federalists ran Republicans for the minor posts of coroner and sheriff.[80] In 1805, a Federalist gained nomination on a Republican-dominated ticket in Gloucester County and as a result won election to the legislature.[81] Finally, in 1807, addressing their appeal to the county's "free and independent electors," Monmouth County Federalists listed a Republican as their ticket's candidate for coroner.[82]

In addition to sometimes combining with them on electoral tickets, the New Jersey Federalists of 1803–1807 evinced good will toward the moderate New Jersey Republicans in two other ways. First, the Federalists rejoiced when moderates gained election over "that part of the democratic party denominated revolutionists."[83] By the same token, they chided the Republicans when they passed over these men and instead preferred "violent democrats."[84]

Secondly, the Federalists were known to lend their support to moderate Republicans in joint meeting. It was the sole Federalist member of the Cumberland County delegation who was responsible for the nomination of Republican Ebenezer Elmer, said by Republicans to be "too moderate a man."[85] Between 1805 and 1807 the Federalists put up no Federalist candidate for governor but unequivocally supported for that post Republican Joseph Bloomfield, whom they denominated a "third party-man."[86]

Yet another indication of the New Jersey Federalists' flexibility and energy during their minority years was their growing acceptance of party after 1801. As early as 1802 the state's Federalists began publicly to defend organization. Replying to the Republicans' account of the way in which the Hunterdon County Federalists had organized for the October, 1802, election, which the opposition had handled in the manner of an exposé, the Federalists stated that their organizational efforts represented nothing more than "common practice with all parties" to the end that they might prevent being "easily overthrown and dispersed." Moreover the *Federalist* encouraged party members to ignore the vehemence with which Republicans greeted every measure of the Federalists which indicated any *"regular plan of conduct"* and to be systematic rather than

any longer suffer a wicked cause to triumph from the superior zeal and organization of its supporters.[87]

The minority Federalists' electioneering techniques indeed revealed that they were zealous, so much so that the New Jersey party appeared rather more concerned with winning elections than staying within the bounds of propriety. Certainly many of its efforts to amass votes may be categorized as persuasive but others definitely were deceptive and coercive.

One of the ways New Jersey Federalists tried to persuade people to their viewpoint after 1801 was by providing them with Federalist propaganda. Especially, but not solely, at election time "swarms of federal[ist] publications" were distributed liberally throughout the state. Even Sussex, the northernmost county in the state, was not forgotten. According to the Republicans, that county's Newton post office alone received gratuitously 100 copies of the Trenton *Federalist* each week.[88]

Monmouth County Federalists took the persuasive technique a step further with their annual observance of the "Monmouth Saddle Bags" custom. Each year one Federalist traveled about the county at election time with saddle bags full of hard cider. All along the way, citizens were offered the beverage "for the purpose of toasting Federalism."[89]

An instance of Federalist electioneering of the deceptive sort occurred in 1810. That year Federalists colored their tickets similar to Republican ones so that they could be mistaken for Republican ballots.[90]

Coercion of voters by the Federalists occurred particularly in Burlington County, according to the Republicans. At one point Federalists there formed an employers' association which vowed to discharge or refuse to hire any workman who had voted contrary to the will of the association.[91]

But whereas the Burlington Federalists threatened Republican voters with economic punishment, the Gloucester Federalists threatened them with bodily harm. In 1803 the Republicans of Galloway Township, Gloucester County, charged that they had been driven away from the polling place by a Federalist mob which had threatened their lives.[92]

Even though minority Federalist electoral activity was notable,[93] it never equaled that of the Republicans. In fact, after 1800 the New Jersey Federalists entered no Congressional or presidential elections for a period of seven years. Having been unsuccessful in their attempt to secure district elections for federal contests, the Federalists did not choose to contest these elections, for they did not believe they could win in a general canvass.[94]

All of this changed in 1808. The Federalists now had the embargo as an issue, and they believed that its exploitation could carry them to victory in the statewide as well as the county contests for the legislature. Therefore, in 1808 the New Jersey Federalists entered the national contests with gusto.[95]

In preparation for these statewide contests of November 1–2, 1808, New Jersey Federalist leaders caucused in Trenton in July.[96] Next, nominating conventions were held, the first in Hunterdon County in August, 1808. This meeting nominated 70 percent of the Federalist candidates for Congress and the electoral college, most nominees being from northern New Jersey.

A second nomination meeting, held in New Brunswick on September 2, named the remaining 30 percent of the national tickets; most of its nominees were South Jerseyans. Together, the two Federalist tickets exhibited perfect north-south balance, each section of the state having seven of the fourteen candidates. However, on the Congressional ticket northern men predominated, while on the presidential elector ticket southern men predominated.[97]

Further statewide organizational efforts grew out of the New Brunswick meeting. Here a state committee of correspondence was appointed. This committee issued a form letter containing suggested organizational and electioneering techniques. It was sent to each county chairman, who was requested to report back to the committee on his endeavors and prospects for success.[98]

At least for Burlington and Middlesex counties, substantial documentary evidence remains of the New Jersey Federalists' organizational efforts below the county level.[99] A printed form letter of instructions from Burlington County chairman Joshua Wallace to that county's township committees clearly establishes that in Burlington such committees were held responsible for "bring[ing] out every vote" in their areas.[100] For Middlesex County surviving documents show that in this county there were vote-seeking committees that operated even below the township level. Here district committees were responsible for each portion of a township and, as part of their efforts, they issued electioneering propaganda.[101]

All three of the 1808 contests in New Jersey were lost only narrowly by the Federalists. Not only in the legislative election but in the Congressional and presidential canvasses as well, the Federalists fell short of winning by only seven percentage points.[102]

In 1809, however, the New Jersey party's performance dropped significantly as once again the New Jersey party exhibited its characteristic pattern of uneven electoral effort and success.[103] In 1810 the Federalists' downturn continued as they lost yet another 3 percent of the legislative seats and failed even to enter the Congressional contest. Then in October, 1811, the

New Jersey Federalists fell to their all-time low point to date.[104]

When the minority party had so declined over a period of three years that it held only 29 percent of the state legislature, the Republicans felt safe in declaring,

Federalism has declined, is declining, and WILL [CONTINUE TO] DECLINE.[105]

The Republicans, however, had spoken too soon as they would learn the following year.

NOTES

1. Prince, *New Jersey's Jeffersonian Republicans,* p. 104; Noble E. Cunningham, *The Jeffersonian-Republicans in Power: Party Operations, 1801–1809* (Chapel Hill: University of North Carolina Press, 1963), pp. 7, 9; Roger H. Brown, *The Republic in Peril: 1812* (New York: W. W. Norton & Company, Inc., 1971), pp. 158–59.

2. Cunningham, *The Jeffersonian-Republicans in Power,* p. 260; William Griffith to Elisha Boudinot, July 30, 1803, Stimson-Boudinot Collection, Princeton University Library; James Giles to Garret D. Wall, October 14, 1814, Wall Papers, Rutgers University Library; Fischer, *The Revolution of American Conservatism,* p. xx; Elmer, *The Constitution and Government of the Province and State of New Jersey,* p. 151; Fee, *The Transition from Aristocracy to Democracy,* pp. 169, 129, 139; *True American,* September 15, 1806; September 3, 1810; *Centinel of Freedom,* October 17, 1809; October 19, 1813; Joseph Bloomfield to Ebenezer Elmer, July 6, 1802, Ely Collection, New Jersey Historical Society; Sher, "Party Battles in Middlesex County," p. 72; Carl Prince, "James J. Wilson: Party Leader, 1801–1824," *Proceedings of the New Jersey Historical Society* LXXXIII (January, 1965): 29; Prince, *New Jersey's Jeffersonian Republicans,* pp. 104–5; *Federalist,* February 2, 1803. Indeed, most years until the advent of the Era of Good Feelings the New Jersey Federalists publicly indicated that their aim was to win the state legislature and asserted that they could do so. See, for example, *Centinel of Freedom,* November 10, 1802; September 10, 1816; *Newark Gazette,* September 27, 1803; *Federalist,* September 30, 1805; September 29, 1806; October 2, 1809; October 14, 1811; October 14, 1816; *True American,* September 24, 1810; *Guardian,* September 27, 1804; *Palladium of Liberty,* October 23, 1810; Richard Stockton to ? , February 9, 1802, Gratz Collection, Historical Society of Pennsylvania; Joseph Bloomfield to Dear Doctor [Ebenezer Elmer], January 25, 1802, Gratz Collection, Historical Society of Pennsylvania; *To the Federal Electors of the County of Somerset,* n.p., Septem-

ber, 1811; Pasler, "The Federalist Party in Burlington County, New Jersey," p. 191; Rodgers, "Some Phases of New Jersey History in the Jeffersonian Period," p. 11.

3. Similarly, James Banner notes regarding Massachusetts, "Apostasy made staunch Federalists almost apoplectic with anger and resentment." Banner, *To the Hartford Convention*, p. 78.

4. *Guardian*, April 26, 1804; Lucius H. Stockton, *An Address Before the Convention of the Friends of Peace* (Trenton, July 4, 1814), p. 26.

5. *Federalist*, October 4, 1802; *Proceedings and Address of the Second Convention of Delegates Held at the City of Trenton, on the Fourth of July, 1814, to the People of New Jersey* (n.p., July 4, 1814), p. 18; Fischer, *The Revolution of American Conservatism*, p. 331; Marshall Smelser, *The Democratic Republic, 1801–1815* (New York: Harper & Row, 1968), p. 322. Dissatisfaction with the Republican government was properly expressed only via the ballot according to the New Jersey Federalists, and in 1808 they so informed their fellow anti-embargoists in other states who had taken to the streets and were rioting. *Federalist*, May 16, 1806; Rodgers, "Some Phases of New Jersey History in the Jeffersonian Period," p. 66. Very early in their history as the minority the New Jersey Federalists had evinced an unwillingness to frustrate the will of the people. "Jefferson was the choice (if not wise) of the people" and ought to be so treated, Elias Boudinot stated, expressing scorn for those Congressional Federalists who were attempting to elect Burr. (New Jersey's vote had been cast for Jefferson.) Elias Boudinot to Elisha Boudinot, January 7, 1801, Stimson-Boudinot Collection, Princeton University Library; Eugene H. Roseboom, *A History of Presidential Elections* (New York: Macmillan Co., 1964), p. 45. Later, in 1807, the New Jersey Federalists voted, along with the Republicans, to liberalize the franchise in the state. *New Jersey Laws*, 32nd Session, 1st Sitting, pp. 14–15; J. R. Pole, "The Suffrage in New Jersey, 1790–1807," *Proceedings of the New Jersey Historical Society* LXXI (January, 1953); 58.

6. Commenting on the nation during the Early Republic period, James Banner has stated, "The frenzied political climate . . . continued unabated after 1800." Banner, *To the Hartford Convention*, p. xi.

7. See, for example, *Federalist*, October 24, 1801; February 14, March 14, 1803; March 25, 1805; "The Founding of the Trenton *True American*," *Trenton Times*, , October 16, 1932; *True American*, October 27, 1801.

8. *Guardian*, November 22, 1803.

9. Ibid., April 22, 1813; *Fredonian*, January 16, 1812.

10. Fischer, *The Revolution of American Conservatism*, p. 185.

11. Prince, "New Jersey's Democratic Republicans," p. 480; *True American*, March 20, 1802; Pasler, "The Federalist Party in Burlington County, New Jersey," p. 135; Gaillard Hunt, "Office-Seeking during Jefferson's Administration," *American Historical Review* III (1898): 168. Tucker recently had assailed Coxe and Pearson, as well as other Burlington Federalists, in the broadside, *A Dialogue between Quacko and Sambo; Addressed to the New Jersey Federalists,*

Particularly those of Burlington County, n.p., n.d. [c. Nov., 1801]. Later, in 1803, Tucker charged that Federalist Job Lippincott struck him when Tucker refused his challenge to a duel. *True American,* July 25, August 29, 1803; Pasler, "The Federalist Party in Burlington County, New Jersey," p. 148.

12. *Federal Republican,* August 2, 1803; *Federalist,* September 29, 1801; July 25, August 1, 1803; "Mr. Democrat" to Garret D. Wall, July 20, 1803, Wall Papers, Princeton University Library; Pasler, "The Federalist Party in Burlington County, New Jersey," p. 149; Prince, "New Jersey's Democratic Republicans," p. 144. For some years Wilson evidently had been expecting an attack. In 1801 the *Federalist* stated that because of cowardice Wilson went about the streets at night armed with a sword-cane in his hand and a brace of pistols in his pocket. *Federalist,* September 29, 1801. Initiation of physical battles by New Jersey Republicans was not unknown, either. In 1803 Republican Jonathan Coperthwaite was found guilty of assaulting Federalist judge Edward French, an outcome Republicans deplored for "poor Coperthwaite got much bruised in the battle." *True American,* August 29, 1803; Pasler, "The Federalist Party in Burlington County, New Jersey," p. 148.

13. Prince, "New Jersey's Democratic Republicans," p. 383; Prince, *New Jersey's Jeffersonian Republicans,* p. 92; *Centinel of Freedom,* January 2, 1810; *Paladium of Liberty,* October 23, 1810.

14. Of course, other, more localized factors played their parts in keeping these counties Federalist, but the attempt here, has been to discover common causes for these counties' allegiance to the New Jersey Federalist party.

15. Fischer, *The Revolution of American Conservatism,* pp. 213–16; Banner, *To the Hartford Convention,* p. 173; Sher, "Party Battles in Middlesex County," pp. 8, 124; Walter Robert Fallow, "The Rise of the Whig Party in New Jersey," Ph.D. diss., Princeton University, 1967, pp. 87–88; James Giles to Garret D. Wall, October 15, 1814, Wall Papers, Rutgers University Library.

16. Prince, "New Jersey's Democratic Republicans," p. 479; James J. Wilson to William Darlington, October 23, 1820, Darlington Papers, Library of Congress; Pasler and Pasler, "Federalist Tenacity in Burlington County," pp. 198–200, 210–12; Glover Moore, *The Missouri Controversy, 1819–1821* (Lexington: University of Kentucky Press, 1953), p. 70.

17. Prince, *New Jersey's Jeffersonian Republicans,* pp. 74, 80, 132; Prince, "New Jersey's Democratic Republicans, pp. 217, 210, 289–90, 485, 499, 502, 299, 321.

18. *Federalist,* September 19, 1808; Prince, "New Jersey's Democratic Republicans," pp. 382, 377, 366, 324, 326, 361–62; *Centinel of Freedom,* September 11, 1810; *True American,* October 15, 1810; Prince, *New Jersey's Jeffersonian Republicans,* p. 87. The Republican press did not dispute this fact. Rather, it even used similar wording to describe the situation. *Centinel of Freedom,* September 12, 1815.

19. *Centinel of Freedom,* August 23, 1808; *Federalist,* September 11, 25, 1809; September 10, October 15, 1810; *True American,* October 8, 1810; *Paladium of Liberty,* October 23, 1810.

20. Elias Boudinot to Lewis Pintard, February 3, 1801, Ford Papers, New York Public Library; Samuel S. Smith to Jonathan Dayton, December 22, 1801, Miscellaneous Papers, Princeton University Library; Fee, *The Transition from Aristocracy to Democracy*, pp. 122–23.

21. James Schureman to Andrew Kirkpatrick, February 9, 1801, Ely Collection, New Jersey Historical Society; Elmer, *The Constitution and Government of the Province and State of New Jersey*, p. 150; James Venza, "Federalists in Congress, 1800–1812," Ph.D. diss., Vanderbilt University, 1967, p. 329; Lucius H. Stockton to John Adams, February 25, 1801, Adams Papers, quoted in Kathryn Turner, "The Judiciary Act of 1801," Ph.D. diss., University of Wisconsin, 1959, p. 264; Oliver Wolcott to Mrs. Wolcott, January 22, 1801 in George Gibbs, ed., *Memoirs of the Administrations of Washington and Adams Edited from the Papers of Oliver Wolcott*, vol. 2, p. 468; Jonathan Dayton to Aaron Ogden, January 21, 1801, Aaron Ogden Letters, Rutgers University Library.

22. Richard Hofstadter, *The American Political Tradition* (New York: Vintage Books, 1957), p. 33; White, *The Federalists*, p. 515.

23. Frederick Frelinghuysen accepted appointment as United States Attorney in Stockton's stead, and, in place of Schureman, Aaron Ogden became United States Senator, holding that post until the expiration of the term in 1803. When the Republicans replaced Ogden with one of their own party, they fully expected that the other senator, Federalist Jonathan Dayton, would resign now that he found himself the sole member of his party in the New Jersey Congressional delegation. However, he did not, but rather held his post until the last. Thus, New Jersey Federalists had some representation in Congress until 1805 when Dayton's term expired. Turner, "Judiciary Act of 1801," p. 264; Joseph Bloomfield to Dear Doctor [Ebenezer Elmer], January 25, 1802, Gratz Collection, Historical Society of Pennsylvania; Elmer, *The Constitution and Government of the Province and State of New Jersey*, p. 150; Rodgers, "Some Phases of New Jersey History in the Jeffersonian Period," pp. 7–8; *Centinel of Freedom*, November 8, 1803; Venza, "Federalists in Congress, 1800–1812," p. 134.

24. William Griffith to Elisha Boudinot, October 10, 1801; William Griffith to Elisha Boudinot, April 10, 1802, Stimson-Boudinot Papers, Princeton University Library. New Jersey Federalism did revive in 1802. That year the Federalists won 50 percent of the state legislature.

25. Lucius H. Stockton to John Adams, February 25, 1801, Adams Papers, quoted in Turner, "Judiciary Act of 1801," p. 264; Joseph Bloomfield to Dear Doctor [Ebenezer Elmer], January 25, 1802, Gratz Collection, Historical Society of Pennsylvania.

26. McCormick, *The Second American Party System*, p. 166; Fischer, *The Revolution of American Conservatism*, p. 324.

27. James Banner has made a similar observation regarding Massachusetts. Banner, *To the Hartford Convention*, pp. 136, 252, 141, 145–146, 235, 138. As with Massachusetts, in New Jersey there was no sharp dissociation between the two generations of Federalist party leaders. Prince, "The Leadership of New Jersey's First Party System," p. 6. Young and old New Jersey Federalists shared

the same backgrounds, and, in general, they worked side by side. Even in 1812, when young Federalists in New Jersey truly came into their own, the chairman of the New Jersey Federalists' state convention was old Federalist John Neilson. *Proceedings and Address of the Delegates of the People of New-Jersey* (Trenton: September 15, 1812), p. 11. To be sure, the two generations of New Jersey Federalists were not indistinguishable. Likewise, they were not inseparable. To illustrate: for the July 4, 1803, celebration, the young Federalists met apart from the old Federalists, and for the July 4, 1804, Society of the Cincinnati meeting they did likewise. *Federalist,* July 11, 1803; July 9, 1804.

28. Sher, "Party Battles in Middlesex County," pp. 74, 77; *Guardian,* November 26, 1801; September 30, 1802; September 27, 1804; *Federalist,* September 16, 30, 1811; James Giles to Garret D. Wall, Wall Papers, Rutgers University Library; Fischer, *The Revolution of American Conservatism,* p. 58.

29. Alexander Hamilton to Samuel Bayard, April, 1802, Bayard Letterbook, New York Public Library; Venza, "Federalists in Congress, 1800–1812," p. 71; Miller, *Alexander Hamilton,* p. 550.

30. *Guardian,* March 18, 1802.

31. Richard Stockton to ? , February 9, 1802, Gratz Collection, Historical Society of Pennsylvania.

32. William Griffith worked with old Federalist Elisha Boudinot in forming a committee to manage the *Federalist* as well as to see to its distribution among the "benighted." William Griffith to Elisha Boudinot, December 20, 1802, Stimson-Boudinot Papers, Princeton University Library.

33. That same year the New Brunswick *Guardian* began to feature the columnist "Yorick." Because of his satiric wit, he probably qualifies as the outstanding columnist in either the *Federalist* or the *Guardian. Guardian,* 1804–1806; Sher, "Party Battles in Middlesex County," pp. 81–90.

34. Visually speaking, the *Federalist*'s best effort probably was the front page of the October 4, 1814, issue. It featured a drawing of a ship named the "good old Federal Ship, New-Jersey," whose banners contained electioneering slogans such as "No War, No Democrats," and "Farmers, Mechanics and Sailor's Rights, equally protected." "Madison & Co." were pictured as being thrown overboard. Framing the ship were the Federalists' electoral tickets for the legislature and for Congress. *Federalist,* October 4, 1814; *New York Evening Post,* October 4, 1814; Fee, *The Transition from Aristocracy to Democracy,* p. 202. Fischer has described the development of visual impact by Federalist newspapers on a nationwide basis. Fischer, *The Revolution of American Conservatism,* pp. 143–44.

35. *Federalist,* January 12, October 4, 1802.

36. See, for example, *Guardian,* July 28, 1803; *Newark Gazette,* February 2, 1802.

37. See, for example, *Federalist,* January 12, February 9, 1802.

38. *New Jersey Journal,* September 14, 1813.

39. *New York Evening Post,* October 6, 1802.

40. These were the *Federal Republican,* Elizabeth, Essex County, January, 1803–1804; the *Impartial Register,* Hackensack, Bergen County, August, 1804–1805; the *New Jersey Telescope,* Newark, Essex County, November, 1808–November, 1809; the *Essex Patriot,* Elizabeth, Essex County, December, 1812–December, 1813; and the *Spirit of Washington,* Freehold, Monmouth County, May, 1814–February, 1815. The existing Federalist newspapers, especially the *Federalist,* always publicly welcomed the new prints and urged that they be supported. But in 1803, the embattled editor of the Federalist *Newark Gazette* was perhaps happiest of all to welcome the *Federal Republican* to Republican Essex County. *Federalist,* December 7, 1812, June 12, 1814; *Newark Gazette,* February 1, 1803; Rodgers, "Some Phases of New Jersey History in the Jeffersonian Period," pp. 19–20.

41. *Centinel of Freedom,* October 17, 1809; Thayer, *As We Were: The Story of Old Elizabethtown,* p. 200.

42. *Newark Gazette,* February 1, 1803; *Federal Republican,* January 17, 1804; *New Jersey Journal,* March 5, 1804; Rodgers, "Some Phases of New Jersey History in the Jeffersonian Period," pp. 19–20; *New Jersey Telescope,* November 4, 1808; May 5, 1809; Sabine, "Antecedents of the Newark Public Library," p. 65; *True American,* November 7, 1808; *Federalist,* November 4, 1808; December 7, 1812; June 12, 1814; Urquhart, *A History of the City of Newark, New Jersey,* Vol. 1, pp. 780–781; *Centinel of Freedom,* November 21, 1809; Prospectus of *Essex Patriot,* November 6, 1812 and *New Brunswick Daily Fredonian,* November 12, 1860 in Elmer T. Hutchinson Papers, Rutgers University Library.

43. *Federalist,* September 29, 1801; January 12, 1802; November 28, 1803.

44. *Centinel of Freedom,* July 19, 1803.

45. Banner, *To the Hartford Convention,* p. 145.

46. *Federalist,* January 12, 1802; James Broussard, "The Federalists in the South Atlantic States," Ph.D. diss., Duke University, 1969, p. 117; Fischer, *The Revolution of American Conservatism,* pp. 153, 161, 172, xx; Smelser, *The Democratic Republic, 1801–1815,* p. 247. In 1814 older Federalist Richard Stockton would declare in Congress, "I am the defender of the rights and liberties of the people. . . ." *Annals of Congress,* 13th Congress, 2nd Session (January 10, 1814), p. 881. Still, even after 1801 the New Jersey Federalists' public statements occasionally were couched in the old elitist rhetoric. *Centinel of Freedom,* September 21, 1813; *True American,* November 29, 1813.

47. Shaw Livermore, *The Twilight of Federalism: The Disintegration of the Federalist Party, 1815–1830* (Princeton: Princeton University Press, 1962), p. 23; Prince, "New Jersey's Democratic Republicans," p. 612; Prince, *New Jersey's Jeffersonian Republicans,* pp. 237, 239; *Federalist,* January 12, October 4, 1802; March 7, November 7, 1803; April 2, 16, June 25, July 23, December 24, 1804; November 4, 1805; November 23, 1807; November 4, 18, 1811; Elmer, *The Constitution and Government of the Province and State of New Jersey,* pp. 279–80; *Centinel of Freedom,* September 9, 1804; Sickler, *The History of Salem*

County, New Jersey, p. 178; *Guardian,* July 8, 1802; November 15, 1804; Carl Prince, "The Passing of the Aristocracy: Jefferson's Removal of the Federalists, 1801–1805," *Journal of American History* LVIII (December, 1970): 568, 571; Hunt, "Office-Seeking during Jefferson's Administration," p. 288; *Newark Gazette,* November 17, 1801; August 17, 1802; *New York Evening Post,* October 6, 1802; Andrew Bell Papers, New York Historical Society.

48. *Federalist,* May 7, 1804.

49. *Federalist,* January 19, 1802; Pasler, "The Federalist Party in Burlington County, New Jersey," p. 154; Harold F. Wilson, *Outline History of New Jersey* (New Brunswick, N. J.: Rutgers University Press, 1950), p. 92. In citing the incompetence of Republican appointees, the Federalists found their firmest ground in the judicial category. Very few Republicans of the day did possess formal training in the law, and those who were trained had inferior qualifications compared to the New Jersey Federalists. Many years after the fact, a New Jersey Republican confirmed that, particularly in the early 1800s, the Federalists were correct in stating that even Republican justices of the New Jersey Supreme Court had little legal knowledge and experience. Elmer, *The Constitution and Government of the State and Province of New Jersey,* pp. 161, 311.

50. *Federalist,* October 4, 1802; January 3, 1803; *Guardian,* October 1, 1801; January 7, 1802; *New York Evening Post,* October 6, 1802; Livermore, *The Twilight of Federalism,* p. 10.

51. *Federalist,* March 2, 1802.

52. Ebenezer Elmer to ? , January 29, 1802, Gratz Collection, Historical Society of Pennsylvania; Thayer, *As We Were: The Story of Old Elizabethtown,* p. 199; Venza, "Federalists in Congress, 1800–1812," pp. 56, 58; Richard Stockton to ? , February 9, 1802, Gratz Collection, Historical Society of Pennsylvania; Rosenberg, "The Political Thought of William Paterson," pp. 225–26; *New Jersey Journal,* March 3, 1801; Adams, *The Works of John Adams,* v. 9, pp. 94–95; Joseph Bloomfield to Ebenezer Elmer, March 3, 1802, Ely Collection, New Jersey Historical Society; Ebenezer Elmer to George Burgin, March 5, 1802, Ely Collection, New Jersey Historical Society; William Griffith to Elisha Boudinot, January 6, 1802, Stimson-Boudinot Papers, Princeton University Library; Turner, "Judiciary Act of 1801," pp. 262, 259–60, 263.

53. Venza, "Federalists in Congress, 1800–1812," pp. 131–32. During the 1801–1802 legislative session, the New Jersey Republicans brought unsuccessful impeachment proceedings against John Lacey, Federalist justice of the peace in Burlington County. *New York Evening Post,* October 6, 1802; William Darlington Papers, Historical Society of Pennsylvania; *Federalist,* January 1, 19, October 4, 1802; Prince, "New Jersey's Democratic Republicans," p. 176; *Guardian,* November 12, 19, 1801; *Newark Gazette,* February 9, 16, 1802; *True American,* December 1, 1801; *A Dialogue between Quacko and Sambo; Addressed to the New Jersey Federalists, Particularly Those of Burlington County,* n.p., n.d. [c. November, 1801]; Pasler, "The Federalist Party in Burlington County, New Jersey," pp. 132, 134; *Votes and Proceedings of the General*

Assembly of the State of New Jersey, 22nd Session, 1st Sitting (Nov. 17, 1801).

54. *Federalist,* September 10, 1804; *A Candid Appeal to the Honest Yeomanry of Essex, Morris, and Sussex Counties, in the State of New Jersey, on the Subject of the Approaching Presidential and Congressional Election,* n.p., October, 1808, p. 131.

55. *Serious Considerations Addressed to the Electors of New Jersey Concerning the Choice of Members of the Legislature for the Ensuing Year,* n.p., 1803.

56. *Guardian,* October 1, 1801; *Federalist,* October 4, 1802; *New York Evening Post,* October 6, 1802.

57. *Federalist,* September 6, 1802.

58. *Guardian,* December 1, 1802; January 5, 1804.

59. *Federalist,* September 10, 1804; Broussard, "The Federalists in the South Atlantic States," p. 118. The New Jersey Federalists recognized the efficacy of the Republicans' mass versus class appeal, and as the minority party they tried to counter it. *Federalist,* November 29, 1813; August 7, 1815. First they tried to transfer the stigma of aristocracy to the Republicans. For example, at one point the New Jersey Federalists referred to the Republicans as the "monied aristocracy." *Federalist,* April 5, 1813. Another time they described a Republican parade as a "select party of *fashionables,* rigged out in a coach and six with outriders, postillions and footmen, if we understand the dialect." *Federalist,* August 16, 1824. Secondly, more and more, the New Jersey Federalists evinced concern and respect for the people as well as a desire for their support. One 1803 electioneering pamphlet constituted an appeal to farmers and the poor. *Serious Considerations Addressed to the Electors of New Jersey Concerning the Choice of Members of the Legislature for the Ensuing Year,* n.p., 1803. Also, when the Republicans passed a law increasing the fine for nonattendance at militia duty, the Federalists scored the law for the burden it placed on "plain men and mechanics." *Federalist,* September 29, 1806. Finally, by late in the Era of Good Feelings, the Federalists could write a hymn to the "poor man." refer to the dignity of a laborer, and in public so reject the standard of nobility as to declare that " . . . if heraldry were guided by reason, a plough in a field arable would be the most noble and ancient arms." *Federalist,* July 14, 1823; June 28, November 8, 1824.

60. *Federalist,* November 4, December 9, 1811; Cadman, *The Corporation in New Jersey: Business and Politics, 1791–1875,* p. 63. Besides the Republican legislature's creation of state banks, the local banking issue contained a second facet, the placing of a tax upon privately owned bank stock. Here the New Jersey Federalists were hard pressed to show how the "common man" would be injured by such a move. However, still they managed to couch one of their objections in democratic terms. The "principle of equality in taxation" was being trampled upon, the Federalists said, since other types of stock were not taxed. Rodgers," Some Phases of New Jersey History in the Jeffersonian Period," p. 32; *Federalist,* November 20, 1809. The banking issue, probably the most influential state issue of the period, raged in New Jersey from 1809 to 1812. For

further discussion of the Federalist viewpoint on the matter, see such issues of the *Federalist* as September 18, 25, October 2, November 20, 1809; November 19, 1810; August 26, November 4, December 9, 16, 1811; January 20, February 3, 10, 1812.

61. *Newark Gazette*, March 8, 1803; *Federalist*, September 29, 1801; July 11, 1803; November 4, 1805; August 25, 1806; *Philadelphia Gazette*, December 13, 1802; Fischer, *The Revolution of American Conservatism*, p. 167; Miller, *Alexander Hamilton*, p. 553.

62. *Federalist*, February 9, 1802.

63. Hofstadter, *The Idea of a Party System*, p. 95.

64. *Federalist*, September 29, 1806; Prince, *New Jersey's Jeffersonian Republicans*, p. 129. Of course, if anything, New Jersey Federalist party machinery was even less democratic than that of the Republicans.

65. *True American*, December 1, 1806; January 11, 1808; *Federalist*, November 7, 1803; March 17, 1806; November 5, 1807; February 14, 1814, Prince, *New Jersey's Jeffersonian Republicans*, pp. 226–28; Pasler, "The Federalist Party in Burlington County, New Jersey," p. 173. The Federalists had little success in gaining appointments from Republican-dominated joint meetings of the legislature. In 1805, when the Federalists held 36 percent of the legislative seats, they received about 5 percent of the appointments dispensed by the joint meeting. Prince, *New Jersey's Jeffersonian Republicans*, p. 225.

66. Joseph Bloomfield to Ebenezer Elmer, March 12, 1802, Ely Collection, New Jersey Historical Society; *Centinel of Freedom*, March 15, 1815; David Thompson to Samuel Southard, November 15, 1814, Samuel Southard Papers, Princeton University Library.

67. G. B. Vroom to Peter D. Vroom, Jr., November 22, 1802, Peter D. Vroom Papers, Rutgers University Library; *Federalist*, November 1, 15, 29, 1802; *New Jersey Journal*, November 2, 23, December 7, 1802; *New York Evening Post*, October 29, 1802; *Guardian*, November 18, December 9, 16, 1802; Fee, *The Transition from Aristocracy to Democracy*, pp. 130–31; *Minutes of the Joint Meeting*, 27th Session, 1st Sitting (October 28, 1802); MSS Minutes of the Governor's Privy Council, December 2, 1802, New Jersey State Library.

68. David Thompson to Samuel Southard, November 15, 1814, Samuel Southard Papers, Princeton University Library; *Centinel of Freedom*, March 14, 1815.

69. Cunningham, *The Jeffersonian-Republicans in Power*, p. 7; Prince, *New Jersey's Jeffersonian Republicans*, p. 105; *True American*, October 15, 1808.

70. Morton Borden, *Parties and Politics in the Early Republic, 1789–1815* (New York: Thomas Y. Crowell Company, 1967), p. 61; Joseph Bloomfield to Silas Dickerson, March 19, 1804, Ely Collection, New Jersey Historical Society; *Federalist*, September 10, October 22, 1804; September 30, 1805.

71. *Federalist*, April 8, 1805.

72. Ibid., December 2, 1805.

73. Ibid., November 30, 1807.

74. Joseph Bloomfield to Silas Dickerson, March 19, 1804, Ely Collection, New Jersey Historical Society.

75. *Federalist*, October 20, 1806; Prince, *New Jersey's Jeffersonian Republicans*, p. 130; Sher, "Party Battles in Middlesex County," p. 82; Rodgers, "Some Phases of New Jersey History in the Jeffersonian Period," p. 12; Fee, *The Transition from Aristocracy to Democracy*, pp. 142–43.

76. In 1806 the New Jersey Federalists won 49 percent of the state legislature.

77. Noble E. Cunningham, "Who Were the Quids?" *Mississippi Valley Historical Review* L (September, 1963); 254.

78. *Federalist*, October 22, 1804; Fee, *The Transition from Aristocracy to Democracy*, p. 141.

79. *True American*, October 26, 1806.

80. *Federalist*, October 3, 1803.

81. Ibid., September 9, 30, 1805; Pasler, "The Federalist Party in Burlington County, New Jersey," p. 156.

82. *True American*, October 5, 1807. Earlier, in 1805, James Imlay, Federalist leader in Monmouth County, had been unsuccessful in his attempt to gain a place for himself and one other Federalist on the Republican ticket. *True American*, May 5, 1806.

83. *Federalist*, October 21, 1805.

84. Ibid., October 29, 1804; September 22, 1806.

85. Ibid., March 17, September 22, 1806.

86. Ibid., October 21, 1805; *New Jersey Journal*, October 29, 1805; *Minutes of the Joint Meeting*, 30th Session, 1st Sitting (October 30, 1805); *True American*, November 30, 1806; *Guardian*, November 15, 1801; *Minutes of the Joint Meeting*, 32nd Session, 1st Sitting (October 30, 1807); Deshler, "Governor Joseph Bloomfield of New Jersey."

87. *True American*, October 4, 1802; *Federalist*, October 11, 1802; Hofstadter, *The Idea of a Party System*, p. 149; Banner, *To the Hartford Convention*, p. 66; Fischer, *The Revolution of American Conservatism*, p. 192. Elsewhere, Fischer has noted that later such young New Jersey Federalists as Joseph Hornblower and Lucius H. Stockton became outspoken apologists for Federalist party organization. Fischer, *The Revolution of American Conservatism*, pp. 330–31.

88. *True American*, February 6, 1809. Speaking of the nation as a whole, Fischer has observed that ". . . whole editions of . . . [Federalist electioneering] papers were distributed free." Fischer, *The Revolution of American Conservatism*, p. 143.

89. Prince, "New Jersey's Democratic Republicans," pp. 379–80.

90. *True American*, October 8, 1810.

91. Prince, "New Jersey's Democratic Republicans," pp. 479, 481; Pasler, "The Federalist Party in Burlington County, New Jersey," p. 146; *True American*, July 25, 1803.

140   THE NEW JERSEY FEDERALISTS

92. Pole, "The Suffrage in New Jersey," p. 50; Prince, "New Jersey's Democratic Republicans," p. 460.

93. New Jersey Federalists even tried using new party designations after 1800. Between 1801 and 1811 they variously referred to themselves as Federal Republicans, Republican Federalists, Washingtonians, and Federal Americans. *Federalist*, September 22, 1801; April 4, September 12, 1803; October 2, 1809; Sher, "Party Battles in Middlesex County," p. 106; *Newark Gazette*, September 27, 1803; Cunningham, *The Jeffersonian-Republicans in Power*, p. 296; Fischer, *The Revolution of American Conservatism*, p. 34.

94. *True American*, November 23, 1802; November 26, 1804; *National Intelligencer*, December 3, 1802; *Guardian*, November 25, December 16, 1802; Pole, "The Reform of Suffrage and Representation in New Jersey," pp. 174–75; Manning Dauer, "Election of 1804," *History of American Presidential Elections*, v.1, edited by Arthur M. Schlesinger, Jr. (New York: Chelsea House Publishers, 1971), pp. 164, 166, 168, 173; Fischer, *The Revolution of American Conservatism*, p. 84; Zahniser, *Charles Cotesworth Pinckney*, p. 244; McCormick, *The Second American Party System*, p. 126; Fee, *The Transition from Aristocracy to Democracy*, p. 137; Prince, "New Jersey's Democratic Republicans," pp. 187, 655; Prince, *New Jersey's Jeffersonian Republicans*, p. 122; *Federal Republican*, December 20, 1803; Joseph Bloomfield to Jonathan Dayton, November 12, 1804 in William Richardson, "The Federalist Fathers and the Founding of Jersey City," *Historical Society of Hudson County Magazine* V (1927); 46.

95. *Centinel of Freedom*, May 3, August 2, 23, 1808; Fee, *The Transition from Aristocracy to Democracy*, pp. 151–54; Zahniser, *Charles Cotesworth Pinckney*, p. 249; Smelser, *The Democratic Republic, 1801–1815*, p. 174; Cunningham, *The Jeffersonian-Republicans in Power*, pp. 288, 291; Chambers, *Political Parties in a New Nation*, pp. 122, 190; *True American*, August 15, 1808; *Federalist*, September 19, 1808; McCormick, *The Second American Party System*, p. 128; Prince, *New Jersey's Jeffersonian Republicans*, p. 164. In 1808 the New Jersey Federalists even took the unusual step of directing special propaganda to the three staunchest Republican counties. *A Candid Appeal to the Honest Yeomanry of Essex, Morris and Sussex Counties . . . New Jersey . . . on . . . the Approaching Presidential and Congressional Elections*, n.p., October, 1808. However, for unknown reasons, the New Jersey Federalists did not send representatives to the 1808 presidential nominating meeting in New York. Samuel Eliot Morison, "The First National Nominating Convention, 1808," *American Historical Review* XVII (1911–1912): 756; Fischer, *The Revolution of American Conservatism*, pp. 86–87.

96. *Centinel of Freedom*, July 19, 1808.

97. *Ibid.*, August 23, September 13, 1808; *Federalist*, November 21, 1808.

98. William Lawson, et al., Federalist state committee of correspondence, to Sir [County Chairman], printed form letter, October 21, 1808.

99. As Fischer has said, "The full extent of [New Jersey Federalists'] local

organization [in 1808] is not known, but committees . . . were organized in all townships in Burlington County, [and] similar committees are known to have existed in Bergen, Hunterdon, Middlesex, Monmouth, Salem, Somerset, and Sussex counties." Fischer, *The Revolution of American Conservatism*, p. 67.

100. Joshua Wallace to _____ Township Committee, printed form letter, October 26, 1808.

101. Nicholas Bodine, et al., 4th District Committee, to Gentlemen, printed form letter, October 21, 1808. On all levels of Federalist committees, from the state committee of correspondence down to the district committee, young Federalists predominated in 1808. However, most of the candidates for national office that year were old Federalists. William Lawson, et al., Federalist state committee of correspondence, to Sir, printed form letter, October 21, 1808; Joshua Wallace to_____Township Committee, printed form letter, October 26, 1808; Nicholas Bodine, et al., 4th District Committee, to Gentlemen, printed form letter, October 21, 1808; *New Jersey Telescope*, November 8, 1808; Fischer, *The Revolution of American Conservatism*, pp. 62–63.

102. MSS Minutes of the Governor's Privy Council, November 12, 1808, p. 53, New Jersey State Library; Fee, *The Transition from Aristocracy to Democracy*, p. 158; Louis Martin Sears, *Jefferson and the Embargo* (North Carolina: Duke University Press, 1927), p. 204; Prince, "New Jersey's Democratic Republicans," pp. 545, 656; Prince, *New Jersey's Jeffersonian Republicans*, p. 164.

103. Unevenness of effort has been noted by Broussard in the behavior of the South Atlantic Federalists and by Fischer in the behavior of Federalists throughout the nation. Broussard, "The Federalists in the South Atlantic States," p. 56; Fischer, *The Revolution of American Conservatism*, p. 69.

104. Prince, "New Jersey's Democratic Republicans," p. 656; *Paladium of Liberty*, October 23, 1810; *True American*, September 24, 1810; October 14, November 14, 1811; Prince, *New Jersey's Jeffersonian Republicans*, p. 170; *Fredonian*, October 16, 1811; Rodgers, "Some Phases of New Jersey History in the Jeffersonian Period," p. 13. Besides the New Jersey Federalists disaster at the polls in 1811, that year they also lost their "single remaining [state officer] of the old Washington School" when the Republican legislature removed former state attorney general Aaron Woodruff from appointive office. *Pennsylvania Gazette*, November 13, 1811.

105. *True American*, October 21, 1811.

7

NEW JERSEY FEDERALISTS JOURNEY TOWARD THE SECOND PARTY SYSTEM

Contrary to the Republicans' expectation, the New Jersey Federalists revived in 1812. Again that year they fielded candidates for the national as well as the local elections.

As in 1808, the Federalists' impetus to contest the national elections originated with their belief that in the Republicans' foreign policy they possessed a statewide winning issue. This time they were correct, and in 1812 New Jersey again became Federalist.

According to the New Jersey Federalists, the choice before the electorate in 1812 amounted to a choice between war candidates and peace candidates. Their opposition was the war interest, and they were the peace men, giving up the name of Federalists to campaign as "Friends of Peace."[1]

Although the New Jersey Federalists brandished a bipartisan shield in 1812, the Republicans correctly divined that the peace party was little more than an "alias" for the Federalist party.[2] For, while the Federalists assiduously sought bipartisan support, control of the peace group was firmly in their hands.[3]

The most notable aspect of New Jersey Federalist campaign activity in 1812 was the party's unusual effort at organization.[4] That year the Federalists not only erected statewide machinery of a type that had been absent since 1800, but they even surpassed their best efforts of a dozen years earlier.[5]

Catching the Republicans unaware, the New Jersey Federalists seized the initiative in the campaign by holding their organizational meetings early.[6] The first reported meeting occurred in May in the state capital. That caucus called for a statewide conclave of the Friends of Peace to be held on the Fourth of July. Moreover, it asked that local meetings select representatives to attend what was the New Jersey Federalists' first delegate convention.[7]

Meeting some two weeks following the declaration of war, the Independence Day peace convention addressed the public on the "alarming state of affairs." Inasmuch as the attainment of peace demanded a "change of Men," the conclave of representatives from eleven counties arranged for the nomination of Federalist candidates for national offices. First, it appointed a state committee of correspondence to participate with representatives of other states in choosing candidates for President and Vice President. Secondly, it called another statewide meeting of delegates to choose New Jersey's peace candidates for congressmen and for presidential electors.[8]

On September 15, 1812, the delegates of the New Jersey Friends of Peace from all thirteen counties met in Trenton and named their candidates for federal offices.[9] Their choice of presidential electors did not excite Republican comment, but their selection of Congressional nominees did. Three of the six were the Republican Congressmen who had voted with the Federalists against war being declared. When these Republicans accepted the peace party's nomination, the Republican press retorted that their names were

ever to be blotted out of the tablet of Republicanism.[10]

On the same day that some New Jersey Federalists were attending the state peace convention, others were attending the New York conclave convened to choose the party's presidential and vice presidential candidates. In all, there were twelve New Jersey delegates, more than from any other state except New York, the size of each state's delegation having been left up to the individual state.

As with the other states, New Jersey's delegation had been

selected by its state committee of correspondence. Among the Jerseyans chosen to attend were Elias Boudinot, William Griffith, Richard Stockton, and Jonathan Rhea. Originally, New Jersey Federalists evidently had favored Judge Bushrod Washington for president. This nephew of George Washington was well known to Jerseyans, for since 1798 New Jersey had been part of the circuit to which he was assigned as a justice of the United States Supreme Court. However, at the national nominating meeting the New Jersey Federalists received a letter of declination from Judge Washington in which he counseled that rather than allow James Madison to be reelected, he felt DeWitt Clinton should be supported, a stand the Federalists as a whole eventually took.[11]

Besides erecting statewide machinery in 1812, the New Jersey Federalists did something even more unusual that year. Though earlier they had soundly denounced the clubs formed by Republicans, they now began to found their own political clubs, called Washington Benevolent Societies.[12] Clearly, the appearance of such a society in New Jersey at this time was part of the New Jersey Federalists' all-out effort to win the state in 1812.[13]

Coinciding with the first state peace convention, the initial public appearance of the Washington Benevolent Society in New Jersey occurred in Trenton on July 4, 1812. That day the Washington Society presented a parade consisting of over 200 participants and viewed by spectators from neighboring towns and other parts of the state as well as from Trenton itself. Considerable pomp, designed to mobilize the electorate, marked the occasion. The Society possessed its own banner and marched under the superintendence of three marshals of the day, who rode on horseback. These officials carried wands bearing the motto, "For Our Country," and every member of the association wore the badge of the Society,

a striking likeness of the beloved Washington printed upon satin, surmounted with the motto "Pro Patria" (for our country).[14]

The promise of participation in the parade and receipt of the badge of the Society had been used as part of the Trenton Society's membership drive, for the Federalists were interested in gaining as many members as possible. Both the night before the parade and from 9:00 A.M. until marching time on the day itself, the officers of the Society, mainly young Federalists, were busy admitting new members. As indicated by the speed with which membership was conferred, this was no exclusive society. Anyone who would cast a Federalist vote was welcome.[15]

Although the Washington Societies did perform acts of benevolence in New Jersey, their primary function was as an arm of the Federalist party organization. Their very name indicated the party's aim of exploiting the prestige of George Washington for electioneering purposes. In their apotheosis of Washington, the New Jersey Federalists did not hesitate even to announce that the *"shade* of Washington . . . our political father and saviour" counseled a return to "measures of peace," cautioning,

If ye be my disciples and love me, keep my commandments.
. . . *These things do,* and ye *shall yet live.*[16]

It is difficult to gauge the electoral impact of New Jersey's Washington Benevolent Societies, especially because Federalist efforts of all kinds were at an all-time high in 1812 as was the peace sentiment in New Jersey. Yet it is true that in 1812 the Federalists won both houses of the state legislature by adding to their camp three counties hitherto wholly or partially Republican, and that in all of these counties there were Washington Societies.[17]

Following their success in the October state legislative election, the Federalists faced two more canvasses in 1812. Congressmen and presidential electors were yet to be chosen. Control of the state legislature gave the Federalists the power to arrange for the holding of these contests in a manner advantageous to themselves, and at a caucus convened the evening before the 1812–1813 legislative session began, the Federalists determined to use this power to its utmost, believing that only through the election of proper candidates for President and Congress could the desired change in national policy be effected.[18]

The Federalists realized they had but little time to accomplish their ends since both contests were scheduled to be decided on November 3–4 via a popular election. So, once the legislative session began on October 27, the Federalists moved swiftly, and within two days they had secured New Jersey's eight electoral votes for DeWitt Clinton. Over the protests of the helpless Republicans, the Federalists repealed the 1804 law providing for the popular election of presidential electors and returned this power to the state legislature, wherein it had lodged during the Federalist era. Then it only remained for the Federalists to choose the particular men who ultimately would cast the Clinton ballots.[19]

The Federalists' approach to the problem of the Congressional election also featured an alteration of electoral law. After repealing the law mandating a general election for November 3–4, 1812, the Federalists replaced it with one authorizing a district election for January 12–13, 1813.

Next, the Federalists created Congressional election districts so arranged as to make it likely that the peace party would win a majority of the state's six-man Congressional delegation.[20] Republican strength was isolated in a single district—the northern one, composed of Bergen, Essex, and Morris counties— which was empowered to elect only two of the six Congressmen. Both the central district—Monmouth, Middlesex, Somerset, and Hunterdon—which had delivered a Federalist majority earlier that month, and the southern district of Burlington, Gloucester, Cape May, Salem, and Cumberland, normally Federalist, were expected to elect peace men. They did, and thus the New Jersey peace party controlled the state's thirteenth Congressional delegation, possessing four of the six seats.[21]

With electoral success behind them, the New Jersey Federalists turned their attention toward securing the state's appointive offices. Once again the Federalists were able to accomplish their aim as a consequence of controlling the legislature.

In the 1812–1813 joint meetings of that body the Federalists dismissed many Republicans and appointed members of their own party in the Republicans' stead. Thus, offices as high as the governorship and as humble as that of the doorkeeper returned to Federalist hands.[22]

Some Federalists were considered by the legislature as having a prior, binding claim on certain offices. These were the men who had been turned out of those offices by the opposition and replaced with Republicans, for the New Jersey Federalist party considered it

> not only a political but also a moral duty, to restore to office
> men who . . . [had] . . . been wrongfully displaced. . . .[23]

Despite all their electoral activity during the early days of the thirty-seventh legislature, by November 11, 1812, the New Jersey Federalists also had formally stated their administration's policy regarding the war. This was accomplished through a set of resolutions, passed by both houses of the legislature.

The New Jersey government was unalterably opposed to the war with England, which it considered "inexpedient, ill-timed and most dangerously impolitic." Yet, although it desired that the war be ended immediately, until peace did come New Jersey would perform those "Constitutional duties" that war conferred upon the state.[24]

Subsequently the New Jersey Republicans accused the Federalist state government of not supporting the war. According to the Republicans, the Federalists were guilty of such acts as discouraging enlistments, opposing loans to the United States government, and objecting to the fitting out of privateers to harrass England's commerce.[25]

However, true to their word, the New Jersey Federalists did contribute to the war effort. For example, members of the party served in key positions in the state militia. Also, both the governor and the legislature gave attention to military matters.

At one point, as commander-in-chief of the New Jersey mi-

148   THE NEW JERSEY FEDERALISTS

litia, Governor Ogden directed that there was to be full compliance with a United States law governing the militia. Brigade inspectors were to insure that every militiaman had armed and equipped himself as described in the law. Earlier, Ogden had called the legislature's attention to certain deficiencies in the state's military preparedness. To deal with them, the Assembly formed a military committee, and ultimately the legislature voted a $5,000 appropriation to rectify the particular problems Ogden had mentioned.[26]

Still, although the New Jersey Federalist government did contribute to the war effort, it did so only in a nominal fashion. Notably, the Federalists provided that the resources of New Jersey be expended only in defense of the state. Not only the activities of the militia proper, but those of the governor were to be confined to New Jersey.[27]

After 1812 the New Jersey Federalists continued to campaign as the peace party for several years. In 1813, 1814, and even in 1815, when the war had ended, the Federalists' electoral tickets bore the designation, "Friends of Peace."[28]

However, never again did the peace issue carry the Federalists to victory.[29] Still, between 1813 and 1815 the New Jersey Federalists enjoyed considerable electoral success.[30]

In 1813, when they returned to minority status in the state, the Federalists won 43 percent of the New Jersey legislature. And, in contrast to their earlier seesaw pattern of the 1801–1811 period, they held this high percentage for three consecutive years.[31]

Moreover, the New Jersey Federalists made an impressive showing in the 1814 Congressional election, the last one they entered.[32] Exceeding their percentage in the legislature by four points, the Federalists captured 48 percent of the vote in that general election, leaving the Republicans shaken.[33]

At the 1814 Peace Convention, held to nominate their Congressional candidates, the New Jersey Federalists had expressed sympathy for the New England Federalists.[34] And their attitude did not change following the Hartford Convention. Rather, the New Jersey Federalists approved of the Convention and its proceedings. At one point, for example, they referred to the "wisdom of the men at Hartford."[35]

When Governor Pennington's January, 1815, message to the New Jersey legislature attacked the Convention as a

> combination . . . hostile to the Constitution and Government of the Union. . . .

the Federalists protested. First they moved that the message be returned to the Governor for reconsideration. That motion being defeated, they next moved, again unsuccessfully, to strike the objectionable parts of the message from the minutes.[36] Later, in February, the Federalist legislators voted in favor of the Connecticut legislature's resolutions, proposing the adoption of the Constitutional amendments recommended by the Hartford Convention.[37]

The Federalist-Republican battles over the Hartford Convention and the Connecticut resolutions which resulted from it constituted the two parties' last major issue-oriented confrontations on the floor of the New Jersey legislature. By the election of 1816 it became evident that a new era was being entered. Party ideology and party spirit were diminishing, and party organization was disintegrating, trends which increasingly affected the dominant Republicans as well as the eclipsed Federalists.[38] But it was the Federalists' electoral strength, and not that of the Republicans, that would dwindle as the period wore on.[39]

The year 1816 found the New Jersey Federalists making a capitulatory declaration they would repeat for the remainder of the first party system period: they would make no attempt to win the legislature.[40] Yet, New Jersey Federalists by no means wholly passed from the scene then or any time during the Era of Good Feelings.[41]

In 1816 and thereafter they did not campaign above the county level,[42] yet in 1816 for the last time they carried five of the thirteen New Jersey counties. Thereafter until 1819 they held four counties. And, to the end of the first party system period, Cape May Federalists, at least, never failed to deliver a wholly Federalist legislative delegation, even in 1824, while in Burlington the Federalists controlled the county equally long, allowing only a few legislative seats to go to the Republicans between 1820 and 1822. Bergen was wholly Federalist as late as 1818, and Gloucester, which had gone partially Republican since 1816, returned a full Federalist delegation to the legislature in 1823, bringing to three the number of counties the Federalists carried that year in their best election since 1817.[43]

During the years 1816 through 1820 the Federalists' principal legislative strength, such as it was, derived from their usually reliable counties. But starting in 1821, when their strength further dwindled in the traditional Federalist counties,[44] the Federalists began to win an equal or nearly equal number of seats in former Republican bastions. In fact, in 1821, the Federalists even gained one representative from New Jersey's foremost Republican county, Essex.[45]

Sometimes the victories of Federalists in former Republican strongholds resulted from their having run as independents. In Sussex County, for example, where perhaps the zenith in nomination chaos was reached in 1821, no less than twenty-six tickets were fielded, and one of the four winning candidates was a Federalist.[46]

The other route Federalists used to gain election in traditionally Republican counties was the union ticket.[47] As early as 1815 New Jersey Federalists began to run on electoral tickets with dissident Republicans, their common meeting ground being opposition to the Republican caucus which had kept both groups out of office.[48] Thereafter union tickets remained a part of the political scene for the duration of the first party system.[49]

During the Era of Good Feelings Federalists hungered for appointive office just as they did for elective office. In joint meeting, even more than at the polls, Federalist success depended upon Republican cooperation.

Such cooperation did exist, but to a far lesser extent than would have satisfied the Federalists.[50] Probably the most important post gained by a Federalist during the period was that of state attorney general, which went to Theodore Frelinghuysen in 1817. Garnering the votes of every Federalist legislator plus those of six Republicans, Frelinghuysen won by one vote.[51] The rest of the appointments gained by the Federalists during the period were rather minor ones, a fact the Federalists lamented in one of their many complaints over being virtually a proscribed sect.[52]

In 1819 Federalist Burlington County launched a movement which Republicans claimed had been designed by the Federalists as a means to regain political power. It became known as the "Anti-Missouri Crusade."[53]

On August 30, 1819, Federalists Elias Boudinot and William Newbold led what probably was the first public meeting held in the nation for the purpose of opposing the extension of slavery into Missouri. That meeting, which occurred in Burlington City, called for a statewide conclave to take place in the state capital.[54]

Well-attended, the October 29 Trenton meeting also was Federalist dominated in its leadership. William Griffith served as secretary, and the six-member correspondence committee contained five Federalists.

It was the task of the correspondence committee, led by Elias Boudinot, to obtain the cooperation of others in furthering the anti-slavery cause. To do so, the committee issued a printed circular which by the middle of November had been distributed to influential persons in all of the Eastern states.[55]

As one result of the correspondence committee's work, additional public meetings occurred in New Jersey as well as in other parts of the country. Local meetings held in New Jersey, in accordance with the committee's recommendations, included those of New Brunswick, Salem, Bridgeton, Woodbury, Freehold, Hunterdon County, Mount Holly, and Monmouth County. Like the state conclave, all of these lower level meetings in New Jersey were dominated by Federalists, at least insofar as their leadership was concerned.[56]

Beginning with the initial gathering in Burlington, each New Jersey meeting recommended that Congress prohibit slavery not only in Missouri but in any new state admitted to the Union. Then, in January, 1820, this sentiment was enunciated in the name of the entire state by the New Jersey legislature. Brought to the floor via the report of a committee chaired by Federalist William Griffith, the anti-extension resolutions had passed easily.[57]

Each New Jersey senator and Congressman, every one a Republican, was sent a personal copy of the legislature's resolutions. Still, when the vote was taken, half of the state's Congressmen voted against restriction.

Widely attacked for this act, the anti-restrictionist Congressmen defended themselves by saying that they had been forced to vote against restriction in order to frustrate a Federalist plot, for

> the Federalists have seized upon . . . [the Missouri question] and are seeking to turn it to their advantage in order to regain their former influence and power.

This charge the Federalists heartily denied.[58]

Abolitionism, the reason for the anti-Missouri stance of most of the New Jersey Federalists, was not the only manifestation of Federalist desires for social betterment during the Era of Good Feelings. Prominence in religious and moralistic societies was another.[59]

For example, Federalists constituted the principal leaders of the New Jersey Bible Society, which supported missionary and benevolent activities. By 1817 they had founded local chapters of that Society in at least three counties—Gloucester, Somerset, and Middlesex. On the county as on the state level, Federalists dominated the Bible societies, such Federalists as Andrew Kirkpatrick, James Neilson, Peter Dumont, and Joseph V. Clark assuming the presidency of the various local chapters.[60]

Federalists were also conspicuous in the leadership of the New Jersey Society for the Suppression of Vice and Immorality. Among not only the officers of the November 11, 1817, meeting in Trenton, which established the Society, but also among the permanent officers of the Society elected by that meeting, Frederalists predominated.[61]

New Jersey Federalists of the Era of Good Feelings period further demonstrated their concern for social reform in the state legislature, where most Federalist members voted in favor of reform bills, occasionally in somewhat larger percentages than the Republicans.[62] Moreover, two of the handful of reform measures passed by the state legislature during the Era of Good Feelings were sponsored by Federalists, although these were not party measures. In 1817 James Parker successfully steered through the legislature a bill to establish a free school fund,[63] and in 1819 William Griffith, of Burlington County, introduced a bill to abolish imprisonment for debt. Unsuccessful for several years, Griffith continued his efforts to secure such a measure until 1823, when the bill finally passed.[64]

That same year the final erosion of the first American party system began in earnest. Underway by 1823, the party realignment that eventually resulted was a true one. It sent New Jersey Federalist leaders as well as the party's rank and file into different camps, where together with Republicans they formed new parties.[65]

The immediate catalyst for realignment was the forthcoming presidential election. New Jersey Federalists evinced increasing interest in that election after 1823 as it became clear that the Republican party would not be able to agree on a candidate.[66] More and more as the election neared, men of the Federalist as well as the Republican party lined up behind one of several Republican candidates for president and stated their political orientation in these terms.[67]

At the outset, the most popular candidate among New Jersey Federalist leaders was John C. Calhoun.[68] Soon, however, the 1824 race, and later that of 1828, narrowed to a contest between John Q. Adams and Andrew Jackson, and many Federalist leaders chose one of these two men as their candidate, each man's choice being based largely upon his conception of which candidate would gratify his political ambition.[69]

On that basis, a number of Federalist leaders became Adams

men. They included Theodore Frelinghuysen; Richard, Lucius, and Robert Stockton; several Burlington Federalists like William Griffith, William and Richard Coxe, Richard Beatty, John Evans, Jonathan Hough, William Irich and William Pearson; Samuel Bayard; Samuel Edgar; Theodore Parker; Aaron Leaming; the Ewings; the Kinneys; and the Hornblowers.[70]

Other New Jersey Federalists declared for Jackson.[71] Among them were Garret D. Wall, Peter D. Vroom, the Lloyds, Aaron Ogden Dayton, John Beatty, James Green, James Parker, William Chetwood, Joseph W. Scott, Aaron Ogden, Elias B. D. Ogden, Thomas Ryerson, D. J. Hardenbergh, James Neilson, the Daytons, William T. Anderson, Peter I. Clark, Thomas Gordon, and Jacob R. Thompson.[72]

However, it was in the Jacksonian camp that ex-New Jersey Federalists achieved the greater importance, and they did so quite early. In June of 1824 ex-Federalists Merriman Smith and Aaron Ogden Dayton were the leaders of the public meeting which set the Jackson candidacy in motion in New Jersey.[73] Then, at the September, 1824, Jackson state convention called for by the June meeting, ex-Federalists again were prominent, notably Aaron Ogden Dayton, who served as secretary.[74]

In October, a second Jacksonian state meeting was held. On this occasion a former Federalist presided, and the electoral ticket chosen at this convention contained the name of ex-Federalist James Parker.[75]

During the 1824 campaign, ex-Federalist Garret D. Wall served as chairman of the Jackson party's state correspondence committee.[76] While Wall coordinated the Jackson campaign throughout South Jersey, other ex-Federalists were responsible for campaign activity in smaller geographic areas—James Parker in Middlesex County, William Chetwood in Essex County, and James Green in Somerset County.[77]

The only apparent evidence of ex-Federalist participation in the Adams organization in 1824 was the presence of William Halstead, Jr., on the list of Adams convention delegates and the publication of an Adams organ by Robert Stockton.[78] Only in 1826 did the Adams camp begin to welcome ex-New Jersey

Federalists as the Jacksonians had in 1824.[79]

Still, by 1828, there was no question but that ex-New Jersey Federalists were important in the Adams organization as well as among the Jacksonians.[80] The 1828 Adams convention not only included many former Federalists as delegates but appointed ex-Federalist Joseph Hornblower as one of the convention's three chairmen. Together with the other chairmen, Hornblower also drew up that convention's address.[81]

At the 1828 Jackson state convention too, the importance of ex-Federalists in that party was emphasized. Besides many former Federalists who were present as delegates to the convention, two of the five members of the address committee were ex-Federalists, as were four of the thirteen state correspondence committeemen and one of the six officers of the meeting.[82] Moreover, the Jackson convention appointed ex-Federalist Garret D. Wall to head its central state committee, and control of that committee became the mechanism whereby the Wall-Federalist faction continued to hold great power in the New Jersey Jacksonian party.[83]

The year 1828–1829 also saw the names of ex-Federalists, whether Jacksonians or Adams men, being linked with high office. At the 1828 Adams convention two former Federalists, Aaron Leaming and Theodore Frelinghuysen, were named as electors. Both parties' 1828 Congressional tickets contained former Federalists. Furthermore, in January of 1829, an Adamsite, Theodore Frelinghuysen, was appointed United States senator by the New Jersey legislature.[84]

But Jacksonians were more fortunate than Adams men at this time, for their candidate had won the presidency. Jackson proceeded to bestow federal patronage rather freely upon those of his supporters who were ex-New Jersey Federalists. For instance, Garret D. Wall was appointed United States Attorney for the district of New Jersey, being replaced later that year by ex-Federalist James Green. James Parker, Aaron Ogden, and Henry Low all received posts as collectors of customs, and Francis B. Ogden was appointed United States consul at Liverpool, England.[85]

After October, 1829, New Jersey Jacksonians gained control of many state offices since they had won the legislature. For instance, Peter D. Vroom became governor following fellow ex-Federalist Garret D. Wall's refusal of that post,[86] and former Federalists Joseph W. Scott, Robert Armstrong, and Elias Van Aradale were appointed prosecutors of the pleas in their counties.[87]

Ex-New Jersey Federalists' achievement of high positions in political party organization continued after 1830. In 1831 two ex-Federalists were prominent enough in the National Republican party to be selected as part of an eight-member delegation to that party's 1832 presidential nominating convention. The Wall-Federalist faction remained in control after the Jacksonian party developed into the Democratic party, and Theodore Frelinghuysen and Charles Ewing emerged as leaders of the New Jersey Whig party as did William Halstead, Jr., who served as New Jersey Whig party chairman from 1834 to 1836. By 1840 ex-Federalists Frederick Frelinghuysen, Jr., Edward Q. Keasbey, John J. Chetwood, Thomas H. Hughes, Thomas P. Hughes, and Charles Kinsey also had served as state Whig party officials.[88]

Similarly, ex-Federalists continued to win high elective and appointive office after 1830. Former Federalist Joseph Hornblower was appointed chief justice of New Jersey in 1832 and held that office for many years afterward. In 1832 former Federalist James Parker was elected to Congress, where he remained until 1837. Garret D. Wall received an appointment as United States senator in 1834, while in 1836 both Democrat William Chetwood and Whig William Halstead, Jr., were elected to Congress. Peter D. Vroom, Democrat, gained a Congressional seat the following term, which began in 1838, and in 1843 Democrat Daniel Haines became governor of New Jersey. Then, in 1844, Theodore Frelinghuysen received the Whig party's nomination for vice president of the United States. Finally, in 1851, Robert Stockton became a United States senator.[89]

Nearly forty years earlier, when the Federalists had lost the state for the last time, the *Essex Patriot* expressed the hope that the "Sun of Federalism . . . [had] not set forever."[90] But it had.

Still, from the foregoing, it can be seen that even the total disappearance of the party did not permanently remove from power those men who had been New Jersey Federalism's leaders.

NOTES

1. Prince, *New Jersey's Jeffersonian Republicans,* pp. 170, 173; Norman K. Risjord, "Election of 1812," *History of American Presidential Elections,* vol. I, edited by Arthur M. Schlesinger, Jr. (New York: Chelsea House Publishers, 1971), p. 250; Wilson, *Outline History of New Jersey,* p. 88; Peter Levine, "The New Jersey Federalist Party Convention of 1814," *The Journal of the Rutgers University Library* XXXIII (December, 1969): 1; Beckwith, "Mahlon Dickerson of New Jersey," p. 181; *Federalist,* October 26, 1812; *Proceedings and Address of the Delegates of the People of New Jersey,* Trenton, 1812. The peace issue was not new in 1812 as a New Jersey Federalist appeal. Rather, It was more the case of an appeal whose time had come. As early as 1807 the Federalists had begun to articulate the peace issue in the very terms they would use in 1812 but to no avail. Even the phrase "Friends of Peace," used by the Federalists to great advantage in 1812, dated from 1807. *Federalist,* October 5, 1807, September 21, 1807, September 11, 1809, September 16, 1811, July 6, 1812; *Centinel of Freedom,* October 17, 1809; Pasler, "The Federalist Party in Burlington County, New Jersey," p. 162; Rodgers, "Some Phases of New Jersey History in the Jeffersonian Period," p. 89; Wilson, *The Jersey Shore,* vol. I, p. 331; Fee, *The Transition from Aristocracy to Democracy,* p. 174; Smelser, *The Democratic Republic,* p. 217; Prince, *New Jersey's Jeffersonian Republicans,* p. 171; Brown, *The Republic in Peril,* p. 114.

2. *Centinel of Freedom,* October 19, 1813.

3. Risjord, "Election of 1812," pp. 257, 272; Lynn W. Turner, "Elections of 1816 and 1820," *History of American Presidential Elections,* vol. I, edited by Arthur M. Schlesinger, Jr. (New York: Chelsea House Publishers, 1971), p. 309; Elmer, *The Constitution and Government of the Province and State of New Jersey,* p. 151; *Federalist,* June 1, 1812; Fee, *The Transition from Aristocracy to Democracy,* p. 182; Sher, "Party Battles in Middlesex County," p. 100.

4. Levine, "The New Jersey Federalist Party Convention of 1814," p. 21; Risjord, "Election of 1812," p. 250.

5. McCormick, *The Second American Party System,* p. 127.

6. Risjord, "Election of 1812," pp. 257, 264; Levine, "The New Jersey Federalist Party Convention of 1814," p. 1. Following the Federalists' July 4 meeting, the Republicans hastily called one for July 10, and while the Federalists' state nominating convention occurred on September 15, the Republicans did not hold theirs until October 20. Prince, *New Jersey's Jeffersonian Republicans,* pp.

158   THE NEW JERSEY FEDERALISTS

173–74; Fee, *The Transition from Aristocracy to Democracy*, p. 178.

7. *True American*, May 25, 1812; Pasler, "The Federalist Party in Burlington County, New Jersey," pp. 173–74; *Guardian*, May 21, 1812; *Federalist*, May 18, 25, June 1, 8, 15, 29, 1812; Pasler and Pasler, "Federalist Tenacity in Burlington County," p. 202. The Trenton meeting had requested only that county meetings choose the delegates to the July state peace convention. But Burlington County, at least, began the delegate selection process at the grassroots level. There, township meetings selected delegates to attend the county meeting. The members of the county meeting then chose delegates to the state meeting. *Federalist*, May 18, 25, 1812.

8. *Proceedings and Address of the Convention of Delegates to the People of New Jersey*, Trenton, July 4, 1812; Samuel Eliot Morison, *The Life and Letters of Harrison Gray Otis, Federalist, 1765–1845*, vol. I (Boston: Houghton Mifflin Company, 1913), p. 309; Fee, *The Transition from Aristocracy to Democracy*, pp. 175–76; Pasler, "The Federalist Party in Burlington County, New Jersey," pp. 175–76; Pasler and Pasler, "Federalist Tenacity in Burlington County," p. 202. According to at least one source, it is probable that the Massachusetts peace convention occurred as an offshoot of New Jersey's Morison, *The Life and Letters of Harrison Gray Otis*, vol. II, p. 59.

9. *Federalist*, July 27, August 24, September 21, 1812; Fischer, *The Revolution of American Conservatism*, p. 329. Men with legislative and/or legal backgrounds predominated at the convention; 65 percent of the delegates had served in the state legislature and 69 percent were lawyers. *Proceedings and Address of the Delegates of the People of New Jersey*, Trenton, September 15, 1812.

10. *Federalist*, July 6, 1812; Prince, *New Jersey's Jeffersonian Republicans*, pp. 171, 174; Fee, *The Transition from Aristocracy to Democracy*, pp. 174–75; Smelser, *The Democratic Republic*, p. 217; Brown, *Republic in Peril*, p. 114. Later, the Congressional peace ticket was revised. All but one of the Republicans were dropped and replaced by Federalists, indicating once again that in its leadership the New Jersey peace party was the Federalist party in disguise. *Federalist*, January 4, 1813.

11. Morison, *The Life and Letters of Harrison Gray Otis*, vol. I, pp. 308–9; Smelser, *The Democratic Republic*, p. 245; Risjord, "Election of 1812," pp. 254, 290–91; John S. Murdock, "The First National Nominating Convention," *American Historical Review*, I (1895–1896):682; Fischer, *The Revolution of American Conservatism*, p. 88; H. M. Wagstaff, ed., *The Papers of John Steele* (Raleigh, North Carolina: North Carolina Historical Commission, 1924), p. 687; Elmer, *The Constitution and Government of the Province and State of New Jersey*, p. 281.

12. Eugene Link, *Democratic-Republican Societies, 1790–1800* (New York: Columbia University Press, 1942), pp. 208–9; Hofstadter, *The Idea of a Party System*, p. 95.

13. The first Washington Benevolent Society had been founded in nearby

New York City some three years earlier and before 1812 the idea had spread to states a good deal farther from New York than New Jersey. Fischer, *The Revolution of American Conservatism*, p. 116; Risjord, "Election of 1812," p. 251.

14. *Federalist*, June 29, July 6, 1812. The Washington Benevolent Societies remained a part of the New Jersey scene until 1817. By then there were county or town associations in at least nine of the thirteen New Jersey counties. In addition to those on the Fourth of July, public ceremonies also were held on Washington's birthday. "A handsome and plentiful dinner" sometimes was featured, as after 1812 the public exercises grew more elaborate. In 1813 the New Brunswick Society's commemoration of the Fourth of July included the dedication of "Washington-Hall," while both the New Brunswick and Princeton societies' Washington's Birthday celebration comprised a parade, an oration, music and prayers as well as a dinner. Then, the year 1815 saw the first appearance of the new Washington band in Trenton and that Society's participation in an elaborate ceremony involving the presentation of a new standard fashioned by the ladies of Trenton. Fischer, *The Revolution of American Conservatism*, pp. 118, 122, 128; New Brunswick *Times*, June 29, 1815; March 7, 1816; Fee, *The Transition from Aristocracy to Democracy*, pp. 200–201; Prince, "New Jersey's Democratic Republicans," p. 420; Sher, "Party Battles in Middlesex County," p. 104; *Federalist*, June 21, July 12, 1813; February 14, 28, March 7, June 20, July 19, 1814; February 27, June 19, July 24, August 14, 1815; February 9, June 24, 1816; *Guardian*, February 18, 25, June 10, 1813.

15. *Federalist*, June 29, July 6, 1812; Lewis Deare to Garret D. Wall, February 16, 1813, Wall Papers, Rutgers University Library; Banner, *To the Hartford Convention*, p. 264; Fischer, *The Revolution of American Conservatism*, pp. 119–120, 126; Smelser, *The Democratic Republic*, p. 247. Prominent among the young Federalists who dominated the state's Washington Benevolent Societies were Garret D. Wall, Lucius H. Stockton, Joseph W. Scott, and Richard Coxe. *Guardian*, February 18, 1813; *Federalist*, June 21, 1813; Fischer, *The Revolution of American Conservatism*, p. 331; Pasler and Pasler, "Federalist Tenacity in Burlington County," p. 204.

16. James Imlay, *An Oration Delivered Before the Washington Benevolent Society of the County of Burlington* (Mount Holly, New Jersey, February 22, 1814), pp. 15–16; George L. Roth, "Verse Satire on Faction, 1790–1815," *William and Mary Quarterly*, Third Series, XVII (October, 1960), 481; Victor Sapio, "Maryland's Federalist Period, 1808–1812," *Maryland Historical Quarterly* LXIV (Spring, 1969): 3; Banner, *To the Hartford Convention*, p. 264; Risjord, "Election of 1812," p. 251; Fischer, *The Revolution of American Conservatism*, pp. 121–22, 126. As they often were, the Republicans again were angered by the Federalists' appropriation of Washington on this occasion. In response to it they conjured up a vision of Washington saying to the Federalists, "Ye are not my disciples; I utterly disclaim and disown you." Fee, *The Transition from Aristocracy to Democracy*, p. 201. Also, partly in protest, the Cumber-

land County Republicans organized a Washington Whig Society. Lucius Elmer, *History of . . . Cumberland County. . . .* (Bridgeton, New Jersey: George Nixon Company, 1869), p. 57; *Constitution of the Washington Whig Society of the County of Cumberland, in the State of New Jersey,* n.p., 1815.

17. Fischer, *The Revolution of American Conservatism,* p. 118; Fee, *The Transition from Aristocracy to Democracy,* pp. 179–80; *True American,* October 16, 1812; *New York Evening Post,* October 17, 1812; Thayer, *As We Were: The Story of Old Elizabethtown,* p. 202; Rodgers, "Some Phases of New Jersey History in the Jeffersonian Period," p. 88; Elmer, *The Constitution and Government of the State and Province of New Jersey,* p. 151; Prince, *New Jersey's Jeffersonian Republicans,* p. 181.

18. Fee, *The Transition from Aristocracy to Democracy,* p. 182. As a result of the October, 1812 election, the New Jersey Federalist party had more than doubled its representation in the legislature. *True American,* October 14, 1811; *Federalist,* October 22, 1812; Elmer, *The Constitution and Government of the State and Province of New Jersey,* p. 151.

19. Fee, *The Transition from Aristocracy to Democracy,* pp. 182–183; *Essex Patriot,* December 1, 1812; Pole, "Jeffersonian Democracy and the Federalist Dilemma in New Jersey," p. 279; Smelser, *The Democratic Republic,* p. 248; *Federalist,* November 23, 1812; Elmer, *The Constitution and Government of the State and Province of New Jersey,* p. 152; Sher, "Party Battles in Middlesex County," p. 101; Prince, "New Jersey's Democratic Republicans," p. 378; Rodgers, "Some Phases of New Jersey History in the Jeffersonian Period," p. 98; *Niles' Weekly Register,* November 7, 1812. Although the Federalists moved swiftly, the interval of only several days between the enactment of the new law and the day previously scheduled for the election proved insufficient time in which to notify all counties of the change. Voting already had commenced in some counties when express riders arrived with the news. Elmer, *The Constitution And Government of the State and Province of New Jersey,* p. 152; Fee, *The Transition from Aristocracy to Democracy,* p. 184.

20. Now, with victory in the Congressional race seemingly assured, the New Jersey Federalists dropped two of the three Republicans from the peace ticket and replaced them with Federalists. Therefore, the half-Federalist half-Republican peace ticket, chosen at the September 15, 1812 peace convention, was no more, and in its place an all but Federalist slate was presented to the voters. *Federalist,* September 12, 1812; January 4, 25, 1813; *Proceedings and Address of the Delegates of the People of New Jersey,* Trenton, September 15, 1812, p. 5.

21. *Niles' Weekly Register,* November 7, 1812; Prince, "New Jersey's Democratic Republicans," pp. 518–19; Fee, *The Transition from Aristocracy to Democracy,* pp. 183, 185; Prince, *New Jersey's Jeffersonian Republicans,* pp. 179–81; Rodgers, "Some Phases of New Jersey History in the Jeffersonian Period," pp. 90–95; Francis Lee, *New Jersey as a Colony and as a State,* vol. III (New York, 1902), pp. 87–88; Elmer, *The Constitution and Government of the*

State and Province of New Jersey, p. 412; *Guardian,* November 19, 1812; *Federalist,* December 7, 14, 1812; January 4, 18, 25, 1813; J. Simpson to Samuel Southard, January 18, 1813, Samuel Southard Papers, Princeton University Library. The New Jersey Federalists also used their legislative powers to rid themselves of the state-owned banks they had described a year earlier as "engines [designed] to perpetuate the Democratic party in New Jersey." By law the Federalists provided for the immediate sale of the state's subscription rights in each of the banks. Also, an alteration in the banks' charters placed the choice of presidents and directors in the hands of the stockholders. When the Republicans returned to power in 1813, the Federalists rejoiced that the Republicans no longer could appoint Democrats to these "good, snug, fat, easy [bank] offices" as formerly they had. In fact, the Republicans never again established a state-owned or managed bank. Thus, the change the Federalists had made in the banking system stood as the outstanding example of an 1812-1813 Federalist measure that was not overturned by the thereafter dominant Republicans. Cadman, *The Corporation in New Jersey,* pp. 65–66, 423; *Federalist,* March 15, April 5, 1813; Fee, *The Transition from Aristocracy to Democracy,* p. 193; Rodgers, "Some Phases of New Jersey History in the Jeffersonian Period," pp. 34–36.

22. Prince, "New Jersey's Democratic Republicans," p. 615; Pasler, "The Federalist Party in Burlington County, New Jersey," p. 177; Rodgers, "Some Phases of New Jersey History in the Jeffersonian Period," p. 90; Pasler and Pasler, "Federalist Tenacity in Burlington County," p. 203; Fee, *The Transition from Aristocracy to Democracy,* p. 185; *Minutes of the Joint Meeting,* 37th Session, *passim.*

23. Richard Stockton to Governor [Aaron] Odgen, December 12, 1812, Morristown National Historical Park; *Federalist,* March 15, 22, 1813; Franklin Davenport to Jonathan Rhea, December 7, 1812, Gratz Collection, Historical Society of Pennsylvania; Lucius Elmer, MS. Diary, July 13, 1813, Rutgers University Library.

24. Rodgers, "Some Phases of New Jersey History in the Jeffersonian Period," p. 99; Pasler and Pasler, "Federalist Tenacity in Burlington County," p. 204; Wilson, *Outline History of New Jersey,* p. 94; Fee, *The Transition from Aristocracy to Democracy,* pp. 188–89; *Niles' Weekly Register,* November 21, 1812; *Centinel of Freedom,* November 31, 1812; Pasler, "The Federalist Party in Burlington County, New Jersey," p. 179; *Minutes of the Legislative Council,* 37th Session, 1st Sitting (November 1, 1812). Not all New Jersey Federalist leaders agreed with their party's stance against the war. In fact, several war Federalists broke with their party over this issue. Among them were the Strykers of Somerset County and Isaac Williamson and Jonathan Dayton of Essex County. Livermore, *The Twilight of Federalism,* p. 38; Elmer, *The Constitution and Government of the State and Province of New Jersey,* p. 75; *New Jersey Journal,* October 14, 1814; Fee, *The Transition from Aristocracy to Democracy,* pp. 223–24.

162 THE NEW JERSEY FEDERALISTS

25. *New Jersey Journal*, April 20, 1813; *Centinel of Freedom*, March 23, 1813.
26. Fee, *The Transition from Aristocracy to Democracy*, pp. 190–92; *General Orders for the Militia of New Jersey*, March 24, 1813, [signed] Aaron Ogden, Commander in Chief; *Centinel of Freedom*, January 26, 1813.
27. Pasler and Pasler, "Federalist Tenacity in Burlington County," p. 204; Rodgers, "Some Phases of New Jersey History in the Jeffersonian Period," p. 106; Wilson, *Outline History of New Jersey*, p. 94; *Federalist*, October 11, 1813. Because of a new law passed by the Federalists, had the present governor accepted a United States appointment, such as a generalship in the United States Army, as Governor Bloomfield had before him, Ogden automatically would have ceased to be governor. Fee, *The Transition from Aristocracy to Democracy*, p. 191; Elmer, *The Constitution and Government of the State and Province of New Jersey*, pp. 134–35; Deshler, "Governor Joseph Bloomfield of New Jersey;" Edward Wagner, "Relations of State and Federal Government in the War of 1812," Ph.D. diss., Ohio State University, 1963, p. 103. Indeed, Governor Ogden was nominated by President Madison for a major-generalship in the Army, but he declined the appointment. Irving Brant, ed., *James Madison: Commander in Chief*, vol. VI (New York: Bobbs Merrill, 1961), pp. 166–67; Elmer, *The Constitution and Government of the State and Province of New Jersey*, p. 153; Rodgers, "Some Phases of New Jersey History in the Jeffersonian Period," p. 116.
28. Prince, *New Jersey's Jeffersonian Republicans*, p. 204; *New Jersey Journal*, September 23, 1813; Fee, *The Transition from Aristocracy to Democracy*, pp. 194, 208; Levine, "The New Jersey Federalist Party Convention of 1814," pp. 3–4; *Proceedings and Address of the Convention of Delegates Held at the City of Trenton, on the Fourth of July, 1814, to the People of New Jersey*, n.p. July, 1814; *Federalist*, August 3, September 13, 27, 1813; March 7, June 12, August 9, 16, 30, September 20, October 14, 1814; August 14, 21, September 11, 25, October 9, 1815; Pasler, "The Federalist Party in Burlington County, New Jersey," p. 185; *Pennsylvania Gazette*, September 29, 1813, October 6, 1813. In 1815 the main thrust of the New Jersey Federalists' anti-war stand consisted of assertions that the war had brought nothing but losses, documented by detailed discussions of the ill effects resulting from the Republicans' bungling of foreign policy. Fee, *The Transition from Aristocracy to Democracy*, p. 207; *Federalist*, February 27, June 12, 19, October 15, 1815. Also that year, the New Jersey Federalists' use of the designation, "Friends of Peace" on their electoral tickets was not universal. In some counties, reversion to the Federalist label already had occurred by the election of 1815. *Federalists*, August 14, September 11, 1815.
29. In 1814, Federalist James Giles opined that, "If the war had been felt in this part of the country as it had been in other parts of the country, we should have no difficulty in carrying a federal ticket." James Giles to Garret D. Wall, October 15, 1814, Wall Papers, Rutgers University Library.
30. Levine, "The New Jersey Federalist Party Convention of 1814," p. 299;

Rodgers, "Some Phases of New Jersey History in the Jeffersonian Period," p. 134; Turner, "Elections of 1816 and 1820," p. 299; *New York Evening Post*, October 25, 1814; Livermore, *The Twilight of Federalism*, p. 11; McCormick, *The Second American Party System*, p. 126; Prince, "James J. Wilson," p. 29.

31. *Centinel of Freedom*, October 19, 1813, October 17, 1815; Rodgers, "Some Phases of New Jersey History in the Jeffersonian Period," p. 106; Fee, *The Transition from Aristocracy to Democracy*, p. 203; *Fredonian*, October 20, 1814, October 19, 1815; *New Jersey Journal*, October 17, 1815; *Federalist*, October 23, 1815. In 1816, the Federalists dipped only to 39 percent of the New Jersey legislature and then, in 1817, to 38 percent. *Fredonian*, October 24, 1816; *New Jersey Journal*, October 15, 1816, October 28, 1817; *Centinel of Freedom*, October 21, 1817; *True American*, October 21, 1816, October 27, 1817; *Federalist*, October 27, 1817.

32. Just as 1814 marked the last occasion on which the New Jersey Federalists entered a Congressional election, it also was the last occasion on which the Federalists held a statewide convention. In 1814, the Federalists' conclave again was of the delegate type. Ninety-six delegates from all thirteen New Jersey counties met in Trenton on July 4 and nominated Congressional candidates to be voted for by the "Friends of Peace" in the state. *Federalist*, May 23, June 13, 27, August 9, 23, September 20, 1814; Levine, "The New Jersey Federalist Party Convention of 1814," pp. 2–4, 6–7; Pasler and Pasler, "Federalist Tenacity in Burlington County, New Jersey," p. 205; Fee, *The Transition from Aristocracy to Democracy*, pp. 198–99; McCormick, *The Second American Party System*, p. 127; William Nelson, "The Election of Congressmen from New Jersey," *Proceedings of the New Jersey Historical Society*, Third Series VIII (July, 1913): 82.

33. Levine, "The New Jersey Federalist Party Convention of 1814," p. 7; Pasler, "The Federalist Party in Burlington County, New Jersey," pp. 182, 184; Prince, *New Jersey's Jeffersonian Republicans*, p. 207; *New York Evening Post*, October 25, 1814. The New Jersey Republicans had realized that the election would be very close. Loss of the Salem and Cumberland militia's votes might be decisive in those counties they feared, so the Republicans sent the men home to vote. Even so, they won Cumberland County by only 117 votes and Salem County by only 142. However, Republican efforts to win Cape May by calling out that county's militia resulted in total failure. As usual, Cape May County went Federalist in 1814. *Federalist*, November 21, 1814; James Giles to Garret D. Wall, October 15, 1814, Wall Papers, Rutgers University Library.

34. Lucius H. Stockton, *An Address Delivered Before the Convention of the Friends of Peace*, Trenton, July 4, 1814.

35. *Federalist*, January 16, 23, 1815; Richard Stockton to Samuel Bayard, December 29, 1814, Stockton Family Papers, Princeton University Library; Fee, *The Transition from Aristocracy to Democracy*, p. 206; Livermore, *The Twilight of Federalism*, p. 11.

36. Pasler and Pasler, "Federalist Tenacity in Burlington County," p. 205;

164   THE NEW JERSEY FEDERALISTS

Fee, *The Transition from Aristocracy to Democracy*, pp. 204–5; Fallow, "The Rise of the Whig Party in New Jersey," p. 37; *Votes and Proceedings of the General Assembly of the State of New Jersey*, 39th Session, 2nd Sitting (January 14, 1815).

37. *Federalist*, February 6, 27, 1815; Fee, *The Transition from Aristocracy to Democracy*, p. 207; *Votes and Proceedings of the General Assembly of the State of New Jersey*, 39th Session, 2nd Sitting (February 10, 1815).

38. Livermore, *The Twilight of Federalism*, pp. 14, 265; Thomas Ward to General [Jonathan] Dayton, November 18, 1814, Moore Collection, Princeton University Library; James Parker to Brigadier General Henry Dearborn, December 1, 1814, Princeton University Library, Prince, "New Jersey's Democratic Republicans," pp. 535, 511, 296, 406, 670; Fee, *The Transition from Aristocracy to Democracy*, p. 210; Turner, "Elections of 1816 and 1820," p. 325; Sher, "Party Battles in Middlesex County," p. 100; *True American*, October 7, 1816; Prince, *New Jersey's Jeffersonian Republicans*, pp. 183, 205, 199, 202, 207; *Centinel of Freedom*, September 17, 1816; Herbert Ershkowitz, "The Origins of the Whig and Democratic Parties in New Jersey," paper presented at the Second Annual New Jersey History Symposium, Trenton, New Jersey, December 5, 1970, p. 2; William J. Dunham, "Mahlon Dickerson: A Great But Almost Forgotten Jerseyan," *Proceedings of the New Jersey Historical Society* LXVII (October, 1950): 311; Beckwith, "Mahlon Dickerson of New Jersey," p. 192; *Centinel of Freedom*, January 30, 1816; New Brunswick *Times*, November 9, 1815; April 11, 1816; July 9, September 3, 1818; *Federalist*, February 9, 1816; July 14, 1817; *New Jersey Journal*, June 10, August 8, 1817; September 18, 1818; *Fredonian*, October 17, 1817; October 22, 1818; Henry Southard to Judge [Samuel] Southard, n.d. [c.1817] Samuel Southard Papers, Princeton University Library; Fee, *The Transition from Aristocracy to Democracy*, pp. 211–14; Wallace, "Changing Concepts of Party in the United States," p. 475; Wilson, *Outline History of New Jersey*, p. 95; *Federalist*, September 8, 1821; February 23, 1824. However, political strife did not cease; rather, it often took the form of intraparty conflict. Still, as party unity declined, disinterest among the electorate increased. Prince, *New Jersey's Jeffersonian Republicans*, pp. 71, 215; Ershkowitz, "New Jersey Politics During the Era of Andrew Jackson, 1820–1837," p. 2; *Centinel of Freedom*, November 14, 1820; New Brunswick *Times*, October 7, 1819; Chambers, *Political Parties in a New Nation*, p. 197.

39. In 1816 the Federalists held 39 percent of the legislature. By 1820 their legislative strength had fallen to 23 percent. *Fredonian*, October 24, 1816; *True American*, October 21, 1816; *New Jersey Journal*, October 15, 1816; October 28, 1817; *Centinel of Freedom*, October 21, 1817; *True American*, October 27, 1817; *Federalist*, October 27, 1817; Fee, *The Transition from Aristocracy to Democracy*, pp. 227–28; *Centinel of Freedom*, October 27, 1818; *Federalist*, October 26, 1818; *True American*, November 2, 1818; *New Jersey Journal*, October 20, 1818; *Centinel of Freedom*, October 26, 1819; *True American*, October 26, 1819; *Federalist*, November 8, 1819; New Brunswick *Times*, Octo-

ber 21, 1819; *True American*, October 21, 1820; *Centinel of Freedom*, October 23, 1820; *New-Jersey Mirror*, October 28, 1820; *New Jersey Journal*, October 16, 1820.

40. *Federalist*, October 14, 1816; September 21, 1818; September 18, 1820; October 7, 1822; October 27, 1823; *True American*, October 7, 1816; *New-Jersey Mirror*, October 2, 1822. New Jersey Federalists had last contested a presidential election in 1812 and a Congressional race in 1814. Turner, "Elections of 1816 and 1820," p. 307; Livermore, *The Twilight of Federalism*, p. 34; Ershkowitz, "New Jersey Politics During the Era of Andrew Jackson, 1820–1837," p. 17; Prince, *New Jersey's Jeffersonian Republicans*, p. 208.

41. Livermore, *The Twilight of Federalism*, pp. viii, 265–66, passim; Fee, *The Transition from Aristocracy to Democracy*, pp. 221–22, 244; McCormick, *The Second American Party System*, p. 161; Pasler and Pasler, "Federalist Tenacity in Burlington County," p. 205; Ershkowitz, "New Jersey Politics During the Era of Andrew Jackson, 1820–1837," p. 18; Ershkowitz, "The Origins of the Whig and Democratic Parties in New Jersey," p. 14; Prince, "New Jersey's Democratic Republicans," p. 258; Fallow, "The Rise of the Whig Party in New Jersey," pp. 40–41; *Minutes of the Legislative Council*, 42nd Session, 2nd Sitting (January 19, 1818); *Votes and Proceedings of the General Assembly of the State of New Jersey*, 42nd Session, 2nd Sitting (January 26, 1818); *Federalist*, August 25, September 15, 1817; April 27, August 3, October 5, 1818; August 23, September 13, 1819; October 2, 1822; *True American*, September 27, October 11, 1823; September 18, 1824; Clarence Brigham to Elmer T. Hutchinson, November 1, 1940, Elmer T. Hutchinson Papers, Rutgers University Library; *Fredonian*, October 22, 1818; Fischer, *The Revolution of American Conservatism*, p. 80; Henry Southard to General [Ebenezer] Elmer, January 25, 1819, Gratz Collection, Historical Society of Pennsylvania; Wilson, *Outline History of New Jersey*, p. 89.

42. Prince, "New Jersey's Democratic Republicans," p. 566; McCormick, *The Second American Party System*, p. 126.

43. In 1823 the New Jersey Federalists briefly held 38 percent of the legislature, a figure they had not reached or even approached since 1817. Livermore, *The Twilight of Federalism*, pp. 85, 124; Turner, "Elections of 1816 and 1820," p. 309; Fee, *The Transition from Aristocracy to Democracy*, pp. 244–46; *Emporium*, October 11, 1823; *New Jersey Journal*, October 24, 1823; *Fredonian*, October 23, 1823; McCormick, *The Second American Party System*, p. 27.

44. Bergen County was wholly Republican between 1820–1822 and elected a total of only two Federalist legislators in the years 1823 and 1824; Burlington's legislative delegation was two-fifths Republican between 1820 and 1822; Middlesex usually sent at least half Republicans to the legislature between 1821 and 1824; and Somerset was all Republican between 1820 and 1822 and half Republican in 1823 and 1824. *True American*, October 21, 1820; October 20, 1821; October 12, 1822; October 16, 1823; October 23, 1824; *Centinel of Freedom*, October 23, 1820; *New Jersey Journal*, October 20, 1820; October 16, 1821;

October 15, 1822; *Federalist,* October 21, 1822; October 27, 1823; October 14, 1824.

45. *Fredonian,* October 18, 1821; October 17, 1822; *Federalist,* October 17, 1822; Fee, *The Transition from Aristocracy to Democracy,* pp. 216–17; *True American,* October 20, 1821; Prince, "New Jersey's Democratic Republicans," p. 300. Federalists had begun to infiltrate the Essex County Republican organization after 1814 when, to the chagrin of some Republicans, they started appearing at nominating meetings. By 1816 two men who had not denounced their former Federalist connections were appointed to the county nominating committee. Also in that year, the *Centinel of Freedom* went so far as to say that one-third of the nominating meeting's delegates from Newark were Federalists. *Centinel of Freedom,* September 17, 1816; Prince, New Jersey's Democratic Republicans, p. 300. Federalists had begun to infiltrate the Essex County Republican organization after 1814 when, to the chagrin of some Republicans, they started appearing at nominating meetings. By 1816 two men who had not denounced their former Federalist connections were appointed to the county nominating committee. Also in that year, the *Centinel of Freedom* went so far as to say that one-third of the nominating meeting's delegates from Newark were Federalists. *Centinel of Freedom,* September 17, 1816; Prince, New Jersey's Democratic Republicans," pp. 242, 254; Fee, *The Transition from Aristocracy to Democracy,* p. 216; *New Jersey Journal,* September 24, 1816. However, it was in other traditionally Republican counties that the Federalists came to enjoy the greatest success at the polls. As early as 1816 the Federalists won two legislative seats in Sussex County and thereafter, except for 1820, they won at least one Sussex seat each year. In 1819 the Federalists won one seat each in Salem and Cumberland counties, a pattern they also continued for the duration of the first party system period. And beginning in 1821, the Federalists won several seats yearly in Morris and Monmouth counties. Thus, by the end of the Era of Good Feelings, Federalists had been elected to the legislature at least once from every Republican county in New Jersey and had dominated the Morris delegation in 1823 and 1824.

46. *Emporium,* October 6, 1821.

47. Fallow, "The Rise of the Whig Party in New Jersey," p. 42; Ershkowitz, "New Jersey Politics During the Era of Andrew Jackson, 1820–1837," pp. 19–20; Fee, *The Transition from Aristocracy to Democracy,* pp. 210, 217; Richard McCormick, "Party Formation in New Jersey in the Jackson Era," *Proceedings of the New Jersey Historical Society,* LXXXIII (July, 1965), 162; McCormick, *The Second American Party System,* p. 126; *Emporium,* September 29, 1821; *Fredonian,* October 17, 1817; Henry Southard to General Ebenezer Elmer, January 25, 1819; Gratz Collection, Historical Society of Pennsylvania.

48. *Centinel of Freedom,* September 19, 26, 1815; *Sussex Register,* October 9, 1815; Livermore, *The Twilight of Federalism,* p. 129; Ershkowitz, "The Origins of the Whig and Democratic Parties in New Jersey," p. 2; Prince, "New Jersey's Democratic Republicans, p. 315; *Federalist,* October 8, 1821; Septem-

ber 1, 1823; *True American*, February 9, 1822; Ershkowitz, "New Jersey Politics During the Era of Andrew Jackson, 1820–1837," pp. 19–20.

49. *Sussex Register*, September 30, 1816; Prince, "New Jersey's Democratic Republicans," pp. 315, 344, 446; Ershkowitz, "New Jersey Politics During the Era of Andrew Jackson," pp. 20–21; William Pennington to Samuel Southard, August 11, 1818, Samuel Southard Papers, Princeton University Library; J. T. Blackwell to Samuel Southard, September 21, 1818, Samuel Southard Papers, Princeton University Library; *Fredonian*, October 22, 1818; September 20, 1819; October 17, 1822; *True American*, September 13, 20, 27, 1819; Elmer, *The Constitution and Government of the State and Province of New Jersey*, pp. 211, 426; *Federalist*, September 30, October 17, 1822. Republicans, however, did state that the Federalists' desire for a union of parties was not sincere and constituted mere opportunism on the Federalists' part, for their wish for amalgamation was confined to Republican counties. In the traditionally Federalist areas, the Republicans charged, the Federalists labored to keep their organization intact. There was a good deal of truth in the Republicans' accusation, and in no county did the Federalists work harder to maintain their machine than in Burlington, but even here they ultimately failed. Faced after 1817 with opposition from the "News," a coalition of dissident Federalists and Republicans, the old Federalists' repeated efforts to bring the party back together finally succeeded in 1819, but the following year the party factionalized once more. Likewise, except for Cape May, all the other Federalist counties experienced similar factionalization. *Address of Charges Against the Old Party of Burlington*, n.p., 1817; *True American*, October 13, 1817; October 5, 1822; *Federalist*, October 8, 1821; New Brunswick *Times*, September 12, 19, October 3, 1816; *Federalist*, August 25, September 15, 1817; August 31, 1818; *Fredonian*, October 22, 1818; *True American*, September 27, October 11, 1823; October 18, 1824; Fee, *The Transition from Aristocracy to Democracy*, p. 217; Pasler, "The Federalist Party in Burlington County, New Jersey," pp. 189, 197; Prince, *New Jersey's Jeffersonian Republicans*, p. 203; Pasler and Pasler, "Federalist Tenacity in Burlington County," p. 205; Prince, "New Jersey's Democratic Republicans," pp. 477–78; *Federalist*, October 13, 1817; *True American*, September 22, 1817; October 12, 1818; *Federalist*, October 15, 1818; September 13, 1819; August 23, 1819; *New-Jersey Mirror*, September 6, 1820; *Federalist*, September 20, 27, October 11, 23, 1820; Sher, "Party Battles in Middlesex County," pp. 119–21, 123; New Brunswick *Times*, October 18, 1821; October 17, 1822; *Fredonian*, October 22, 1818.

50. Ebenezer Elmer to Jonathan Dayton, January 28, 1815, Gratz Collection, Historical Society of Pennsylvania; Ershkowitz, "The Origins of the Whig and Democratic Parties in New Jersey," p. 14; J. T. Blackwell to Samuel Southard, January 9, 1818, Samuel Southard Papers, Princeton University Library; Pole, "The Reform of Suffrage and Representation in New Jersey," p. 216; *Federalist*, February 10, 1817; Fee, *The Transition from Aristocracy to Democracy*, pp. 212, 223; Elmer, *The Constitution and Government of the State and Province*

168   THE NEW JERSEY FEDERALISTS

of New Jersey, pp. 420–21; Prince, "New Jersey's Democratic Republicans," p. 255.

51. Ebenezer Elmer to Samuel Southard, November 6, 1817, James Fitz Randolph to Samuel Southard, November 5, 1817, Samuel Southard Papers, Princeton University Library; *Minutes of the Joint Meeting,* 42nd Session, 1st Sitting (November 1, 1817); *New Jersey Journal,* October 14, 1817, September 22, 1818; Elmer, *The Constitution and Government of the State and Province of New Jersey,* pp. 210, 444; Ershkowitz, "New Jersey Politics in the Era of Andrew Jackson, 1820–1837," p. 24; Fee, *The Transition from Aristocracy to Democracy,* p. 224; Isaac Southard to Samuel Southard, October 4, 1822, Samuel Southard Papers, Princeton University Library; *True American,* February 17, 1818. Just as during the Era of Good Feelings Republicans were known to aid the election of Federalists in joint meeting, at times Federalists also gave their votes to Republicans, notably those who had not been nominated by their party's caucus. Joseph C. Hornblower to Aaron Ogden Dayton, October 27, 1823, Jonathan Dayton Papers, New Jersey Historical Society; *Minutes of the Joint Meeting,* 40th Session, 1st Sitting (October 26, 1815); *True American,* October 30, November 18, 1815; Fee, *The Transition from Aristocracy to Democracy,* pp. 225–26. Whenever Federalists voted as a bloc on these occasions, the Republicans brandished the instance as proof that the Federalists' oft-expressed desire to see an end to party spirit was a mere ploy. "As a party . . . [they] still keep together . . .," the Republicans would shout. Their shouts would grow even louder when the Federalists, seizing a relatively rare opportunity to do so, would unite behind a Federalist, as in Frelinghuysen's case. In this instance the Republicans' outcry continued longer than usual, for Frelinghuysen proceeded to appoint all Federalist assistants. *New Jersey Journal,* October 13, 1818; Fee, *The Transition from Aristocracy to Democracy,* p. 225; David Thompson to Samuel Southard, February 21, 1818, Samuel Southard Papers, Princeton University Library; *True American,* February 17, 1818.

52. *Federalist,* June 2, 1817. The Federalists' complaints over being proscribed from office included the lament that they had not received federal appointments from President Monroe. *Federalist,* April 27, 1818; Livermore, *The Twilight of Federalism,* pp. 59, 108. In the 1820s the New Jersey Federalists' situation in regard to offices in the gift of the state legislature improved somewhat, for the Republicans then vowed to allow each county's delegation, regardless of party, to make its own appointments in joint meeting, but by then the Federalists controlled very few counties. Elmer, *The Constitution and Government of the State and Province of New Jersey,* pp. 163, 211.

53. *Federalist,* August 21, 1820; Elias Boudinot to Elias E. Boudinot, November 27, 1819 in Boyd, *Elias Boudinot,* p. 290; Turner, "Elections of 1816 and 1820," p. 313; Hofstadter, *The Idea of a Party System,* p. 201; Livermore, *The Twilight of Federalism,* p. 94; Moore, *The Missouri Controversy,* pp. 67–68; George Dangerfield, *The Era of Good Feelings* (New York: Harcourt, Brace, and World, Inc.), p. 119; Pasler and Pasler, "Federalist Tenacity in Burlington County," p. 208.

54. Moore, *The Missouri Controversy*, pp. 66, 70; Pasler, "The Federalist Party in Burlington County, New Jersey," pp. 194, 202; *True American*, October 18, 1819; *New Jersey Journal*, September 7, 1819; Cecil B. Egerton, "Rufus King and the Missouri Question: A Study in Political Mythology," Ph.D. diss., Claremont Graduate School, 1967, p. 71.

55. Moore, *The Missouri Controversy*, pp. 70–73; Egerton, "Rufus King and the Missouri Question," pp. 71–72; Fee, *The Transition from Aristocracy to Democracy*, p. 240; Robert Ernst. *Rufus King: American Federalist* (Chapel Hill: University of North Carolina Press, 1968), p. 371; *Public Meeting Respecting Slavery*, n.p., October 29, 1819. One of the most important Federalists personally contacted by Elias Boudinot was John Jay. He endorsed the movement. Henry P. Johnson, ed., *The Correspondence and Public Papers of John Jay*, vol. IV (New York: G. P. Putnam's Sons, 1893), p. 430; Pasler, "The Federalist Party in Burlingron County, New Jersey," p. 203.

56. Moore, *The Missouri Controversy*, p. 80; *Federalist*, December 20, 1819; February 21, 1820; New Brunswick *Times*, December 2, 16, 1819; January 20, 1820; Fee, *The Transition from Aristocracy to Democracy*, p. 240; *New-Jersey Mirror*, December 29, 1819.

57. Fee, *The Transition from Aristocracy to Democracy*, pp. 240–41; Egerton, "Rufus King and the Missouri Question," p. 142; *Votes and Proceedings of the General Assembly of the State of New Jersey*, 44th Session 1st Sitting (January 14, 1820), (January 15, 1820); *Niles' Weekly Register*, January 22, 1820; Mahlon Dickerson to Governor [Isaac] Williamson, February 10, 1820, Philhower Collection, Rutgers University Library.

58. *New-Jersey Mirror*, February 16, 1820; Fee, *The Transition from Aristocracy to Democracy*, p. 242; *Federalist*, March 13, August 21, September 25, October 8, 1820; Elias Boudinot to Elias E. Boudinot, November 27, 1819 in Boyd, *Elias Boudinot*, p. 290; Livermore, *The Twilight of Federalism*, p. 94. Although Federalist-led, the anti-extension movement had enjoyed bipartisan support in New Jersey. An indication of the unpopularity of the anti-restrictionist stand among New Jersey Republicans was their failure to renominate for another term in the House any of the three Congressmen who had voted against restriction. Fee, *The Transition from Aristocracy to Democracy*, p. 241; Pasler, "The Federalist Party in Burlington County, New Jersey," p. 203.

59. Part of the motivation here also may have been the desire to regulate the public's conduct. No longer hopeful of regaining the political power to do so, Federalists may have turned to the use of moral force to achieve their ends. Fischer, *The Revolution of American Conservatism*, pp. 48–49; Charles Griffin, "Religious Benevolence as Social Control, 1815–1860," *Mississippi Valley Historical Review* XLIV (December, 1957): 426–27.

60. John F. Hageman, *History of Princeton and Its Institutions*, vol. I (Philadelphia: J. B. Lippincott Company, 1879), p. 230; New Brunswick *Times*, March 3, 1811; July 18, 1816; January 2, 1817; *True American*, July 29, 1816; Griffin, "Religious Benevolence," p. 427.

61. Pasler, "The Federalist Party in Burlington County, New Jersey," p. 50;

170   THE NEW JERSEY FEDERALISTS

Joshua Wallace to J. Warren Scott, November 25, 1817, Wallace Papers, Historical Society of Pennsylvania; *Constitution of the New Jersey Society for the Suppression of Vice and Immorality and for the Encouragement of Virtue and Good Morals*, November 11, 1817, Wallace Papers, Historical Society of Pennsylvania; *Address of the Society for the Suppression of Vice and Immorality and for the Encouragement of Virtue and Good Morals*, November 11, 1817, Wallace Papers, Historical Society of Pennsylvania; Thompson, *Colonel James Neilson*, p. 293; New Brunswick *Times*, November 5, 1818. At least one local chapter of the Society was formed. Located in New Brunswick, its first president was Federalist John Neilson.

62. For example, an 1818 act liberalizing the insolvent law was passed by the legislature with the votes of 79 percent of the Federalists but only 63 percent of the Republicans. *Minutes of the Legislative Council*, 41st Session. Still, this act cannot be considered a party measure.

63. Nelson Burr, *Education in New Jersey, 1630–1871* (Princeton: Princeton University Press, 1942), p. 245; *Votes and Proceedings of the General Assembly of the State of New Jersey*, 41st Session, 2nd Sitting (February 12, 1817). Virginia Federalists evinced a similar interest in public education during the Era of Good Feelings. Norman K. Risjord, "The Virginia Federalists," *Journal of Southern History* XXXIII (No. 4, 1967): 516.

64. *Votes and Proceedings of the General Assembly of the State of New Jersey*, 44th Session, 2nd Sitting (January 15, 1820); Michael Lutzker, "Abolition of Imprisonment for Debt in New Jersey," *Proceedings of the New Jersey Historical Society* LXXXIV (October, 1966): 9–10; Elmer, *The Constitution and Government of the State and Province of New Jersey*, p. 297; Boyd, *Elias Boudinot*, p. 287; Lucius Elmer to Samuel Southard, December 10, 1823, Samuel Southard Papers, Princeton University Library. Largely because of these and other legislative attainments on the part of James Parker and William Griffith, it may be said that New Jersey Federalists exercised considerable leadership in the state legislature during the period of their party's final decline. Fee, *The Transition from Aristocracy to Democracy*, pp. 242, 232, 262, 228–29; Elmer, *The Constitution and Government of the State and Province of New Jersey*, pp. 294, 298.

65. Ershkowitz, "New Jersey Politics During the Era of Andrew Jackson," pp. 32, 289; McCormick, *The Second American Party System*, p. 128; Ershkowitz, "The Origins of the Whig and Democratic Parties in New Jersey," p. 4; Fallow, "The Rise of the Whig Party in New Jersey," pp. 409–10. In the presidential election of 1824 the six traditionally Federalist counties divided nearly evenly between Adams and Jackson. Bergen, Burlington, Somerset, and Gloucester went for Jackson; Cape May and Middlesex for Adams. Too, the Federalist organs split. The *Federalist* went for Adams while the New Brunswick *Times* and the *Emporium* supported Jackson. And the two groups noted for their long-time allegiance to Federalism in New Jersey entered different camps. The Quakers supported Adams, the Dutch Jackson. Fallow, "The Whig Party in New

Jersey," pp. 444, 140; Herbert Ershkowitz, "The Election of 1824 in New Jersey," *Proceedings of the New Jersey Historical Society* LXXXIV (April, 1966): 121; Fee, *The Transition from Aristocracy to Democracy*, p. 259; William Chute, "The New Jersey Whig Campaign of 1840," *Proceedings of the New Jersey Historical Society* LXXVII (October, 1959):233; Samuel Allinson, MS. Diary, Rutgers University Library. There was considerable apathy on the part of the electorate in 1824. Only about one-third of the Jerseyans eligible to vote did so. McCormick, *The Second American Party System*, p. 129; *New York Evening Post*, November 9, 1824.

66. *True American*, April 12, 1823; McCormick, "Party Formation in New Jersey in the Jacksonian Era," p. 163.

67. However, not until 1828 were all levels of New Jersey elections run strictly on the new party alignment. Until then traces of the first party system existed in a few localities. Ershkowitz, "New Jersey Politics During the Era of Andrew Jackson," pp. 62, 88, 91, 109, 288; *True American*, September 30, 1826, October 1, 8, 1825; *Fredonian*, September 28, 1825, October 8, 1826, October 25, 1826; *Federalist*, October 25, 1826; McCormick, *The Second American Party System*, pp. 124–25; Lucius H. Stockton to Samuel Southard, October 20, 1827, Samuel Southard Papers, Princeton University Library; Ershkowitz, "The Election of 1824 in New Jersey," pp. 128, 132.

68. Ershkowitz, "New Jersey Politics During the Era of Andrew Jackson," p. 35; Ershkowitz, "The Election of 1824 in New Jersey," p. 115.

69. *True American*, September 11, 1824; Ershkowitz, "New Jersey Politics During the Era of Andrew Jackson," p. 288, 50–51, 55; Sher, "Party Battles in Middlesex County," p. 122; Ershkowitz, "The Election of 1824 in New Jersey," p. 122; Fallow, "The Rise of the Whig Party in New Jersey," p. 48; Livermore, *The Twilight of Federalism*, p. 133. A minority of Federalist leaders did not make a public choice at this time but held aloof, even for many years in some cases. For example, several men did not formally join a party until after 1834, when they became Whigs. Three such individuals were Daniel Elmer, William Sherman, and Andrew Bell. Chute, "The New Jersey Whig Campaign of 1840," p. 231; Elmer, *The Constitution and Government of the State and Province of New Jersey*, p. 345; Livermore, *The Twilight of Federalism*, p. 132; Ershkowitz, "The Election of 1824 in New Jersey," p. 123.

70. Ershkowitz, "New Jersey Politics During the Era of Andrew Jackson," pp. 68, 44–45, 86, 75, 289, 100, 158; James Neilson to Gabriel Tichenor, July 2, 1825, Gabriel Tichenor to James Neilson, April 18, 1825, Neilson Family Papers, Rutgers University Library; Jane Bayard Kirkpatrick, MS. Diary, February 12, 1825, Rutgers University Library; Pasler, "The Federalist Party in Burlington County, New Jersey," p. 213; Ershkowitz, "The Election of 1824 in New Jersey," p. 120. Fee, *The Transition from Aristocracy to Democracy*, p. 256; Pole, "The Reform of Suffrage and Representation in New Jersey," p. 230.

71. Besides their belief that Adams was not the candidate who would end Federalist proscription, many Federalists who became Jacksonians viewed John

Q. Adams with distaste, considering him as a deserter from the party and, in the case of ex-High Federalists, an opponent of their beloved Alexander Hamilton. John Paterson to Samuel Southard, February 5, 1822, Samuel Southard Papers, Princeton University Library; Elmer, *The Constitution and Government of the State and Province of New Jersey*, p. 157; Ershkowitz, "New Jersey Politics During the Era of Andrew Jackson," pp. 45, 60–61; Livermore, *The Twilight of Federalism*, p. 140.

72. Fallow, "The Rise of the Whig Party in New Jersey," pp. 411, 43, 33–34, 45; Fee, *The Transition from Aristocracy to Democracy*, pp. 249, 256, 263; *Federalist*, August 9, 1824; *True American*, August 14, 1824; Ershkowitz, "New Jersey Politics During the Era of Andrew Jackson," p. 163; Elmer, *The Constitution and Government of the State and Province of New Jersey*, pp. 186, 153, 147, 321–22, 324, 352; Aaron Ogden Dayton, MS. autobiography, Jonathan Dayton Papers, Princeton University Library; Pasler, "The Federalist Party in Burlington County, New Jersey," p. 212; *Fredonian*, May 6, 1824; Ershkowitz, "The Election of 1824 in New Jersey," p. 127; Pole, "The Reform of Suffrage and Representation in New Jersey," p. 231. All ex-Federalist leaders did not remain permanently with the party they originally chose, however. Until after 1834, shifts in allegiance were common. In 1826, testifying to the important role hunger for office had played in determining their political allegiance, most members of the important Stockton family left Adams because Richard Stockton did not receive an anticipated federal judgeship. They took with them to the Jackson camp the newspaper published by Robert Stockton and Samuel Bayard, entitled the *New Jersey Patriot*. Again, by 1829, the Adams forces had lost several other ex-Federalist leaders. Some went over to Jackson following Adams' defeat, but others in this group did so just as soon as they decided he would lose. William B. Ewing and Charles Parker were among the 1826–1829 Adams defectors who apparently felt that being in a losing camp would afford them no political advantage. Finally, about 1834, a number of former Federalist leaders left the Jackson-Democratic party and became Whigs because of Jackson's attack on the Bank of the United States. Among them were Robert Stockton, James Parker, Frederick Schenck, William Chetwood, Joseph W. Scott, Alexander Wurts, Merriman Smith, David B. Ogden, and the Richards family. During the 1824–1834 period the bulk of the defunct New Jersey Federalist party exhibited similar shifts in political allegiance. For example, in the 1828 presidential race four of the traditionally Federalist counties, which in 1824 had been Jacksonian, now voted for Adams. Then, in 1832, two of these counties returned to Jackson. Only in 1832 did all six of the formerly Federalist counties begin to vote consistently for a particular party regardless of the office involved. Before then, these counties often would select members of one party to represent them in the state legislature and members of the other to represent them in Congress, even when the two elections had been held simultaneously. McCormick, *The Second American Party System*, pp. 170, 130; McCormick, "Party Formation in New Jersey in the Jackson Era," pp. 171–72; Fallow, "The

Rise of the Whig Party in New Jersey," pp. 10, 407, 103–6, 167–69; Ershkowitz, "New Jersey Politics During the Era of Andrew Jackson," pp. 77, 83–85, 87, 114–17, 284, 209; Elmer, *The Constitution and Government of the State and Province of New Jersey,*" pp. 414, 184, 461; Herbert Ershkowitz, "Samuel L. Southard: A Case Study of Whig Leadership in the Age of Jackson," *New Jersey History* LXXXVIII (Spring, 1970):11; *Federalist,* October 23, 1826; Livermore, *The Twilight of Federalism,* pp. 214–15, 188, 240–42, 250; Robert F. Stockton to Samuel Southard, October 19, 1826, William Prall to Samuel Southard, December 9, 1826, Samuel Southard Papers, Princeton University Library; Chute, "The New Jersey Whig Campaign of 1840," p. 236; Pasler, "The Federalist Party in Burlington County, New Jersey," p. 214; Fee, *The Transition from Aristocracy to Democracy,* p. 259; *Fredonian,* October 18, 1826; *True American,* November 22, 1828.

73. McCormick, *The Second American Party System,* pp. 128–29; *Emporium,* July 3, 1824.

74. McCormick, *The Second American Party System,* p. 164; Ershkowitz, "The Election of 1824 in New Jersey," p. 126; Ershkowitz, "New Jersey Politics During the Era of Andrew Jackson," p. 57.

75. McCormick, *The Second American Party System,* p. 129; Ershkowitz, "New Jersey Politics During the Era of Andrew Jackson," p. 59; Fee, *The Transition from Aristocracy to Democracy,* pp. 255–60.

76. *Address of the State Convention. . . .* [Jackson], Trenton, 1824.

77. Ershkowitz, "New Jersey Politics During the Era of Andrew Jackson," pp. 48, 60; Ershkowitz, "The Election of 1824 in New Jersey," p. 127.

78. Stockton Family Papers, New Jersey Historical Society; *Adams Meeting,* October 19, 1824; *True American,* October 30, 1824; *Fredonian,* October 29, 1824.

79. *Address of . . . a Republican Meeting in the County of Hunterdon Recommending General Andrew Jackson,* Trenton, September, 1824, p. 6; *Fredonian,* November 8, 1826; McCormick, *The Second American Party System,* p. 132.

80. Another change that occurred in 1828 was a resurgence of interest on the part of the electorate. That year about 72 percent of those Jerseyans eligible to vote did so. McCormick, *The Second American Party System,* p. 130; Ershkowitz, "New Jersey Politics During the Era of Andrew Jackson," p. 111; Fallow, "The Rise of the Whig Party in New Jersey," p. 51.

81. Pole, "The Reform of Suffrage and Representation in New Jersey," p. 226; Ershkowitz, "New Jersey Politics During the Era of Andrew Jackson," p. 100; McCormick, "Party Formation in New Jersey in the Jackson Era," p. 166.

82. *Proceedings and Address of the New Jersey State Convention Assembled at Trenton on the Eighth of January, 1828 which Nominated Andrew Jackson for President and John C. Calhoun for Vice-President,* Trenton, Joseph Justice, 1828; Fee, *The Transition from Aristocracy to Democracy,* p. 264.

83. McCormick, *The Second American Party System,* p. 133; McCormick, "Party Formation in New Jersey in the Jackson Era," pp. 166, 172; Ershkowitz,

"New Jersey Politics During the Era of Andrew Jackson," pp. 107, 159–60, 129, 132; Fallow, "The Rise of the Whig Party in New Jersey," pp. 45, 92–93.

84. *True American,* January 12, 1828; Pole, "The Reform of Suffrage and Representation in New Jersey," p. 266; Ershkowitz, "New Jersey Politics During the Era of Andrew Jackson," p. 100; Fallow, "The Rise of the Whig Party in New Jersey," p. 57; Elmer, *The Constitution and Government of the State and Province of New Jersey,* p. 227; McCormick, "Party Formation in New Jersey in the Jackson Era," p. 167.

85. Fallow, "The Rise of the Whig Party in New Jersey," pp. 59–60; Ershkowitz, "New Jersey Politics During the Era of Andrew Jackson," pp. 121–123, 132; Chute, "The New Jersey Whig Campaign of 1840," pp. 232–33; Elmer, *The Constitution and Government of the State and Province of New Jersey,* p. 429; Livermore, *The Twilight of Federalism,* p. 242.

86. Fallow, "The Rise of the Whig Party in New Jersey," p. 34; Ershkowitz, "New Jersey Politics During the Era of Andrew Jackson," pp. 125, 127–28; McCormick, "Party Formation in New Jersey in the Jackson Era," pp. 166–67; Elmer, *The Constitution and Government of the State and Province of New Jersey,* pp. 180–81: Pole, "The Reform of Suffrage and Representation in New Jersey," p. 215; Fee, *The Transition from Aristocracy to Democracy;* p. 267; P. D. Vroom to Peter D. Vroom, Jr., January 28, 1830, Peter D. Vroom Papers, Rutgers University Library.

87. Ershkowitz, "New Jersey Politics During the Era of Andrew Jackson," p. 126; Chute, "The New Jersey Whig Campaign of 1840," pp. 232–33.

88. Ershkowitz, "Samuel L. Southard," p. 22; Chute, "The New Jersey Whig Campaign of 1840," p. 239; Ershkowitz, "New Jersey Politics During the Era of Andrew Jackson," p. 253; McCormick, "Party Formation in New Jersey in the Jackson Era," p. 171; Pole, "The Reform of Suffrage and Representation in New Jersey," p. 244; Livermore, *The Twilight of Federalism,* p. 273. Antimasonry was insignificant in New Jersey, but even in this party two ex-Federalist leaders were important. They were Joseph C. Hornblower and John Rutherfurd. McCormick, *The Second American Party System,* p. 337; Ershkowitz, "New Jersey Politics During the Era of Andrew Jackson," pp. 140, 143, 182, 290; Fallow, "The Rise of the Whig Party in New Jersey," p. 23.

89. Ershkowitz, "Samuel Southard," p. 22; Chute, "The New Jersey Whig Campaign of 1840," p. 224; Ershkowitz, "New Jersey Politics During the Era of Andrew Jackson," pp. 136, 191; Elmer, *The Constitution and Government of the State and Province of New Jersey,* pp. 157, 429, 461, 187, 257, 455, 385.

90. *Essex Patriot,* December 13, 1812.

8

THE NEW JERSEY FEDERALISTS
IN PERSPECTIVE

From faction to party to disintegration and realignment the career of the New Jersey Federalists spanned little more than thirty years. First unquestionably dominant, after 1795 they face an organized opposition which at length wrested control from them in 1801.

For nearly the next dozen years the New Jersey Federalists were the minority, although four times their strength in the state legislature rose to over 40 percent. Then, in 1812, they regained the state only to lose it narrowly the following year. During the next two years a margin of eight percentage points or less separated the party from victory in the state and national elections held in New Jersey. Thereafter, however, the party not only lacked a national base but also a state one. Still, in 1817 the Federalists could win nearly 40 percent of the state legislature and return to this high figure once more in 1823, just as realignment began to occur.

Adjustment to these relatively rapid changes in their circumstances demanded flexibility on the part of the New Jersey Federalists. It must be said that they rose to the challenge.

As the dominant political group, New Jersey Federalists exhibited overt elitism. When thrown out of power, however, they looked to the example of their successful opponents and increasingly modeled themselves on the Republicans. New-style Federalism was the result.

It was this new-style Federalism which, rather inadvertently, aided the development of political democracy. The intense, albeit uneven, competition it offered to the dominant Republicans spurred a rise in voter interest and participation.

In a philosophical moment, one New Jersey Republican leader publicly gave the Federalists credit for this important contribution. The Federalists' competitiveness made for poltiical healthfulness wherever it appeared, said Ebenezer Elmer.[1]

Besides being flexible, the New Jersey Federalists also must be viewed as having been energetic and durable. Through all their setbacks and defeats they continued to battle and garner whatever success they could. Elements of the New Jersey party preserved party dominance well beyond the demise of the Federalist party elsewhere. And these flexible, energetic, durable New Jersey Federalists not only dominated their county strongholds but even the state party for a time and also furthered, however briefly, national Federalist momentum.

Still, despite their public posture, new-style Federalists had not deserted their elitist beliefs. They demonstrated this most forceably in 1812–1813 when they briefly returned to power in the state. While enunciating statements that had become part of the rhetoric of new-style Federalism they took from the people the power to choose presidential electors, returning it to the legislature, wherein it had lodged during the Federalist period.

In plotting the downfall of the Federalists the question of whether they were realists or ideologues often has been raised.[2] Were they politicians who lost because they supported injudicious policies or did they lose because they were ideologues who, after the idea of a deferential society began to crumble, persisted in adhering to the vision of a society governed by an elite? In New Jersey, at least, assuredly the Federalists were both realists and ideologues and at one and the same time.

NOTES

1. Prince, "The Democratic Republicans," p. 497; Carl Prince, "Party Theory and a Party Operative: Ebenezer Elmer Defines the First American Party System," *New Jersey History* LXXXVII (Autumn, 1970): 164.

2. George Athan Billias, ed., *The Federalists: Realists or Ideologues?* (Lexington, Massachusetts: D.C. Heath and Company, 1970), passim.

PARTY AFFILIATION OF NEW JERSEY STATE LEGISLATORS BY COUNTY, 1800–1824

BERGEN COUNTY

Year	Federalists	Republicans
1800	4	0
1801	4	0
1802	4	0
1803	4	0
1804	4	0
1805	4	0
1806	4	0
1807	2	2
1808	4	0
1809	4	0
1810	2	2
1811	2	2
1812	4	0
1813	3	1
1814	4	0
1815	2	2
1816	2	2
1817	4	0
1818	4	0
1819	1	3
1820	0	4
1821	0	4
1822	0	4
1823	1	3
1824	1	3

BURLINGTON COUNTY

Year	Federalists	Republicans
1800	4	0
1801	5	0
1802	5	0
1803	5	0
1804	5	0
1805	5	0
1806	5	0
1807	5	0
1808	5	0
1809	5	0
1810	5	0
1811	5	0
1812	5	0
1813	5	0
1814	5	0
1815	5	0
1816	5	0
1817	5	0
1818	5	0
1819	5	0
1820	3	2
1821	3	2
1822	3	2
1823	5	0
1824	5	0

CAPE MAY COUNTY

Year	Federalists	Republicans
1800	2	0
1801	1	1
1802	2	0
1803	2	0
1804	2	0
1805	2	0
1806	2	0
1807	2	0
1808	2	0
1809	2	0

1810	2	0
1811	1	1
1812	2	0
1813	2	0
1814	2	0
1815	2	0
1816	2	0
1817	2	0
1818	2	0
1819	2	0
1820	2	0
1821	2	0
1823	2	0
1824	2	0

CUMBERLAND COUNTY

Year	Federalists	Republicans
1800	3	0
1801	0	3
1802	0	3
1803	0	3
1804	0	3
1805	0	3
1806	1	2
1807	0	3
1808	0	3
1809	0	3
1810	0	3
1811	0	3
1812	0	3
1813	0	3
1814	0	4
1815	0	4
1816	0	4
1817	0	4
1818	0	4
1819	1	3
1820	1	3
1821	1	3
1822	2	2
1823	2	2
1824	0	4

ESSEX COUNTY

Year	Federalists	Republicans
1800	0	4
1801	0	4
1802	0	4
1803	0	4
1804	0	5
1805	0	5
1806	0	5
1807	0	5
1808	0	5
1809	0	5
1810	0	5
1811	0	5
1812	0	5
1813	0	5
1814	0	5
1815	0	5
1816	0	5
1817	0	5
1818	0	5
1819	0	5
1820	0	5
1821	1	4
1822	0	5
1823	0	5
1824	0	5

GLOUCESTER COUNTY

Year	Federalists	Republicans
1800	4	0
1801	4	0
1802	4	0
1803	0	4
1804	0	4
1805	1	3
1806	3	1
1807	0	4
1808	0	4
1809	2	2

1810	2	2
1811	2	2
1812	4	0
1813	4	0
1814	4	0
1815	4	0
1816	4	0
1817	3	1
1818	1	3
1819	1	3
1820	2	2
1821	3	1
1822	3	1
1823	4	0
1824	0	4

HUNTERDON COUNTY

Year	Federalists	Republicans
1800	0	5
1801	0	5
1802	3	2
1803	0	5
1804	0	5
1805	0	5
1806	0	5
1807	0	5
1808	0	5
1809	0	5
1810	0	5
1811	0	5
1812	3	2
1813	0	5
1814	0	5
1815	0	5
1816	0	5
1817	0	5
1818	0	5
1819	0	5
1820	0	5
1821	0	5
1822	1	4

| 1823 | 0 | 5 |
| 1824 | 0 | 5 |

MIDDLESEX COUNTY

Year	Federalists	Republicans
1800	4	0
1801	4	0
1802	4	0
1803	4	0
1804	4	0
1805	4	0
1806	4	0
1807	4	0
1808	4	0
1809	4	0
1810	4	0
1811	0	4
1812	4	0
1813	4	0
1814	4	0
1815	4	0
1816	4	0
1817	3	1
1818	4	0
1819	0	4
1820	3	1
1821	1	3
1822	2	2
1823	1	3
1824	1	3

MONMOUTH COUNTY

Year	Federalists	Republicans
1800	3	0
1801	0	4
1802	0	4
1803	0	4
1804	0	4

1805	0	4
1806	0	4
1807	0	4
1808	4	0
1809	0	4
1810	0	4
1811	0	4
1812	4	0
1813	0	4
1814	1	3
1815	0	4
1816	0	4
1817	0	4
1818	0	5
1819	0	5
1820	0	5
1821	2	3
1822	2	3
1823	1	4
1824	1	4

MORRIS COUNTY

Year	Federalists	Republicans
1800	4	0
1801	0	4
1802	0	4
1803	0	4
1804	0	4
1805	0	4
1806	0	4
1807	0	4
1808	0	4
1809	0	4
1810	0	4
1811	0	4
1812	0	4
1813	0	4
1814	0	4
1815	0	4
1816	0	4
1817	0	4
1818	0	4

1819	0	4
1820	0	4
1821	0	4
1822	0	4
1823	1	3
1824	1	3

SALEM COUNTY

Year	Federalists	Republicans
1800	4	0
1801	0	4
1802	0	4
1803	0	4
1804	0	4
1805	0	4
1806	0	4
1807	0	4
1808	0	4
1809	0	4
1810	0	4
1811	0	4
1812	0	4
1813	0	4
1814	0	4
1815	0	4
1816	0	4
1817	0	4
1818	0	4
1819	0	4
1820	0	4
1821	1	3
1822	1	3
1823	2	2
1824	1	3

SOMERSET COUNTY

Year	Federalists	Republicans
1800	4	0
1801	4	0

1802	4	0
1803	4	0
1804	0	4
1805	4	0
1806	4	0
1807	4	0
1808	4	0
1809	4	0
1810	4	0
1811	3	1
1812	4	0
1813	4	0
1814	4	0
1815	4	0
1816	4	0
1817	3	1
1818	3	1
1819	3	1
1820	0	4
1821	0	4
1822	0	4
1823	2	2
1824	2	2

SUSSEX COUNTY

Year	Federalists	Republicans
1800	0	5
1801	0	5
1802	0	5
1803	0	5
1804	0	5
1805	0	5
1806	2	3
1807	0	5
1808	0	5
1809	0	5
1810	0	5
1811	0	5
1812	0	5
1813	0	5
1814	0	5

1815	0	5
1816	2	3
1817	1	4
1818	1	4
1819	1	4
1820	0	5
1821	2	3
1822	1	4
1823	1	4
1824	1	4

FEDERALIST STRENGTH IN THE NEW JERSEY LEGISLATURE 1800–1824

	Council	Assembly	Total Legislature
1800	69%	68%	68%
1801	46%	38%	42%
1802	49%	51%	50%
1803	38%	36%	37%
1804	31%	27%	29%
1805	38%	35%	36%
1806	53%	45%	49%
1807	38%	33%	35%
1808	46%	42%	44%
1809	38%	40%	39%
1810	38%	35%	36%
1811	31%	27%	29%
1812	53%	60%	56%
1813	46%	40%	43%
1814	46%	42%	44%
1815	46%	40%	43%
1816	38%	40%	39%
1817	38%	38%	38%
1818	38%	35%	36%
1819	31%	28%	30%
1820	31%	16%	23%
1821	31%	30%	30%
1822	31%	28%	30%
1823	46%	30%	38%
1824	38%	20%	29%

PERCENTAGE OF TOTAL VOTE CAST FOR FEDERALIST CANDIDATE FOR COUNCIL BY COUNTY, 1796–1822

BERGEN COUNTY

Year	Percent Voter Participation	Percent Federalist Vote
1796	**	**
1797	**	**
1798	**	**
1799	**	**
1800	71%	57%
1801	58%	56%
1802	49%	62%
1803	54%	58%
1804	38%	64%
1805	29%	60%
1806	19%	56%
1807	44%	46%
1808	71%	50%
1809	56%	50%
1810	58%	43%
1811	53%	42%
1812	44%	39%
1813	61%	51%
1814	64%	55%
1815	51%	45%

1816	19%	49%
1817	17%	51%
1818	15%	51%
1819	17%	47%
1820	20%	48%
1821	17%	44%
1822	14%	39%

**No record
*No contest

BURLINGTON COUNTY

Year	Percent Voter Participation	Percent Federalist Vote
1796	**	**
1797	**	**
1798	61%	58%
1799	30%	82%
1800	76%	84%
1801	59%	68%
1802	61%	59%
1803	85%	63%
1804	49%	57%
1805	33%	51%
1806	*	*
1807	*	*
1808	65%	69%
1809	43%	66%
1810	**	**
1811	**	**
1812	**	**
1813	**	**
1814	**	**
1815	**	**
1816	*	*
1817	49%	52%
1818	48%	57%
1819	*	*
1820	60%	48%

1821	64%	49%
1822	68%	49%

**No record
*No contest

CUMBERLAND COUNTY

Year	Percent Voter Participation	Percent Federalist Vote
1796	**	**
1797	**	**
1798	76%	55%
1799	**	**
1800	**	**
1801	106% +	42%
1802	*	*
1803	*	*
1804	53%	44%
1805	68%	45%
1806	72%	45%
1807	*	*
1808	*	*
1809	*	*
1810	*	*
1811	*	*
1812	82%	44%
1813	*	*
1814	**	**
1815	**	**
1816	17%	48%
1817	*	*
1818	20%	49%
1819	17%	46%
1820	23%	45%
1821	22%	48%
1822	27%	64%

**No record
*No contest
+Illegal election

ESSEX COUNTY

Year	Percent Voter Participation	Percent Federalist Vote
1796	24%	4%
1797	22%	46%
1798	31%	29%
1799	15%	2%
1800	39%	1%
1801	56%	11%
1802	35%	0%
1803	49%	11%
1804	36%	0%
1805	38%	0%
1806	80%	0%
1807	99%	9%
1808	61%	12%
1809	36%	6%
1810	39%	1%
1811	38%	0%
1812	42%	0%
1813	39%	4%
1814	56%	0%
1815	38%	0%
1816	*	*
1817	*	*
1818	*	*
1819	*	*
1820	*	*
1821	*	*
1822	*	*

*No contest

GLOUCESTER COUNTY

Year	Percent Voter Participation	Percent Federalist Vote
1796	**	**

1797	**	**
1798	**	**
1799	**	**
1800	70%	65%
1801	60%	56%
1802	73%	52%
1803	99%	48%
1804	**	**
1805	**	**
1806	71%	52%
1807	84%	48%
1808	73%	47%
1809	71%	49%
1810	72%	50%
1811	70%	50%
1812	82%	56%
1813	69%	54%
1814	69%	62%
1815	56%	55%
1816	**	**
1817	*	*
1818	59%	47%
1819	45%	53%
1820	43%	60%
1821	49%	64%
1822	43%	49%

**No record
*No contest

HUNTERDON COUNTY

Year	Percent Voter Participation	Percent Federalist Vote
1796	15%	70%
1797	18%	33%
1798	18%	31%
1799	18%	35%
1800	61%	49%
1801	81%	45%
1802	87%	49%

1803	122%+	45%
1804	**	**
1805	**	**
1806	98%	48%
1807	117%+	46%
1808	88%	49%
1809	81%	45%
1810	**	**
1811	**	**
1812	88%	49%
1813	**	**
1814	84%	48%
1815	76%	46%
1816	50%	49%
1817	**	**
1818	62%	48%
1819	*	*
1820	*	*
1821	67%	44%
1822	63%	49%

**No record
*No contest
+Illegal election

MIDDLESEX COUNTY

Year	Percent Voter Participation	Percent Federalist Vote
1796	**	**
1797	**	**
1798	**	**
1799	**	**
1800	71%	66%
1801	58%	56%
1802	47%	58%
1803	86%	55%
1804	43%	54%
1805	47%	52%
1806	39%	61%
1807	56%	51%

1808	74%	55%
1809	56%	53%
1810	54%	53%
1811	61%	49%
1812	79%	55%
1813	69%	55%
1814	70%	59%
1815	59%	54%
1816	58%	52%
1817	55%	51%
1818	53%	45%
1819	49%	48%
1820	51%	51%
1821	59%	49%
1822	60%	53%

**No record

MONMOUTH COUNTY

Year	Percent Voter Participation	Percent Federalist Vote
1796	**	**
1797	**	**
1798	**	**
1799	**	**
1800	47%	50%
1801	58%	42%
1802	70%	45%
1803	59%	32%
1804	**	**
1805	56%	60%
1806	**	**
1807	74%	47%
1808	78%	52%
1809	79%	47%
1810	75%	47%
1811	**	**
1812	81%	50%
1813	**	**
1814	80%	49%

1815	78%	46%
1816	**	**
1817	18%	11%
1818	*	*
1819	*	*
1820	*	*
1821	16%	18%
1822	*	*

**No record
*No contest

MORRIS COUNTY

Year	Percent Voter Participation	Percent Federalist Vote
1796	**	**
1797	20%	37%
1798	28%	17%
1799	40%	43%
1800	**	**
1801	51%	21%
1802	**	**
1803	39%	26%
1804	27%	17%
1805	**	**
1806	28%	11%
1807	32%	**
1808	51%	**
1809	44%	16%
1810	39%	**
1811	49%	**
1812	52%	11%
1813	49%	**
1814	65%	21%
1815	31%	**
1816	22%	09%
1817	26%	32%
1818	**	**
1819	55%	52%
1820	41%	35%

| 1821 | 38% | 24% |
| 1822 | * | * |

**No record
*No contest

SALEM COUNTY

Year	Percent Voter Participation	Percent Federalist Vote
1796	**	**
1797	**	**
1798	**	**
1799	**	**
1800	77%	54%
1801	**	**
1802	**	**
1803	**	**
1804	**	**
1805	**	**
1806	76%	41%
1807	**	**
1808	**	**
1809	**	**
1810	**	**
1811	**	**
1812	**	**
1813	**	**
1814	73%	46%
1815	**	**
1816	**	**
1817	**	**
1818	39%	53%
1819	12%	49%
1820	14%	46%
1821	*	*
1822	41%	57%

**No record
*No contest

SOMERSET COUNTY

Year	Percent Voter Participation	Percent Federalist Vote
1796	**	**
1797	34%	63%
1798	**	**
1799	31%	42%
1800	79%	77%
1801	56%	87%
1802	**	**
1803	**	**
1804	52%	43%
1805	53%	64%
1806	**	**
1807	**	**
1808	82%	60%
1809	62%	60%
1810	**	**
1811	**	**
1812	**	**
1813	**	**
1814	70%	64%
1815	*	*
1816	*	*
1817	*	*
1818	*	*
1819	31%	61%
1820	33%	44%
1821	*	*
1822	*	*

**No record
*No contest

SUSSEX COUNTY

Year	Percent Voter Participation	Percent Federalist Vote
1796	**	**
1797	**	**
1798	**	**
1799	32%	37%
1800	57%	*
1801	57%	48%
1802	**	**
1803	76%	31%
1804	**	**
1805	**	**
1806	**	**
1807	65%	45%
1808	76%	45%
1809	60%	28%
1810	30%	*
1811	47%	38%
1812	73%	36%
1813	61%	35%
1814	58%	38%
1815	57%	38%
1816	58%	51%
1817	52%	39%
1818	60%	55%
1819	44%	46%
1820	42%	41%
1821	53%	24%
1822	*	*

**No record
*No contest

NUMBER OF COUNTIES FOR WHICH STATE LEGISLATIVE ELECTION RESULTS WERE REPORTED IN NEW JERSEY NEWSPAPERS, 1790–1824: AN INDICATION OF ELECTORAL INTEREST

1790–1807

Year	Number of Counties
1790	1
1791	1
1792	3
1793	1
1794	1
1795	2
1796	1
1797	4
1798	4
1799	6
1800	8
1801	10
1802	13
1803	12
1804	6
1805	9
1806	10
1807	12

1808–1824

Year	Number of Counties
1808	11
1809	11
1810	8
1811	10
1812	10
1813	6
1814	10
1815	8
1816	6
1817	6
1818	9
1819	9
1820	10
1821	13
1822	12
1823	13
1824	13

PERCENTAGE OF TOTAL VOTE CAST FOR FEDERALIST CONGRESSIONAL TICKET, 1796–1822

Year	Percent Voter Participation	Percent Federalist Vote
1796	26%	65%
1798	46%	40%
1800	68%	49%
1803	*	*
1806	*	*
1808	70%	44%
1810	*	*
1813	84%	52%
1814	67%	48%
1816	*	*
1820	*	*
1822	*	*

*No contest

APPENDIX 6

BIOGRAPHICAL SKETCHES OF PROMINENT NEW JERSEY FEDERALISTS

In selecting biographees, several indices of prominence were used in an effort to single out individuals who might accurately be termed New Jersey Federalist party leaders. First, for each individual considered for listing, a card was prepared on which was noted the title and number of times each (1) had held Federalist party office, (2) had been nominated for an elective office, and (3) had been appointed to a federal, state or local office. As a result of a tabulation of the above data for each person considered, the most frequent New Jersey Federalist officeholders and candidates for office emerged. Besides the frequency of officeholding, weight was given to the relative importance of the various offices sought and won.

Next, evidence of prominence found in newspapers, political pamphlets, broadsides, and correspondence was noted and weighed, again both quantitatively and qualitatively in each individual case. This method was particularly useful in discovering behind-the-scenes party managers since the search here was broadened beyond officeholding, but still party leaders in this category remained difficult to identify and some may have been overlooked. However, the probability of exclusion is reduced in this particular instance because as Prince says (on page four of an essay on "The Leadership of New Jersey's First Party System" read at the Second Annual New Jersey History Symposium, Trenton, New Jersey, December, 1970),

. . . virtually all party leaders of both camps gained some office, elected or appointed. . . . This was not an era when party managers operated offstage.

Thirdly, weight was given to the individual's mention in certain secondary sources. Included among these are the works of Richard P. McCormick, Carl E. Prince, Walter Fee, J. R. Pole, and the following national and state biographical compilations: *Dictionary of American Biography; Memorial Cyclopedia of New Jersey;* and *The Biographical Encyclopedia of New Jersey of the Nine-*

teenth Century. Besides serving as comparison points for our own listing, the above works provided some data for the sketches. The bulk of the information for the sketches was garnered from a myriad of other sources too numerous to list in their entirety but including abstracts of wills, biographical sketches in manuscript form, correspondence, and card index files of genealogical data and newspaper obituaries at the New Jersey State Library, Newark (New Jersey) Public Library, Jersey City Public Library, the Rutgers University Library Special Collections Department, and various county historical societies in New Jersey. Other secondary sources found helpful were doctoral dissertations, journal articles, several published biographies, and "Appendix II: Federalist Leaders, 1800–1816," in David Hackett Fischer's *The Revolution of American Conservatism.*

The following forty individuals were chosen as the subjects of biographical sketches from an original pool of roughly 2,000. The intent of the sketches is not to provide a balanced view of the individuals but rather to highlight those points about them which are relevant to the visualization of these men as the Federalist party in microcosm.

BAYARD, JOHN (1738–1807). Born Bohemia Manor, Maryland; moved to New Brunswick, New Jersey, in the 1780s; father a large landholder; Presbyterian; educated by a tutor; wealthy merchant; third marriage to Joannah White, sister of General Anthony Walton White, linked Bayard by virtue of his wife's family to Federalists William Paterson and Andrew Bell; daughter married the future Chief Justice of New Jersey Andrew Kirkpatrick; son Samuel became a prominent lawyer and an ultra-Federalist leader; not a strong advocate of independence but was a member of the Sons of Liberty and took part in the Stamp Act protests; a Continental Army officer, he served at the battles of Brandywine, Germantown, and Princeton; 1778—named to the board of trustees of Princeton University; 1790—elected mayor of New Brunswick; after 1790—served in many Middlesex County posts; until his death in 1807 served as chairman of several Middlesex County Federalist party conclaves; promoter of civic betterment programs; hospitality of his luxurious home was extended to the major Federalist political leaders of the day.

John Bayard may be best regarded as typical of the older leadership of the New Jersey Federalist party and his family as typical of the first families of New Jersey.

BAYARD, SAMUEL (1767–1840). Born in Philadelphia; moved in 1806 to Princeton, New Jersey; son of John Bayard (above); father a wealthy merchant and New Jersey Federalist party leader; Presbyterian; Princeton University graduate; lawyer, having studied law under future Attorney General of the United States William Bradford; married the daughter of Lewis Pintard and Susan (Stockton) Pintard; sons became (1) an Episcopalian Bishop, (2) a lawyer and Jacksonian politician; after 1806—served on the town council of Princeton, elected the first mayor of Princeton; 1812—secretary, statewide peace convention; 1814—nominee for the United States Congress; 1813–1815—New Jersey legislator from Somerset County; 1817—leader in the African Colonization Society; co-founder of New-York Historical Society with John Jay, of whom he was a close associate.

Samuel Bayard, whose political connections in New Jersey place him in the top echelon of party leaders in Hunterdon, Somerset, and Middlesex counties from 1806 to 1815, was very much in the tradition of the mainstream Federalist leaders of New Jersey. True to the humanitarian bent of most New Jersey Federalists, he also was active in many religious and intellectual endeavors. His writings reveal his wide range of interests from law and religion to politics.

BEATTY, ERKURIES (1761–1823). Born Princeton, New Jersey; father a Presbyterian minister; read law under Richard Stockton the elder; farmer; younger brother of Federalist leader John Beatty, who politically was the more important of the two; served in the Continental Army (1777–1781) at White Plains, Monmouth, and Yorktown; Middlesex County freeholder (1800–1810, 1815–1822); Middlesex and Somerset County legislator (1801–1805, 1812–1813, 1820 —assemblyman; 1806–1809, 1814–1817, 1822—councilman); land speculator; experimental farmer; 1811–1823—treasurer, Society of the Cincinnati; 1816—chairman of the first meeting of a Hunterdon County African colonization society; 1818–1823—mayor of Princeton.

The life of Erkuries Beatty illustrates once again the wide-ranging interests of the typical New Jersey Federalist party leader and his inclination to promote social welfare progiams. Also, Beatty's lack of prudence in the management of his personal finances is representative of that of an important minority of the New Jersey Federalist party leadership. But Beatty was rare among his fellows in that, at separate times, he represented two different counties in the New Jersey legislature.

BEATTY, JOHN (1749–1826). Born Bucks County, Pennsylvania; moved by 1760 to Princeton; father a Presbyterian minister; studied medicine under Dr. Benjamin Rush of Philadelphia; received M.A. from Princeton; older brother of Erkuries Beatty (above); physician and lawyer; rose to the rank of colonel in the Continental Army, but afterward was dismissed, having been charged with trading with the enemy; president of the New Jersey Medical Society, which he had helped to organize; 1781–1784—councilman; 1784–1786—Continental Congressman; 1787—delegate from Middlesex County to the state's federal Constitution ratifying convention; 1789, 1790—assemblyman; 1789—speaker of the New Jersey General Assembly; 1793—named brigadier general in the New Jersey militia by the state legislature; 1793–1795—United States Congressman; 1795–1805—New Jersey secretary of state; 1800—secretary of New Jersey Federalist party Congressional nominating meeting; 1812, 1814—chaired local peace meetings, attended New Jersey Federalist party conventions; helped form the state's African colonization society; treasurer, Society of the Cincinnati; trustee, Princeton University.

Beside being prominent in politics, John Beatty, like a number of other New Jersey Federalist party leaders, also was active in the business world, serving as director of the Delaware River Bridge Company and later as president of the Trenton Banking Company.

BELL, ANDREW (1757–1843). Born in New Jersey; son of an East Jersey proprietor; residence—Perth Amboy; Episcopalian; read law under David Ogden; brother-in-law of Federalist leader William Paterson (below); lawyer and wealthy land owner; 1800—collector of the port of Perth Amboy.

Andrew Bell is representative of those Federalist leaders, such as James Parker and the Rutherfurds, who surmounted serious charges of Toryism and adjusted to the new order. However, his leadership role in the Federalist party, that of an offstage party manager, marks him as a rarity in New Jersey politics of the day.

BOUDINOT, ELIAS (1740–1821). Born Philadelphia, Pennsylvania; moved to New Jersey by 1760; father a silversmith; Presbyterian; educated in classical schools; read law under Richard Stockton, Sr.; lawyer (early practice—Elizabeth); brother-in-law of Richard Stockton, Jr.; also related to New Jersey Federalist leader Joshua Wallace (below); commissary general of prisoners during the Revolutionary War; 1777, 1781–1783—Continental Congressman; 1782–1783 —President, Continental Congress; 1789–1795—United States Congressman; 1795–1805—director of United States Mint; author, *Age of Revelation*, a reply to the deistic *Age of Reason* written by Thomas Paine; 1772–1821—Trustee, Princeton College; philanthropist; president, American Bible Society; abolitionist.

Particularly because of his activities after retirement Boudinot today is as well known for his religious and humanistic endeavors as he is for his earlier political prominence. He is one of the outstanding examples of a New Jersey Federalist party leader who gained equal prominence in nonpolitical activities.

BOUDINOT, ELISHA (1749–1819). Born Philadelphia, Pennsylvania; father a silversmith; Presbyterian; educated in classical schools; lawyer (Newark, New Jersey); judge; married (1) daughter of wealthy Federalist William Peartree Smith, (2) sister of William Bradford, attorney general in Washington's cabinet; younger brother of New Jersey Federalist leader Elias Boudinot (above); member, Newark committee of correspondence; holder of administrative posts during Revolutionary War; 1798—appointed justice of the New Jersey Supreme Court and became a vigorous enforcer of the Sedition Act; 1804–1819—active, civic and philanthropic endeavors.

After the dominant Republicans removed him from the New Jersey Supreme Court in 1804, Boudinot disappeared from the political scene. Thus, he is representative of that minority of New Jersey Federalist politicians who ceased to challenge the Republicans for power once they had come into full possession of the state and national governments.

COLEFAX, WILLIAM (1756–1838). Born in Connecticut; moved to Bergen County, New Jersey, during the Revolution; joined the Dutch Reformed Church; grammar school education; large landowner; married into one of the wealthiest Dutch families in Bergen County; an officer in the Continental Army

(1777–1781), he served in Washington's personal guard; Bergen County legislator (1806, 1807, 1809–1811—assemblyman; 1808, 1812, 1813—councilman); 1800, 1806, 1812, 1814—judge of the Court of Common Pleas.

Colefax is representative of those New Jersey Federalist leaders who were exceedingly active at party conclaves, for from 1800 to 1812 he served almost continuously as a Bergen County Federalist party officer, often chairman or secretary of meetings. After 1812, however, his participation in party affairs declined, perhaps due to his advanced age.

COXE, RICHARD (1792–1865). Born Burlington City, New Jersey; father New Jersey Federalist party leader William Coxe, Jr. (below); Episcopalian; educated at Princeton; read law under William Griffith (below); lawyer; married daughter of William Griffith; 1812—appointed a militia officer, he rose to the rank of major; author, *A New Pronouncing Dictionary of the English Language Compiled by an American Gentleman.*

Coming to prominence during the War of 1812 while still young, Coxe served as a delegate to the New Jersey Federalist party conventions of 1812 and 1814 along with his father and his father-in-law. At the conclave of 1814, the last year the party functioned at the statewide level, he was a speaker.

COXE, WILLIAM, JR. (1762–1831). Born Philadelphia, Pennsylvania; moved to Burlington City, New Jersey, in 1789; father a Quaker landowner and merchant; Episcopalian; apprenticeship with a Philadelphia merchant; large landowner, pomologist, and speculator; married into the powerful Smith family of Burlington County; father of Richard S. Coxe (above); 1796–1804, 1806–1809, 1816, 1819—assemblyman; 1798–1800, 1802—speaker of the Assembly; 1813–1815—United States Congressman.

Constituting another example of a New Jersey Federalist party leader who engaged in scientific farming, Coxe in 1817 published a nationally accepted book on pomology. But, more than anything else, William Coxe, Jr., is illustrative of those New Jersey Federalist party leaders who remained faithful to the party and locally powerful under its banner until the mid-1820s.

DAYTON, ELIAS (1737–1807). Born Elizabeth, New Jersey; descended from New England stock; Presbyterian; grammar school education; officer in the French and Indian war; wealthy merchant; married an aunt of Federalist leader Aaron Ogden; son Jonathan Dayton (below) became a key figure in state and national politics; served as a Revolutionary army officer, rising to the rank of brigadier-general; held several minor local elective offices prior to the Revolution; 1778–1779—served in Continental Congress; 1789—recorder of Elizabeth; 1791–1792, 1794–1796—assemblyman from Essex County; 1796–1805—mayor of Elizabeth; active in the Society of the Cincinnati.

Elias Dayton was a Federalist of Washington's generation who remained at the helm during the Republican era. Especially during his later years, a large part of Dayton's efforts were devoted to the promotion of the career of his son Jonathan (below).

DAYTON, JONATHAN (1760–1824). Born in Elizabeth; from an old New Jersey family; son of wealthy merchant, Elias Dayton (above); 1776—received A.B. from Princeton; lawyer and land speculator; married into the Ogden family; officer in the Revolution and leader in the Society of the Cincinnati; 1786, 1787, 1788, 1789—assemblyman; delegate to the federal Constitutional Convention; 1790—councilman; 1791–1799—member of the House of Representatives and served as Speaker of the House in the fourth and fifth Congresses; 1799–1805 —elected by the Federalist legislature to the United States Senate; 1814–1815 —assemblyman.

Besides being one of the most politically active members of the New Jersey Federalist party, Jonathan Dayton was one of the most controversial. Intensely ambitious, he sometimes engaged in schemes that bordered on the illegal or treasonous.

DAVENPORT, FRANKLIN (1755–1832). Born in Philadelphia; moved to Woodbury, New Jersey, about 1775; a nephew of Benjamin Franklin; Presbyterian; studied briefly at the University of Pennsylvania and was admitted to the bar in New Jersey; combined a florishing law practice with land speculation; married a sister of Richard Howell (below) and after Howells' early demise, undertook the care of one of his minor children; held rank of major-general in the militia and served at the battles of Princeton and Trenton; 1785—surrogate of Gloucester County; 1786–1789—assemblyman; 1792 and 1796—presidential elector; 1798–1799—United States Senator; 1799–1801—served in the United States House of Representatives; brigadier-general in the state militia during the War of 1812. Unlike some of his peers in the Federalist party, such as Jonathan Elmer, Davenport did not retire from politics after the War of 1812. Rather, thereafter he frequently chaired county party meetings and offered himself as a nominee for elective office.

ELMER, JONATHAN (1745–1817). Born in Cumberland County; son of well-to-do parents with deep family roots in the county; Presbyterian; graduated from the University of Pennsylvania in 1771; physician and self-taught lawyer; brother of Ebenezer Elmer, moderate Republican leader in Cumberland County; married the daughter of a prominent Federalist family; on the eve of the Revolution Elmer was royal high sheriff of Cumberland County but thereafter joined the Continental Army; 1775—captain, Continental Army; 1776–1778, 1781–1784, 1787–1788—Continental Congressman; 1780, 1785— member, New Jersey legislature; 1789–1791—United States Senator; 1784– 1802, 1812–1817—surrogate of Cumberland County.

The state peace meeting of July 4, 1812, named Elmer chairman and requested him to draw up an address. It was a resounding expression of confidence in the mass of voters. "Most unequivocally . . . do we declare our confidence in the great body of citizens, whatever may have been our distrust or dissatisfaction in regard to the men in office, and the measures they have pursued."

EWING, CHARLES (1780–1823). Born in Trenton; father James Ewing (below) was a merchant and state legislator; Presbyterian; Princeton, class of 1798; a classmate of William Bell Paterson (below); read law under Federalist lawyer Samuel Leake; began law practice in Trenton in 1802, the same year his father was mayor of the city; married sister of Federalist leader and lawyer Garret D. Wall (below); 1824–1832—chief justice of the state supreme court.

Ewing was one of those younger men who did not enter the party until after the Federalist era had ended. His efforts to rebuild the party in Hunterdon County having failed, Ewing ultimately joined with some of his fellows and some dissident county Republicans to form a coalition group.

EWING, JAMES (1754–1823). Born in Bridgeton, New Jersey; son of a Scotch-Irish immigrant farmer; Presbyterian; apprenticed to a printer; later became a merchant in Trenton; married a wealthy widow; father of Charles Ewing (above); during the Revolution he served as auditor of public accounts, a commissioner for the Continental loan office, and a pension agent for the Continental Congress; held many local appointive posts up to 1801; 1794—Hunterdon County Assemblyman; 1797–1803—mayor of Trenton.

James Ewing is representive of those New Jersey Federalist party leaders who founded important political families.

FRELINGHUYSEN, FREDERICK (1753–1804). Born in Somerset County; son of a Dutch Reformed minister; A.B., Princeton, 1770; lawyer; married the daughter of a wealthy New Brunswick merchant; son Theodore (below) became a leading Federalist after 1812; sons John and Frederick, Jr. also served as Federalist party workers and held numerous minor elective and appointive posts; officer in the Continental Army; 1778–1779, 1782–1783—Continental Congressman; 1784, 1800–1804—assemblyman; 1787—attended New Jersey federal Constitutional ratifying convention; 1790–1792—councilman; 1793–1796 —United States Senator; major-general during the Whiskey Insurrection.

Frelinghuysen's inclinations were toward the old-fashioned, elitist-militarist wing of the party also represented by Anthony W. White and Richard Howell.

FRELINGHUYSEN, THEODORE (1787–1862). Born in Somerset County; after 1808 resided in Newark; father (above) a lawyer and Federalist politican; Dutch Reformed; A.B., Princeton, 1804; read law under Richard Stockton; established law practice in Republican-controlled Newark; married the daughter of wealthy Federalist merchant Archibald Mercer of Trenton; several of their children became prominent political leaders; militia captain in the War of 1812; 1817–1829—attorney general of the state; 1828—presidential elector; 1829–1835—United States Senator; 1837–1839—mayor of Newark; 1844—unsuccessful candidate for Vice-President of the United States; 1839–1850—chancellor of New York University; 1850–1862—president of Rutgers.

Theodore Frelinghuysen stands as an example of those younger Federalists who entered the party ranks during the War of 1812 and were political leaders in the state during the pre-Civil War period.

GILES, JAMES (1759–1825). Born in New York City; moved to Bridgeton in 1788; father an Episcopalian minister; studied law with Joseph Bloomfield; lawyer and banker; married sister of ex-Federalist Joseph Bloomfield; officer in the New York militia during the Revolution and member of the Society of the Cincinnati; 1789–1799—county clerk of Cumberland County; 1792–1804—state adjutant general; served as a delegate to every one of the Federalist state party conventions.

Giles typified those New Jersey Federalists who lived in an aristocratic manner. His lucrative law practice enabled him to build a large home in Bridgeton and to maintain one of the largest private libraries in South Jersey.

GRIFFITH, WILLIAM (1766–1826). Born in Somerset County; settled in Burlington County in 1789; son of a physican; not a church member; read law under Elisha Boudinot; lawyer and land speculator; married a Boudinot; daughter married Richard Coxe, (above); one of John Adams' "midnight" appointees to the bench; 1818–1819, 1823–1824—assemblyman; 1824–1826—mayor of Burlington City; 1825—clerk of the United States Supreme Court; author of *Eumenes*, a polemic advocating the revision of the state constitution, and of numerous legal treatises.

Griffith was one of the few Federalists who were influential in the formulation of legislation during the Era of Good Feelings. His most important contribution during this period, when he served as minority leader of the Assembly, was the development of debtor relief legislation.

HORNBLOWER, JOSEPH C. (1777–1864). Born in Belleville in Essex County; son of Joshua Hornblower, a member of the New Jersey legislature (1779–1784) and of the Continental Congress (1785); Presbyterian; read law under Federalist lawyer David Ogden; 1803—married the daughter of Dr. William Burnet, an important Newark Federalist; 1829—assemblyman; 1832–1846—chief justice of the New Jersey Supreme Court; 1845–1864—first president of the New Jersey Historical Society; 1847–1855—professor of law at Princeton; 1860—Republican presidential elector; active in the American Bible society and in the New Jersey Colonization society.

As a county Federalist leader after 1800, Hornblower learned the art of politics, but he did not achieve his greatest prominence until the advent of the second party system.

HOWELL, RICHARD (1754–1802). Born in Newark, Delaware; moved to Cumberland County, New Jersey, while a youth; father was a farmer; originally a Quaker, Howell became an Episcopalian during the Revolution; privately educated; lawyer; married the daughter of Joseph Burr, a Federalist politician and large landowner; 1775–1778—Continental army officer; aide to Washington; 1788–1793—clerk of the New Jersey Supreme Court; 1794—led New Jersey troops into Pennsylvania to help quell the Whiskey Rebellion; 1793–1801—governor of New Jersey.

Howell always thought of himself more as a soldier than as a politician. Like such New Jersey Federalist leaders as Anthony White, he was tied to the cavalier tradition.

KINSEY, JAMES (1733–1803). Born in Philadelphia; moved to Burlington City about 1750; Quaker; father was chief justice of Pennsylvania (1743–1750); A.B.,

Princeton, 1750; lawyer; 1772–1775—assemblyman; 1774–1775—member of the committee of correspondence for Burlington County; July 23, 1774–November, 22, 1775—Continental Congressman; 1789–1803—chief justice of the New Jersey Supreme Court.

Kinsey was representive of those New Jersey Federalists against whom the Republican charge of Toryism could be made with good effect. He had assumed a pacifist position during the Revolution and in 1776 had refused to take an oath to support the new state constitution.

KIRKPATRICK, ANDREW (1756–1831). Born in Somerset County; son of a Presbyterian minister and state legislator; A.B., Princeton, 1775; read law under William Paterson; minister, tutor, lawyer; married into the Bayard family of New Brunswick; 1797—assemblyman; 1798–1803—associate justice of the New Jersey Supreme Court.

Kirkpatrick was rare among the Federalists because he not only received an important state post from the Republicans but was repeatedly reappointed to it by the opposition party over a twenty-year period. Yet, while he obviously retained the good will of the Republicans, his personal life revolved around his Federalist friends and family members.

LACEY, JOHN (1755–1814). Born in Bucks County, Pennsylvania; moved to Burlington in 1782; father was a miller; disowned by the Society of Friends, he turned Episcopalian; by his own admission he was poorly educated; land speculator and iron master; married the daughter of wealthy Federalist Colonel Reynolds of Burlington; 1776–1777—officer in the Continental army; 1777–1782—served in the Pennsylvania militia and attained the rank of brigadier-general; 1801–1803—member of the New Jersey legislature.

Lacey was representative of several New Jersey Federalists whose malfeasance in office came to light between 1800 and 1801. Along with discovery of the unsavory acts of Jonathan Dayton and Governor Richard Howell, the disclosure of attempted bribery on the part of John Lacey hurt the party during these years.

MARTIN, EPHRAIM (1733–1806). Born in New Brunswick, New Jersey; father was a large landowner; Baptist; privately educated; land speculator and farmer; acquired estates in Middlesex, Somerset and Sussex counties; 1774—member of the committee of safety of Sussex County; attended the 1776 New Jersey constitutional convention; 1776–1779—militia officer; 1779–1790—member of the legislative council from Somerset County; 1795–1806—member of the legislative council from Middlesex County.

Martin was atypical among New Jersey Federalists leaders on three counts. First, he was a Baptist; secondly, his service in the legislature spanned an unusually long period; and, thirdly, at separate times, he represented two different counties in the New Jersey legislature.

OGDEN, AARON (1756–1839). Born in Elizabeth; great-grandson of the town's founder and son of a prominent lawyer and member of the assembly; Presbyterian; A.B., Princeton, 1773; a tutor in one of the most prestigious schools in the state; admitted to the bar after the Revolution; married the daughter of Judge John Chetwood, an influential Federalist; during the entire course of the Revolution he occupied an important staff post in the Revolutionary Army; 1796—presidential elector; 1785–1803—clerk of Essex County; 1801–1803— United States Senator; 1802—candidate for governor; 1804—candidate for chief justice of the state; 1808—candidate for Congress; 1803–1839—trustee of Princeton; 1812–1813—governor of New Jersey; 1830–1839—collector of customs for the port of Jersey City; 1824–1839—president of the New Jersey Society of the Cincinnati.

Ogden is representative of a group of very prominent New Jersey Federalist leaders who resided in Elizabeth. After 1796 their path to office became a difficult one, for by then their county, Essex, had emerged as the cradle of New Jersey Republicanism.

PARKER, JAMES (1776–1868). Reared in Perth Amboy; the son of James Parker, Sr., a member of the colonial council and a loyalist; Episcopalian; graduated from Columbia in 1793; land speculator and lawyer; married the sister of important Federalist David Ogden; 1806–1811, 1812–1813, 1815–1816, 1818—assemblyman; 1815—mayor of Perth Amboy; 1824—presidential elector; 1829–1833—collector of customs for the port of Perth Amboy; 1833–1837—Congressman; 1844—delegate to the New Jersey state constitutional convention.

Especially in the later years of the party Parker stood as something of a maverick. While he remained a Federalist, in 1812 he attacked the peace stand of his party. Later, toward the end of the Era of Good Feelings, he angered those Federalists who still were laboring to maintain their local organizations by announcing publicly that the Federalist party had ceased to exist and that he therefore refused to run for office under its banner.

PATERSON, WILLIAM (1745–1806). Born in Antrim, Ireland; brought to America in 1747; son of a Princeton merchant and large landowner; Presbyterian; A.B., Princeton, 1763; read law under Richard Stockton; lawyer; married into the wealthy Federalist Bell family of Perth Amboy; 1775–1776—delegate and secretary to the Provincial Congress; 1776–1778—councilman; delegate to the New Jersey constitutional convention; 1776–1778—attorney-general of New Jersey; delegate to the United States Constitutional Convention; 1789–1790— United States Senator; 1790–1793—governor; 1793–1806—justice of the United States Supreme Court.

Paterson well typifies the legal bent exhibited by many New Jersey Federalist leaders. However, in Paterson's case and that of a lesser number of Federalist leaders, this inclination went even deeper. For them the most desirable post of all was a judicial one.

PATERSON, WILLIAM BELL, (1771–1833). Born in New Brunswick; son of William Paterson (above) and Cornelia Bell Paterson, the sister of Andrew Bell (above); Presbyterian turned Episcopalian, A.B., Princeton, 1801; lawyer; newspaper essayist; never sought elective office; chaired numerous party meetings.

Chronologically a young Federalist, Paterson's statements from the first label him as an old Federalist. At a time when older Federalists publicly were making democratic utterances and exhibiting party loyalty, Paterson was publishing newspaper pieces with such titles as the "Fallacies of Government Based on the Popular Vote" and "France Must Return to Monarchy" and expressing not only a deep distrust of aliens and immigrants but contempt for the calling of a politican. Nowadays "every grog-shop is a caucus of red-hot patriots and red-hot democrats," he said, for since the adoption of the federal Constitution, politics had been "conducted on a cheap scale" with financial gain at its heart. Office-holders ought not to expect compensation, he believed, but rather ought to serve out of sense of duty and a love of honor. ("Addison," *Guardian*, 1808–1810; Paterson Papers, Princeton and Rutgers Universities.)

SCHUREMAN, JAMES (1756–1824). Born in New Brunswick; father a wealthy merchant; member of the Dutch Reformed church; A.B., Queen's College, 1775; became a partner in his father's general store; officer in the Revolution; 1783–1785, 1788—assemblyman; 1786–1787—Continental Congressman; 1789–1791, 1797–1799, 1813–1815—U.S. Congressman; 1799–1801—United States Senator; 1801–1813, 1821–1824—mayor of New Brunswick; 1808, 1810 —councilman; trustee, Queen's College.

Schureman stands out as a New Jersey Federalist leader who was a consistent officeholder over a long period of time. But his record as a political organizer was even better.

SCOTT, JOSEPH WARREN (1778–1871). Born in Somerset County; father, Moses Scott, was a physican and officer in the Revolution; Episcopalian; A.B., Princeton, 1795; trained as a physican, later read law under Federalist Frederick Frelinghuysen (above); militia officer in the War of 1812; 1820–1871—officer in the New Jersey Society of the Cincinnati; 1824—presidential elector; 1829 —Somerset County prosecutor.

Scott, like some of the other young Federalist leaders, gained his political grounding as a Federalist organizer, but he did not seek office during the period of the first party system.

SMITH, ISAAC (1740–1807). Born in Trenton; father a wealthy landholder; Presbyterian; A.B., Princeton 1755; teacher, physican, lawyer; militia officer during the Revolution; 1795–1797—Congressman; 1800—presidential elector; 1797–1805—justice of the New Jersey Supreme Court.

Like some other Federalists, Smith was apt to exhibit partisanship while on the bench. A number of his grand jury charges that have been published are replete with pro-Federalist views.

STOCKTON, LUCIUS H. (1767–1835). Born in Princeton; son of Richard Stockton, the elder, one of the most prominent lawyers and political figures in New Jersey on the eve of the Revolution; younger brother of Richard Stockton (below); nephew of the prominent Federalists Elias and Elisha Boudinot (above); A.B., Princeton, 1787; lawyer; served as United States Attorney for New Jersey until 1801; nominated by outgoing President Adams for the post of Secretary of War, but, at Stockton's request, Adams withdrew the nomination;

July 4, 1814—speaker, New Jersey Friends of Peace Convention; organizer, Washington Benevolent Society of Trenton.

Of all the New Jersey Federalists Stockton probably made the most visible, rapid, and dramatic transition to new-style Federalism.

STOCKTON, RICHARD (1764–1828). Born in Princeton, New Jersey; son of Richard Stockton, the elder, one of the most prominent lawyers and political figures in New Jersey on the eve of the Revolution; of Episcopalian background but attended Presbyterian services; A.B. Princeton, 1779; read law under his uncle Elisha Boudinot; became the leading lawyer in the state by 1790; married the daughter of a wealthy Burlingtonian; their sons became active in Jacksonian politics; 1792, 1800—presidential elector; 1796–1799—United States senator; 1801, 1802, 1803, 1804—candidate for governor; 1813–1815—United States Congressman; 1791–1828—trustee Princeton College.

Vocal and articulate during the thirteenth Congress, the "haughty and imperious" Richard Stockton acted as the spokesman for the majority contingent of the New Jersey delegation. Largely as a consequence of his efforts, between 1813 and 1815 the voice of New Jersey Federalism in national councils was a strong one.

VROOM, PETER (1791–1873). Born in Somerset County; son of a wealthy landowner and Federalist politician; Dutch Reformed; graduated from Columbia College; studied law under Federalist politician George McDonald; lawyer; married (1) a Frelinghuysen (2) a Wall; militia officer in the War of 1812; 1821, 1823—candidate for New Jersey Assembly; 1826–1827, 1829—assemblyman; 1830–1836—governor; 1838–1840—Congressman; 1853–1859—minister to Prussia; 1860, 1864, 1868—presidential elector.

Vroom was one of a group of young New Jersey Federalists who labored mightily to revive the party after 1812 in the face of overwhelming odds.

WALL, GARRET D. (1783–1850). Born in Middletown (Monmouth County), New Jersey; lived in Trenton from 1803 to 1827 and Burlington City from 1828 to 1850; father a Revolutionary war officer and large landowner; Presbyterian; studied at a classical school in Woodbridge; read law under leading Federalist lawyer Jonathan Rhea; admitted to the bar in 1804; married Rhea's daughter; served as a militia officer in the War of 1812; officer, Washington Benevolent Society; 1812–1817—clerk of the New Jersey Supreme Court; 1815–1837— quartermaster general of the state; 1822, 1827—assemblyman; 1829—elected governor but declined to serve; 1829—accepted federal appointment as United States attorney for the district of New Jersey; 1834–1841—United States Senator; 1848–1850—judge, New Jersey Court of Errors.

Like some other Federalist leaders during the Era of Good Feelings, Wall eventually joined a coalition group composed of Federalists and Republicans. In 1822 he gained an Assembly seat on the fusion ticket offered by this group.

WALLACE, JOSHUA (1752–1819). Born in Philadelphia; moved to Burlington City, New Jersey in 1773; father a well-to-do Scotch immigrant who had married into a leading Philadelphia family; Presbyterian; A.B. College of Philadelphia, 1767; lawyer, land speculator, judge, merchant; married the daughter of a wealthy landholder who had been a royal official in colonial Somerset and Burlington counties; son William, a Federalist, became a Pennsylvania state legislator; 1780s—held many local appointive offices and served several terms in the New Jersey legislature; 1787—member of convention which ratified the federal Constitution on behalf of New Jersey; mid-1790s–1812—chaired many Federalist meetings; 1817—organized New Jersey Society for the Suppression of Vice and Immorality.

Although many older Federalists in New Jersey were active after 1801, Wallace still was outstanding because of the degree to which he engaged in organizational matters. Especially in 1808, he was an important participant in the effort to revitalize the party.

WHITE, ANTHONY WALTON (1750–1803). Born near New Brunswick, New Jersey; father a royal official and large landowner and mother the daughter of Governor Lewis Morris of New York; Episcopalian; educated by private tutors; officer, Continental Army (aide to General Washington, cavalry officer); Federalist era—surveyor, inspector of the port of New Brunswick, adjutant general of New Jersey, surrogate general of Middlesex County; 1794—commanded state cavalry during the Whiskey Rebellion expedition into Pennsylvania; 1798 —brigadier general in the provisional army.

White is representative of that part of the New Jersey Federalist leadership which had strong leanings toward the military. But, as his behavior revealed, probably more than any other he relied heavily upon violence as a solution to political opposition whether the individuals had rioted or had installed liberty caps atop flagpoles. His treatment of prisoners captured during the Whiskey Rebellion brought down charges of brutality upon him, as did his armed rides into Republican areas of New Jersey, during which time his party of men harassed the citizens, cut down their flag staffs, and carried away their liberty caps.

WILLIAMSON, ISSAC (1767–1844). Born in Elizabeth, New Jersey; father a general in the Revolution and a leader in town affairs; Presbyterian; read law with his brother Mathias; admitted to the bar in 1791; commissioner of bankruptcy; c.1802—appointed deputy to Federalist Attorney General Aaron Woodruff; 1808—author of the electioneering pamphlet, *A Candid Appeal to the Honest Yeomanry of Essex, Morris and Sussex Counties;* 1815—elected to the New Jersey Assembly as a Republican; 1817–1829—Republican governor of New Jersey; 1831–1832—assemblyman; 1844—president, New Jersey constitutional convention.

Williamson was one of those New Jersey Federalist leaders who broke with his party over its stance against the War of 1812. However, like most other ex-Federalists, he did not sever all ties with his former fellow party members.

BIBLIOGRAPHY

PRIMARY SOURCES

Manuscripts

Haverford College Library:
  Quaker Collection
  Roberts, Charles, Autograph Collection

Historical Society of Pennsylvania:
  Boudinot Papers
  Dreer, Ferdinand, Collection
  Gratz, Simon, Collection
  Lacey, John, Memoirs
  Meredith Papers
  Pemberton Papers
  Society Collection
  Wallace Papers

Library of Congress:
  Boudinot Collection
  Darlington, William, Papers
  Hamilton, Alexander, Papers
  Paterson, William, Papers

Massachusetts Historical Society:
  Pickering, Timothy, Papers

Morristown National Historical Park:
  Ogden, Aaron, Papers
  Park Collection
  Smith, Lloyd, Collection

New Jersey Historical Society:

Bamberger Collection
Bloomfield, Joseph, MSS.
Dayton, Jonathan, Papers
Dickerson, Mahlon, Diary
Dickerson, Mahlon, Papers
Ely Collection
Leddel, William, Papers
Stockton Family Papers
Wall, Garret D., Papers
Williamson, Isaac, Papers

New Jersey State Library:
Assembly Minutes
Bills and Resolutions, 1806–1824
Minutes of the Governor's Privy Council, 1776–1820

New-York Historical Society:
Bell, Andrew, Papers
Dayton, Jonathan, Papers
King, Rufus, Papers
Pintard, John, Papers
Stockton Family Papers

New York Public Library:
Bayard Letterbook
Boudinot, Elias, Account Book
Duyckinck Collection
Ford Papers

Princeton University Library:
Dayton, Jonathan, Papers
Moore Collection
Paterson, William Bell, Papers
Southard, Samuel, Papers
Stimson-Boudinot Collection
Stockton Papers
Thorne-Boudinot Papers
Vroom, Peter D., Papers
Wall, Garret D., Papers

Rutgers University Library:
Boudinot Letters
Cooper, Benjamin, Papers
Coxe, William and Richard, Papers
Dayton, Jonathan, Papers
Elmer Family Papers
Hutchinson, Elmer T., Papers

Kirkpatrick, Jane Bayard, Diary
Miscellaneous Manuscripts
Neilson Family Papers
New Brunswick Historical Club Papers
New Jersey Letters, 1790–1825
Ogden, Aaron, Letters
Parker, James, Papers
Paterson, William, Papers
Petitions, Memorials, and Remonstrances Received
Stryker Family Papers
United States Letters, 1790–1825
Vroom, Peter D., Papers
Wall, Garret D., Papers
White, Anthony Walton, Papers

Printed Documents and Records

New Jersey. Adjutant General's Office. *Records of the Officers and Men of New Jersey in Wars, 1791–1815.* Trenton, New Jersey: State Gazette Publishing Company, 1909.

New Jersey. Department of State. *Compendium of Censuses, 1726–1905.* Trenton, New Jersey: John Murphy, 1906.

New Jersey. Executive Department. *Executive Records, 1795–1830.* Washington, D. C.: Library of Congress Photoduplicating Service, 1949.

New Jersey. New Jersey General Assembly. *Legislative Council Minutes, 1795–1830.* Washington, D.C.: Library of Congress Photoduplicating Service, 1949.

New Jersey. New Jersey General Assembly. *Votes and Proceedings of the General Assembly, 1795–1830.* Washington, D. C.: Library of Congress Photoduplicating Service, 1949.

New Jersey. *New Jersey Laws, Statutes, and Acts, Session Laws, 1797–1830.* Washington, D. C.: Library of Congress Photoduplicating Service, 1949.

U. S. Bureau of the Census. *Historical Statistics of the United States.* Washington, D. C.: United States Government Printing Office, 1960.

U. S. *Annals of Congress.* Washington, D. C.: various publishers, 1790–1812.

U. S. Department of State. *The Population of the United States from 1790 to 1830.* Washington, D. C.: Duff Green, 1835.

Pamphlets

An Address Delivered at a Meeting of the Democratic Association of the County of Gloucester Held at the Court House at Woodbury on the 31st of August, 1801, James Sloan, President. Trenton, Mann and Wilson, 1801.

Address of the Charges Against the Old Party of Burlington. n.p., 1817.

Address of the Committee Appointed by a Republican Meeting in the County of Hunterdon Recommending General Andrew Jackson of Tennessee to the People of New Jersey. Trenton, September, 1824.

Address of the Republican Committee of the County of Gloucester. n.p.. December 15, 1800.

An Address to the Electors of New Jersey and Now Recommended to the Deliberate and Candid Consideration of the Electors of Pennsylvania. n.p., 1808.

Address to the Federal-Republicans of Burlington County Recommending to Them to Support the Present Members in the Legislature from that County, at the Ensuing Election, by a Committee Appointed at the Court House on August 30, 1800. Trenton, Sherman, Mershon, and Thomas, 1800.

Address to the Federal Republicans of the State of New Jersey, Recommending the Choice of Aaron Ogden, William Coxe, Jr., James H. Imlay, Franklin Davenport, and Peter D. Vroom for Representatives in the 7th Congress of the U. S. Trenton, Sherman, Mershon, and Thomas, November, 13, 1800.

An Address to the Freeman of New Jersey. Trenton, 1812.

A Candid Appeal to the Honest Yeomanry of Essex, Morris, and Sussex Counties, in the State of New Jersey, on the Subject of the Approaching Presidential and Congressional Election. n.p., October, 1808.

Constitution of the Washington Whig Society of the County of Cumberland, in the State of New Jersey. n.p., 1815.

Crane, Daniel. *An Oration, Delivered at Bloomfield, on the Fourth of July, 1801.* Newark, New Jersey, Pennington and Gould, 1801.

Elmer, Ebenezer. *An Address to the Citizens of New Jersey.* Elizabethtown, New Jersey, 1807.

Federal Meeting, In Pursuance of Public Notice a Great Number of Respectable Electors of the County of Burlington Hav-

ing Met on this Day for the Purpose of Nominating a Legislative Ticket. . . . Trenton, August 29, 1801.

Friend of Peace . . . Letter to Judge Rozzel [sic] *in Answer to his Appeal.* Trenton, September 18, 1812.

Froeligh, Solomon. *Republican Government Advocated: A Discourse Delivered on 4th of July, 1794.* Elizabeth-Town, New Jersey, Shepard Kollock, 1794.

Griffith, William. *Address of the President of the New Jersey Society for the Promotion of the Abolition of Slavery to the General Meeting at Trenton.* Trenton, Sherman and Mershon, September 26, 1804.

──────. *Eumenes.* Trenton, 1799.

──────. *An Oration, Delivered to the Citizens of Burlington, on the 22nd of February, 1800 in Commemoration of General George Washington . . . With Comments by Charles Wharton.* Trenton, 1800.

Hunt, Holloway. *Discourse on the Necessity of Unity in America.* Newton, New Jersey, Hopkins and Smith, July, 1798.

Imlay, James. *Address Delivered by James Imlay at the Federal Meeting at Freehold, Monmouth County.* Trenton, James Oram, August 22, 1808.

──────. *An Oration Delivered Before the Washington Benevolent Society of the County of Burlington.* Mount Holly, New Jersey, February 22, 1814.

Linn, William. *Serious Considerations on the Election of a President.* . . . Trenton, Sherman, Mershon, and Thomas, 1800.

Ogden, Rev. Uzal. *The Antidote to Deism.* Newark, New Jersey, 1798.

──────. *The Deist Unmasked.* Newark, New Jersey, 1795.

An Oration Delivered at a Meeting of the Democratic Association of the County of Gloucester. . . . Trenton, Wilson and Blackwell, March, 1802.

Plain Questions to the People of New Jersey in Relation to the Selection of Governor. n.p., n.d.

Plain Truth, Addressed to the Independent Electors of the State of New Jersey. Trenton, James Wilson, 1808.

A Political Catechism Intended for the Use of Children of Larger Growth and Respectfully Dedicated to the Republicans of the Counties of Morris, Essex, and Sussex in the State of New Jersey. Morris Town, Henry P. Rossell, n.d.

Proceedings and Address of the Convention of Delegates to the People of New Jersey. Trenton, July 4, 1812.

Proceedings and Address of the Delegates of the People of N. J. Trenton, Sept. 15, 1812.

Proceedings and Address of the Delegation of the Friends of Peace, Convened at Salem. n.p., September 16, 1812.

Proceedings and Address of the New Jersey State Convention Assembled at Trenton on the Eighth Day of January, 1828 which Nominated Andrew Jackson for President and John C. Calhoun for Vice-President. Trenton, Joseph Justice, 1828.

Proceedings and Address of the Second Convention of Delegates Held at the City of Trenton, on the Fourth of July, 1814, to the People of New Jersey. n.p., July, 1814.

Review of an Address of the Minority in Congress to their Constituents on the Subject of the War with Great Britain. Trenton, James Wilson, 1812.

Serious Considerations Addressed to the Electors of New Jersey Concerning the Choice of Members of the Legislature for the Ensuing Year. n.p., 1803.

Sloan, James. *An address to the citizens of the United States, but more particularly those of the middle and eastern states. . . .* Philadelphia, Thomas T. Stiles, 1812.

————. *The Hypocrite Unmasked.* Philadelphia, 1812.

————. *An oration, delivered at a meeting of the Democratic Association, of the County of Gloucester, held in the courthouse at Woodbury on the fourth day of March, 1802.* Trenton, Wilson and Blackwell, 1802.

Stockton, Lucius H. *An Address delivered Before the Convention of the Friends of Peace.* Trenton, July 4, 1814.

————. *A History of the Steam-Boat Case, Lately Discussed by Counsel Before the Legislature of New Jersey.* Trenton, Printed by the Author, 1815.

Swartwout, Samuel. *Presidential Election: 1776, Independence and Liberty and Glory!* n.p., 1824.

To the Electors of New Jersey. n.p., 1808.

Wilson, James. *New Jersey Convention, 1812, Address to the Freemen of New Jersey.* Trenton, James Wilson, September 2, 1812.

Broadsides

Adams Meeting. October 19, 1824.

Address to the Inhabitants of the County of Gloucester. n.p., 1800.

Address to the People of New Jersey. n.p., September 20, 1826.

At a Meeting of the Inhabitants of the Township of Gloucester. . . . n.p., August 4, 1800.

Bloomfield, Joseph. *To the public.* Burlington, New Jersey, December, 1796.

A Dialogue Between Quacko and Sambo; Addressed to the New Jersey Federalists, Particularly Those of Burlington County. n.p., [c. November, 1801].

Extra. Trenton, State Gazette, October 30, 1798.

Federal Meeting: At a Large and Respectable Meeting of the Inhabitants of the County of Cumberland. n.p., December 16, 1800.

Hardenbergh, Jacob. *Answer.* New Brunswick, New Jersey, September 30, 1811.

The Lancet by Doctor Sangrado, Jun. Newark, Newark Gazette, May 3, 1803.

The Newsboy's Address. Newark, W. Tuttle Company, January 1, 1807.

The Newsboy's Address to the Patrons of the Trenton Federalist. Trenton, January 1, 1813.

Odes For the Fourth of July, 1812. n.p., n.d.

Ogden, Aaron. *General Orders for the Militia of New Jersey.* n.p., March 24, 1813.

————. *A Proclamation.* n.p., December, 1812.

Propositions of the Federal Members of the Legislature of New Jersey, Offered the Democratic Members, for the Purpose of Effecting an Amicable Adjustment of Differences With Respect to the appointment of the officers of Government. . . . Trenton, November 24, 1802.

Public Meeting, Respecting Slavery, Trenton, 29th Oct., 1819. n.p., 1819.

A Superficial View of the Govenment of the United States. Newark: *Woods Newark Gazette,* October 15, 1794.

To the Electors of the County of Essex. n.p., January 20, 1807.

To the Electors of the County of Hunterdon, n.p., 1814.

To the Federal Electors of the County of Somerset. n.p., September, 1811.

To the People of New Jersey. n.p., September 30, 1800.

To the Republican Electors of the State of New Jersey . . . Convened at Trenton, This Day to Confer . . . Upon a Suitable Ticket . . . for Representatives to Congress. Trenton, James Wilson, November 23, 1803.

Whig Societies. n.p., February 13, 1813.

Newspapers

Arnett's New Jersey Federalist (New Brunswick), 1793–1795.

Aurora (Philadelphia, Pennsylvania), 1795–1797, 1800–1801, 1812.

Brunswick Gazette and Weekly Monitor (New Brunswick), 1790–1791.

Burlington Advertiser (Burlington), 1791.

Centinel of Freedom (Newark), 1796–1825.

Emporium (Trenton), 1821–1825.

Essex Patriot (Elizabeth), 1812–1813.

Federalist (Trenton), 1798–1825.

Federal Republican (Elizabeth), January 1, 1803-January 10, 1804.

Fredonian (New Brunswick), 1811–1827.

Genius of Liberty (Morristown), 1799–1808.

Genius of Liberty (New Brunswick), 1795.

Guardian (New Brunswick), 1789–1815.

Impartial Register (Hackensack), 1804–1805.

Independent Gazetteer (Philadelphia, Pennsylvania), December 19, 1795.

Jersey Chronicle (Mount Pleasant), 1795–1796.

National Intelligencer (Washington, D. C.), 1802.

Newark Gazette and New Jersey Advertiser, 1797–1804.

New Jersey Eagle and Newark, Orange and Bloomfield Early Intelligencer, 1821–1824.

New Jersey Journal (Elizabeth), 1793–1824.

New-Jersey Mirror (Mount Holly), 1818–1823.

New Jersey State Gazette (Trenton), 1793–1796, 1799–1800.

New Jersey Telescope (Newark), 1809.

New York Evening Post, 1801–1803, 1812–1814, 1824.

Niles' Weekly Register (Baltimore, Maryland), 1811–1825.

Palladium of Liberty (Morristown), 1810–1811, 1815–1823.

Pennsylvania Gazette (Philadelphia, Pennsylvania), 1811–1813.

Philadelphia Gazette and Daily Advertiser, October, 1793–1801.

Political Intelligencer (Elizabeth), 1786.

Porcupine's Gazette (Philadelphia, Pennsylvania), 1797.

Spirit of Washington (Freehold), 1815.

State Gazette (Trenton), 1796–1799.

Sussex Register (Newton), 1814–1825.

Times (New Brunswick), 1821–1825.

Trenton Times, October 16-November 14, 1932.

True American (Trenton), 1801–1825.

Washington Whig (Bridgeton), 1821–1825.

Woods' Newark Gazette, 1791–1797.

SECONDARY SOURCES

Books

Abernethy, Thomas P. *The Burr Conspiracy.* New York: Oxford University Press, 1954.

Adams, Charles Francis. *The Works of John Adams, Second President of the United States with a Life of the Author.* Vol. I. Boston: Little, Brown and Company, 1854.

Aldridge, Alfred Owen. *Man of Reason: The Life of Thomas Paine.* New York: Lippincott Company, 1959.

Applegate, John S. *Early Courts and Lawyers of Monmouth County.* New York: Middleditch Company, 1911.

Bailyn, Bernard. *The Origins of American Politics.* New York: Alfred Knopf, 1968.

Baldwin, Leland. *Whiskey Rebels: The Story of a Frontier*

Uprising. Pittsburg, Pennsylvania: University of Pittsburgh Press, 1939.

Banner, James M. *To the Hartford Convention: The Federalists and the Origins of Party Politics in Massachusetts, 1789–1815.* New York: Alfred Knopf, 1970.

Barber, John and Howe, Henry. *Historical Collection of the State of New Jersey.* Newark, New Jersey: Benjamin Olds, 1844.

Barnes, Harry E. *A History of the Penal, Reformatory, and Correctional Institutions of the State of New Jersey.* Trenton, New Jersey: MacCrellish and Quigley Company, 1918.

Bassett, John Spencer, ed. *Correspondence of Andrew Jackson.* Washington, D.C.: Carnegie Institution of Washington, 1928.

Bateman, Robert. *History of the Medical Men of the District Medical Society of the County of Cumberland.* Newark, New Jersey: Jennings and Hardham, 1871.

Bayard, Samuel John. *A Sketch of the Life of Commodore Robert F. Stockton.* New York: Derby and Jackson, 1856.

Bemis, Samuel F. *Jay's Treaty: A Study in Commerce and Diplomacy.* New York: Macmillan Company, 1923.

_____. *Pinckney's Treaty: A Study of America's Advantage from Europe's Distress, 1783–1800.* Baltimore: Johns Hopkins University Press, 1926.

Benedict, William. *New Brunswick in History.* New Brunswick, New Jersey: By the Author, 1925.

Benson, Lee. *The Concept of Jacksonian Democracy: New York as a Test Case.* Princeton, New Jersey: Princeton University Press, 1961.

Bill, Alfred Hoyt. *A House Called Morven.* Princeton: Princeton University Press, 1954.

Biographical Directory of the American Congress, 1774–1961. Washington, D. C.: U. S. Government Printing Office, 1961.

The Biographical Encyclopedia of New Jersey of the Nineteenth Century. Philadelphia: Galaxy Publishing Company, 1877.

Bloomfield, Joseph. *Laws of the State of N.J.* Philadelphia: Everts Co., 1820.

Bond, Beverley, ed. *The Intimate Letters of John Cleves Symmes and His Family.* Cincinnati: Historical and Philosophical Society of Ohio, 1956.

226   THE NEW JERSEY FEDERALISTS

Borden, Martin. *Parties and Politics in the Early Republic.* New York: Thomas Crowell, 1967.

Boudinot, Jane, ed. *The Life, Public Service, Addresses, and Letters of Elias Boudinot.* 2 vols. Boston: Houghton Mifflin and Company, 1896.

Boyd, George A. *Elias Boudinot: Patriot and Statesman, 1740–1821.* Princeton: Princeton University Press, 1952.

Brant, Irving. "Election of 1808" *History of American Presidential Elections.* Vol. I. Edited by Arthur M. Schlesinger, Jr. New York; Chelsea House Publishers, 1971.

_____, ed. *James Madison: Commander in Chief, 1812–1836.* Vol. VI. New York: Bobbs Merrill, 1961.

Brown, Roger H. *The Republic in Peril: 1812.* New York: W. W. Norton and Company, 1971.

Brown, Stuart G. *The First Republicans: Political Philosophy and Public Policy in the Party of Jefferson and Madison.* New York: Syracuse University Press, 1954.

Burr, Nelson. *Education in New Jersey, 1630–1871.* Princeton: Princeton University Press, 1942.

Cadman, John W. *The Corporation in New Jersey: Business and Politics, 1791–1875.* Cambridge: Harvard University Press, 1949.

Chambers, William Nisbet. *Political Parties in a New Nation: The American Experience, 1776–1809.* New York: Oxford University Press, 1963.

Charles, Joseph. *The Origins of the American Party System.* Williamsburg, Virginia: Institute of Early American History and Culture, 1956.

Clark, J. Henry. *The Medical Men of New Jersey in Essex District from 1666 to 1866.* Newark, New Jersey: Evening Courier Office, 1867.

Clayton, W. Woodford. *History of Bergen and Passaic Counties, New Jersey.* Philadelphia: Everts and Peck, 1882.

Cole, George Douglas Howard, ed. *Letters from William Corbett to Edward Thornton, 1797–1800.* New York: Oxford University Press, 1959.

Combs, Jerald. *The Jay Treaty.* Berkeley: University of California Press, 1970.

Cunningham, Noble E. Jr. "Election of 1800." *History of Ameri-*

can Presidential Elections. Vol. I. Edited by Arthur M. Schlesinger, Jr. New York: Chelsea House Publishers, 1971.

_____. The Jeffersonian-Republicans: The Formation of Party Organization, 1789–1801. Chapel Hill, North Carolina: The University of North Carolina Press, 1957.

_____. The Jeffersonian-Republicans in Power: Party Operations, 1801–1809. Chapel Hill: The University of North Carolina Press, 1963.

Cushing, Thomas and Sheppard, Charles. History of the Counties of Gloucester, Salem and Cumberland, New Jersey. Philadelphia: Everts and Peck, 1883.

Dangerfield, George. The Era of Good Feelings. New York: Harcourt, Brace, and World, Inc., 1952.

Dauer, Manning. "Election of 1804." History of American Presidential Elections. Vol. I. Edited by Arthur Schlesinger, Jr. New York: Chelsea House Publishers, 1971.

_____. The Adams Federalists. Baltimore: The Johns Hopkins University Press, 1953.

Davis, Matthew. Memoirs of Aaron Burr with Selections from his Correspondence. 2 vols. New York: Harper Brothers, 1837.

De Conde, Alexander. The Quasi-War: The Politics and Diplomacy of the Undeclared War with France, 1797–1801. New York: Charles Scribner's Sons, 1966.

De Cou, George. Burlington: A Provincial Capital. Philadelphia: Harris & Partridge Co., 1945.

Ellis, Frank. History of Monmouth County, New Jersey. Philadelphia: R. T. Peck Company, 1885.

Elmer, Lucius Q. C. The Constitution and Government of the Province and State of New Jersey with Biographical Sketches of the Governors from 1776 to 1845 and Reminiscences of the Bench and Bar During More Than Half a Century. Newark, New Jersey: Martin R. Dennis and Company, 1872.

_____. History of the Early Settlement and Progress of Cumberland County and of the Currency this and Adjoining Colonies. Bridgeton, New Jersey: George Nixon Co., 1869.

Erdman, Charles R. The New Jersey Constitution of 1776. Princeton: Princeton University Press, 1929.

Ernst, Robert. Rufus King: American Federalist. Chapel Hill; University of North Carolina Press, 1968.

Fee, Walter. *The Transition from Aristocracy to Democracy in New Jersey, 1789–1826.* Somerville: Somerset Press, 1933.

Fischer, David Hackett. *The Revolution of American Conservatism: The Federalist Party in the Era of Jeffersonian Democracy.* New York: Harper and Row, 1965.

Fitzpatrick, John C., ed. *The Writings of George Washington.* Washington, D. C.: United States Government Printing Office, 1940.

Foner, Philip, ed. *The Complete Writings of Thomas Paine.* New York: The Citadel Press, 1945.

Ford, Paul L., ed. *The Writings of Thomas Jefferson.* New York: G. P. Putnam's Sons, 1898.

Fox, Dixon Ryan. *The Decline of Aristocracy in the Politics of New York.* New York: Columbia University Press, 1931.

Gibbs, George, ed. *Memoirs of the Administration of Washington and John Adams Edited from the Papers of Oliver Wolcott.* 2 vols. New York: Van Norden Company, 1846.

Goodman, Paul. *The Democratic-Republicans in Massachusetts.* Cambridge, Massachusetts: Harvard University Press, 1964.

―――――, ed. *The Federalists vs. the Jeffersonian Republicans.* New York: Holt, Rinehart and Winston, 1967.

Gordon, Thomas F. *A Gazetteer of the State of New Jersey. . . .* Trenton, New Jersey: Daniel Fenton, 1834.

Hageman, John F. *History of Princeton and Its Institutions.* 2 vols. Philadelphia: J. B. Lippincott Company, 1879.

Hammond, Bray. *Banks and Politics in America from the Revolution to the Civil War.* Princeton, New Jersey: Princeton University Press, 1957.

Hartz, Louis. *The Liberal Tradition in America.* New York: Harcourt Brace, Inc., 1955.

Hixson, Richard F. *Isaac Collins: A Quaker Printer in Eighteenth Century America.* New Brunswick: Rutgers University Press, 1968.

Hofstadter, Richard. *The Idea of a Party System: The Rise of Legitimate Opposition in the United States, 1780–1840.* Berkeley: University of California Press, 1970.

Jamieson, Mary, ed. *The Letters of Moore Furman.* N.P.: Daughters of the American Revolution, 1912.

Jamison, Wallace N. *Religion in New Jersey: A Brief History.* Princeton, New Jersey: Van Nostrand, 1964.

Johnston, Henry P., ed. *The Correspondence and Public Papers of John Jay.* Vol. IV. New York: G. P. Putnam's Sons, 1893.

Keasbey, Edward Q. *The Courts and Lawyers of New Jersey, 1661–1912.* 3 vols. New York: Lewis Historical Publishing Company, 1912.

Kemmerer, Donald. *Path to Freedom: The Struggle for Self-Government in Colonial New Jersey, 1703–1776.* Cos Cob, Connecticut: John Edwards, 1968.

Kerber, Linda. *Federalists in Dissent: Imagery and Ideology in Jeffersonian America.* Ithaca, New York: Cornell University Press, 1970.

Kull, Irving, ed. *New Jersey: A History.* 3 vols. New York: The American Historical Society, Inc., 1930.

Kurtz, Stephen. *The Presidency of John Adams: The Collapse of Federalism, 1795–1800.* Philadelphia: University of Pennsylvania Press, 1957.

Lane, Wheaton. *From Indian Trail to Iron Horse: Travel and Transportation in New Jersey, 1620–1860.* Princeton: Princeton University Press, 1939.

Lee, Francis. *New Jersey as a Colony and as a State.* 4 Vols. New York: Lewis Historical Publishing Company, 1902.

Leiby, James. *Charity and Correction in New Jersey.* New Brunswick: Rutgers University Press, 1967.

Link, Eugene. *Democratic-Republican Societies, 1790–1800.* New York: Columbia University Press, 1942.

Livermore, Shaw. *The Twilight of Federalism: The Disintegration of the Federalist Party, 1815–1830.* Princeton: Princeton University Press, 1962.

Lockard, Duane. *The New Jersey Governor: A Study in Political Power.* The New Jersey Historical Series, Vol. XIV. Princeton: D. Van Nostrand Company, 1964.

Luetscher, George C. *Early Political Machinery in the United States.* Philadelphia: University of Pennsylvania Press, 1903.

Lundin, Leonard. *Cockpit of the Revolution: The War for Independence in New Jersey.* Princeton: Princeton University Press, 1940.

Maclay, William. *Sketches of Debate in the First Senate of the*

United States, 1789–1791. Harrisburg, Pennsylvania: Hart Company, 1880.

McCormick, Richard. *Experiment in Independence: New Jersey in the Critical Period, 1781–1789.* New Brunswick: Rutgers University Press, 1950.

———. *The History of Voting in New Jersey: A Study of the Development of Election Machinery, 1664–1911.* New Brunswick: Rutgers University Press, 1954.

———. *The Second American Party System: Party Formation in the Jacksonian Era.* Chapel Hill: University of North Carolina Press, 1966.

McDonald, Forrest. *We the People: The Economic Origins of the Constitution.* Chicago: The University of Chicago Press, 1958.

McMurtrie, Douglas C. *A History of Printing in the United States.* 2 vols. New York: R. R. Bowker Company, 1936.

Miller John. *Crisis in Freedom: The Alien and Sedition Acts.* Boston: Little, Brown and Company, 1951.

———. *Alexander Hamilton: Portrait in Paradox.* New York: Harper & Row, 1959.

———. *The Federalist Era, 1789–1801.* New York: Harper & Row, 1960.

Moore, Glover. *The Missouri Controversy, 1819–1821.* Lexington: University of Kentucky Press, 1953.

Morison, Samuel Eliot. *The Life and Letters of Harrison Gray Otis, Federalist, 1765–1845.* 2 vols. Boston: Houghton Mifflin Company, 1913.

Morris, Anne Cary, ed. *The Diary and Letters of Gouverneur Morris.* Vol. II. New York: Charles Scribner's Sons, 1888.

Munroe, John A. *Federalist Delaware, 1775–1815.* New Brunswick: Rutgers University Press, 1954.

Nelson, William. *Joseph Coerten Hornblower, 1777–1864.* Cambridge, Massachusetts: John Wilson, 1894.

Nichols, Roy F. *The Invention of the American Political Parties.* New York: Macmillan Company, 1967.

North, S. N. D., ed. *A Century of Population Growth: From the First Census of the United States to the Twelfth, 1790–1900.* Washington, D. C.: United States Government Printing Office, 1909.

Ogden, Mary Depue, ed. *Memorial Cyclopedia of New Jersey.*

BIBLIOGRAPHY

231

3 vols. Newark, New Jersey: Memorial History Company, 1915.

Pierce, Arthur. *Family Empire in Jersey Iron.* New Brunswick: Rutgers University Press, 1964.

Pitney, Henry, Jr., ed. *A History of Morris County, New Jersey.* 2 vols. New York: Lewis Historical Publishing Company, 1914.

Porter, Kirk. *Suffrage in the United States.* Chicago: University of Chicago Press, 1918.

Prince, Carl. *New Jersey's Jeffersonian Republicans: The Genesis of an Early Party Machine, 1789–1817.* Chapel Hill: University of North Carolina Press, 1967.

Remini, Robert V. *The Election of Andrew Jackson.* Philadelphia: J. B. Lippincott Company, 1963.

Reock, Ernest C. *Population Inequality Among Counties in the New Jersey Legislature, 1791–1962.* New Brunswick: Bureau of Government Research, Rutgers University, 1963.

Risjord, Norman K. "Election of 1812." *History of American Presidential Elections.* Vol I, Edited by Arthur Schlesinger, Jr. New York: Chelsea House Publishers, 1971.

Rose, Lisle. *Prologue to Democracy: The Federalists in the South, 1789–1800.* Lexington: University of Kentucky Press, 1968.

Salter, Edwin. *A History of Monmouth and Ocean Counties.* Bayonne, New Jersey: E. Gardner and Son, 1890.

Schlesinger, Arthur M., Jr. *The Age of Jackson.* Boston: Little, Brown and Company, 1945.

Sears, Louis Martin. *Jefferson and the Embargo.* North Carolina: Duke University Press, 1927.

Sickler, Joseph. *The History of Salem County, New Jersey.* Salem, New Jersey: Sunbeam Publishing Company, 1937.

Smelser, Marshall. *The Democratic Republic, 1801–1815.* New York: Harper & Row, 1968.

Smith, James. *Freedom's Fetters.* New York: Cornell University Press, 1956.

Snell, James, ed. *History of Hunterdon and Somerset Counties, New Jersey.* Philadelphia: Everts and Peck, 1881.

_____. *History of Sussex and Warren Counties, New Jersey.* Philadelphia: Everts and Peck, 1881.

Stewart, Donald. *The Opposition Press of the Federalist Period.*

Albany: State University of New York Press, 1969.

Stewart, Frank, ed. *Notes on Old Gloucester County.* 2 vols. Camden, New Jersey: By the Author, 1917.

Stevens, Lewis T. *A History of Cape May County.* Cape May, New Jersey: By the Author, 1897.

Thayer, Theodore. *As We Were: The Story of Old Elizabethtown.* Newark, New Jersey: New Jersey Historical Society, 1964.

Thompson, Marion. *The Education of Negroes in New Jersey.* New York: Teachers College, Columbia University, 1941.

Thompson, Robert T. *Colonel James Neilson: A Business Man of the Early Machine Age in New Jersey, 1784–1862.* New Brunswick: Rutgers University Press, 1940.

Tinkcom, Harry. *The Republicans and Federalists in Pennsylvania, 1790–1801.* Harrisburg, Pennsylvania: Historical and Museum Commission, 1950.

Trumbull, L. R. *A History of Industrial Paterson.* Paterson, New Jersey: Carleton M. Herrick Company, 1882.

Turner, Lynn W. "Elections of 1816 and 1820." *History of American Presidential Elections.* Vol I. Edited by Arthur M. Schlesinger, Jr. New York: Chelsea House Publishers, 1971.

Urquhart, Frank J. *A History of the City of Newark, New Jersey.* 3 vols. New York: Lewis Historical Publishing Company, 1913.

Van Der Linden, Frank. *The Turning Point: Jefferson's Battle for the Presidency.* Washington, D. C.: Luce Company, 1962.

Wagstaff, H. M., ed. *The Papers of John Steele.* 2 vols. Raleigh, North Carolina: North Carolina Historical Commission, 1924.

Wall, John P. *History of Middlesex County, New Jersey, 1664–1920.* 3 vols. New York: Lewis Historical Publishing Company, 1921.

Ward, John W. *Andrew Jackson, Symbol for an Age.* New York: Oxford University Press, 1955.

Weiss, Harry and Ziegler, Grace. *Colonel Erkuries Beatty.* Trenton, New Jersey: Past Times Press, 1958.

Welch, Richard. *Theodore Sedgwick, Federalist.* Middletown, Connecticut: Wesleyan University Press, 1965.

Westervelt, Frances, ed. *History of Bergen County, New Jersey, 1630–1923.* New York: Lewis Historical Publishing Company, 1923.

White, Leonard D. *The Federalists: A Study in Administrative History, 1789–1801.* New York: The Free Press, 1948.

————. *The Jacksonians: A Study in Administrative History, 1829–1861.* New York: The Free Press, 1953.

Wickes, Stephen. *History of Medicine in New Jersey and of its Medical Men to 1800.* Newark, New Jersey: Martin R. Dennis and Company, 1879.

Williamson, Chilton. *American Suffrage: From Property to Democracy, 1760–1860.* Princeton: Princeton University Press, 1960.

Wilson, Harold F. *The Jersey Shore: A Social and Economic History of the Counties of Atlantic, Cape May, Monmouth and Ocean.* New York: Lewis Historical Publishing Company, 1953.

————. *Outline History of New Jersey.* New Brunswick, New Jersey: Rutgers University Press, 1950.

Winfield, Charles. *A Monograph on the Founding of Jersey City.* New York: Caxton Press, 1891.

Woodward, Carl R. *Agriculture in New Jersey.* New York: American Historical Society, 1930.

Young, Alfred. *The Democratic Republicans of New York: The Origins, 1763–1797.* Chapel Hill: University Of North Carolina Press, 1967.

Zahniser, Marvin. *Charles Cotesworth Pinckney.* Chapel Hill: University of North Carolina Press, 1967.

Zilversmit, Arthur. *The First Emancipation: The Abolition of Slavery in the North.* Chicago: University of Chicago Press, 1967.

Articles

Agnew, Daniel. "A Biographical Sketch of Governor Richard Howell of New Jersey." *The Pennsylvania Magazine of History and Biography* XXII (1898, no. 2): 221–30.

Ammon, Harry. "The Genêt Mission and the Development of American Political Parties." *Journal of American History* LII (March, 1966): 725–41.

Anderson, Frank M. "Autobiography of Colonel Aaron Ogden." *Proceedings of the New Jersey Historical Society,* Second Series (1892, no. 1): 15–31.

————. "Contemporary Opinion of the Virginia and Kentucky Resolutions." *American Historical Review* V (1899–1900): 48–61.

Bentley, Esther. "Samuel Southard and Political Patronage." *The Princeton University Chronicle* XXIII (Autumn, 1961): 1–15.

Bogert, Frederick. "Colonial Bergen County." *Proceedings of the New Jersey Historical Society* LXXXI (January, 1963): 17–20.

Boggs, J. Laurence. "The Cornelia (Bell) Paterson Letters." *Proceedings of the New Jersey Historical Society* XV (October, 1930): 508–17.

Brown, Dorothy M. "Maryland and the Federalists: Search for Unity." *Maryland Historical Magazine* LXIII (December, 1968): 1–21.

Burr, Nelson R. "New Jersey: An Anglican Venture in Religious Freedom." *Historical Magazine of the Protestant Episcopal Church* XXXIV (1965, no. 1): 3–34.

Chute, William. "The New Jersey Whig Campaign of 1840." *Proceedings of the New Jersey Historical Society* LXXVII (October, 1959): 223–39.

Cranmer, H. Jerome. "Internal Improvements in New Jersey: Planning the Morris Canal." *Proceedings of the New Jersey Historical Society* LXIX (October, 1951): 324–41.

Cunningham, Noble. "Who Were the Quids?" *Mississippi Valley Historical Review* L (September, 1963): 250–57.

Dennis, Helen Dean. "The Elisha Boudinot House, Newark, New Jersey." *Proceedings of the New Jersey Historical Society* LXVII (October, 1949): 254–60.

Deshler, Charles D. "New Brunswick As It Appeared in 1825–1826." *Proceedings of the New Jersey Historical Society* LXVIII (October, 1950): 322–46.

Dodd, Edward W. "Amzi Dodd's Letters." *Proceedings of the New Jersey Historical Society,* New Series III (January, 1918): 49–52.

————. "Reminiscences of the War of 1812." *Proceedings of the New Jersey Historical Society,* New Series II (January, 1917): 20–6.

Drinker, Sophie. "Vote for Women in Eighteenth Century New Jersey." *Proceedings of the New Jersey Historical Society* LXXX (January, 1962): 31–45.

Dunham, William J. "Mahlon Dickerson: A Great But Almost Forgotten Jerseyan." *Proceedings of the New Jersey Historical Society* LXVII (October, 1950): 297–322.

Ellis, William A., ed. "The Diary of William S. Pennington." *Proceedings of the New Jersey Historical Society* LXIII (October, 1945): 200–18.

Elmer, L. Q. C. "Jonathan Elmer." *The Pennsylvania Magazine of History and Biography* I (1877, No. 4): 443–45.

Ershkowitz, Herbert. "The Election of 1824 in New Jersey." *Proceedings of the New Jersey Historical Society* LXXXIV (April, 1966): 113–31.

————. "Samuel L. Southard: A Case Study of Whig Leadership in the Age of Jackson." *New Jersey History* LXXXVIII (Spring, 1970): 5–24.

————. and Shade, William G. "Consensus or Conflict? Political Behavior in the State Legislatures during the Jacksonian Era." *Journal of American History* LVIII (December, 1971): 591–621.

Farber, Jules B. "A Lost Tribute to Washington." *The Journal of the Rutgers University Library* XIV (December, 1950): 28–29.

Fee, Walter. "The Effect of Hamilton's Financial Policy Upon Public Opinion in New Jersey." *Proceedings of the New Jersey Historical Society* L (January, 1932): 32–44.

Field, Richard. "Address on the Life and Character of the Hon. James Parker." *Proceedings of the New Jersey Historical Society,* Second Series I (1869): 111–29.

————. "Life and Character of Hon. Joseph Hornblower." *Proceedings of the New Jersey Historical Society,* Second Series X (January, 1865): 27–45.

Gardner, D. H. "The Emancipation of Slaves in New Jersey." *Proceedings of the New Jersey Historical Society,* New Series IX (January, 1924): 1–21.

Gerlach, Larry R. "Quaker Politics in Eighteenth Century New Jersey: A Documentary Account." *The Journal of the Rutgers University Library* XXXIV (December, 1970): 1–12.

Goodman, Paul. "Social Status of Party Leadership: The House of Representatives, 1797–1802." *William and Mary Quarterly* XXV (July, 1968): 465–74.

Griffin, Charles. "Religious Benevolence as Social Control,

1815–1860." *Mississippi Valley Historical Review* XLIV (December, 1957): 424–44.

Hale, Henry E. "Princeton and Kingston Branch Turnpike Road." *Proceedings of the New Jersey Historical Society* LXIII (January, 1944): 24–30.

Hartridge, Walter Charlton. "The St. Domingan Refugees in New Jersey." *Proceedings of the New Jersey Historical Society* LXII (October, 1941): 197–206; LXIII (April, 1945): 73–82.

Haskett, Richard C. "Village Clerk and Country Lawyer: William Paterson's Legal Experience, 1763–1772." *Proceedings of the New Jersey Historical Society* LXVI (January, 1948): 155–71.

Hockett, Homer. "The Influence of the West on the Rise and Fall of Political Parties." *Mississippi Valley Historical Review* IV (1917, No. 4): 459–69.

Howe, John R. "Republican Thought and the Political Violence of the 1790s." *American Quarterly* XIX (1967, No. 2): 147–65.

Hunt, Gaillard. "Office-Seeking during Jefferson's Administration." *American Historical Review*, III (1898): 270–91.

Hutchinson, Elmer. "Products of Shepard Kollock's Press, 1801–1818." *Proceedings of the New Jersey Historical Society* LXXXVI (April, 1958): 114–31.

James, Edmund J. "Some Additional Information Concerning Ephraim Martin, Esquire, Colonel of the Fourth New Jersey Regiment." *The Pennsylvania Magazine of History and Biography* XXXVI (1912): 143–61.

"Jonathan Dayton, 1760–1824, Patriot and Statesman and Founder of Dayton, Ohio." *New Jersey Genesis* VI (October, 1956): 113–16.

Keasbey, Edward. "William Griffith." *The New Jersey Law Journal* II (September, 1879): 287–88.

Keesey, Ruth. "New Jersey Legislation Concerning Loyalists." *Proceedings of the New Jersey Historical Society* LXXIX (April, 1961): 75–94.

Lane, Wheaton. "The Turnpike Movement in New Jersey." *Proceedings of the New Jersey Historical Society* LIV (January, 1936): 19–52.

Lawton, Frederick. "Fourth of July Orations." *The Journal of the Rutgers University Library* XVII (June, 1954): 63–64.

Lerche, Charles. "Jefferson and the Election of 1800: A Case

Study in the Political Smear." *William and Mary Quarterly,* Third Series V (1948): 467–91.

"Letters from Richard Stockton to John Rutherfurd." *Proceedings of the New Jersey Historical Society,* Second Series III (1873, no. 3): 180–90.

"Letters of Frederick Frelinghuysen." *Magazine of American History* X (December, 1883): 509–10.

Levine, Peter. "The New Jersey Federalist Party Convention of 1814." *The Journal of the Rutgers University Library* XXXIII (December, 1969): 1–8.

Lobdell, Jared. "Two Letters to Cornelius Zabriskie." *Proceedings of the New Jersey Historical Society* LXXXIII (October, 1965): 289–91.

Lutzker, Michael. "Abolition of Imprisonment for Debt in New Jersey." *Proceedings of the New Jersey Historical Society* LXXXIV (October, 1966): 1–29.

McCormick, Richard. "New Jersey's First Congressional Election, 1789: A Case Study in Political Skulduggery." *William and Mary Quarterly,* Third Series VI (April, 1949): 237–50.

_____. "Party Formation in New Jersey in the Jackson Era." *Proceedings of the New Jersey Historical Society* LXXXIII (July, 1965): 161–73.

_____. The Political Essays of William Paterson." *The Journal of the Rutgers University Library* XVIII (June, 1955): 38–49.

_____. "Suffrage, Classes, and Party Alignments: A Study in Voter Behavior." *Mississippi Valley Historical Review* XLVI (December, 1959): 397–410.

_____. "The Unanimous State." *The Journal of the Rutgers University Library* XXIII (December, 1959): 4–8.

Marsh, Philip M. "Philip Freneau and His Circle." *Pennsylvania Magazine of History and Biography* LXIII (January, 1939): 37–59.

_____. "Philip Freneau and James Madison, 1791–1793." *Proceedings of the New Jersey Historical Society* LXV (July, 1947): 189–94.

_____. "Philip Freneau's Fame." *Proceedings of the New Jersey Historical Society* LXXX (April, 1962): 202–19.

McWhorter, George. "Brief Sketch of the McWhorter Family of New Jersey." *Proceedings of the New Jersey Historical Society* X (1865, No. 2): 52–4.

Mahony, W. H. "The Irish Element in Newark, New Jersey." *The Journal of the American Irish Historical Society* XXI (1922): 131–45.

Miller, William. "First Fruits of Republican Organization: Political Aspects of the Congressional Election of 1794." *Pennsylvania Magazine of History and Biography* LXII (April, 1939): 118–43.

Mitchell, Broadus. "Alexander Hamilton in New Jersey." *Proceedings of the New Jersey Historical Society* LXXVI (April, 1958): 84–111.

Morse, Anson D. "Causes and Consequences of the Party Revolution in 1800." *American Historical Association Annual Report* (1894): 531–40.

Moss, Simeon. "The Persistence of Slavery and Involuntary Servitude in a Free State." *Journal of Negro History* XXXV (1950): 289–314.

Nadworny, Milton J. "New Jersey Workingmen and the Jacksonians." *Proceedings of the New Jersey Historical Society* LXVII (January, 1949): 185–98.

Nash, Gary. "The American Clergy and the French Revolution." *William and Mary Quarterly,* Third Series XXII (July, 1965): 392–412.

Nelson, William. "Biographical Sketch of William Colefax." *Proceedings of the New Jersey Historical Society* IV (1876, No. 3): 145–52.

———. "The Election of Congressmen from New Jersey." *Proceedings of the New Jersey Historical Society,* Third Series VIII (July, 1913): 80–2.

———. "The Founding of Paterson." *Proceedings of the New Jersey Historical Society,* Second Series IX, (1883, no. 3): 177–91.

———. "Some New Jersey Printers and Printing in the Eighteenth Century." *Proceedings of the American Antiquarian Society,* New Series XXI (April, 1911): 15–56.

Pasler, Rudolph J. and Pasler, Margaret C. "Federalist Tenacity in Burlington County, 1810–1824." *New Jersey History* LXXXVII (Winter, 1969): 197–210.

Philbrook, Mary. "Women's Suffrage in New Jersey Prior to 1807." *Proceedings of the New Jersey Historical Society* LVII (April, 1939): 87–98.

Pole, J. R. "Election Statistics in Pennsylvania, 1790–1840." *Pennsylvania Magazine of History and Biography* LXXXII (April, 1958): 217–19.

_____. "Jeffersonian Democracy and the Federalist Dilemma in New Jersey, 1798–1815." *Proceedings of the New Jersey Historical Society* LXXIV (October, 1956): 260–92.

_____. "The Suffrage in New Jersey, 1790–1807." *Proceedings of the New Jersey Historical Society* LXXI (January, 1953): 39–61.

_____. "Suffrage Reform and the American Revolution in New Jersey." *Proceedings of the New Jersey Historical Society* LXXIV (July, 1956): 173–94.

Potter, William. "A Sketch of the Life of Lucius Quintius Elmer." *Proceedings of the New Jersey Historical Society*, Second Series VIII (1884): 25–45.

Prince, Carl. "James J. Wilson: Party Leader, 1801–1824." *Proceedings of the New Jersey Historical Society* LXXXIII (January, 1965): 24–39.

_____. "Party Theory and a Party Operative: Ebenezer Elmer Defines The First American Party System." *New Jersey History* LXXXVII (Autumn, 1970): 161–68.

_____. "The Passing of the Aristocracy: Jefferson's Removal of the Federalists, 1801–1805." *Journal of American History* LVIII (December, 1970): 563–75.

_____. "Patronage and a Party Machine: New Jersey Democratic-Republican Activists, 1801–1816." *William and Mary Quarterly*, Third Series XXI (October, 1964): 571–78.

Pumpelly, Josiah. "Mahlon Dickerson, Industrial Pioneer and Old Time Patriot." *Proceedings of the New Jersey Historical Society*, Second Series XI (1890): 133–56.

Purcell, Richard. "Irish Settlers in Early New Jersey." *New Jersey Genesis* VI (April, 1959): 224–27.

Rankin, John L. "Newark Town Government from 1666–1833." *Proceedings of the New Jersey Historical Society* X (July, 1915): 116–27.

Richardson, William. "The Federalist Fathers and the Founding of Jersey City." *Historical Society of Hudson County Magazine* V (1927): 3–47.

Risjord, Norman K. "The Virginia Federalists." *Journal of Southern History* XXXIII (1967, No. 4): 486–517.

Rogers, Fred. "Dr. Nicholas Belleville (1755–1831)—Aristocratic Physician." *Journal of the Medical Society of New Jersey* LV (February, 1958): 71–7.

――――. "General John Beatty (1749–1826): Patriot and Physician." *Bulletin of the History of Medicine* XXXII (February, 1958): 39–45.

Roth, George L. "Verse Satire on Faction, 1790–1815." *William and Mary Quarterly,* Third Series XVII (October, 1960): 471–85.

Ryan, Mary P. "Party Formation in the United States Congress, 1789 to 1796: A Quantitative Analysis." *William and Mary Quarterly* XXVIII (October, 1971): 523–42.

Sapio, Victor. "Maryland's Federalist Period, 1808–1812." *Maryland Historical Quarterly* LXIV (Spring, 1969): 1–17.

Schmidt, George. "The First Congressional Election in New Jersey." *Journal of the Rutgers University Library* IV (June, 1941): 45–50.

Schmidt, Hubert. "Slavery and Attitudes on Slavery in Hunterdon County, New Jersey." *Proceedings of the New Jersey Historical Society* LVIII (October, 1940): 240–53.

Shelley, Fred. "Travel Contrasts: Chancellor Kent's Impressions of New Jersey, 1793–1821." *Proceedings of the New Jersey Historical Society* LXXVI (October, 1955): 300–305.

"Sketch of Colonel Ephraim Martin of the New Jersey Continental Line." *The Pennsylvania Magazine of History and Biography* XXIV (1910, No. 4): 480–83.

Smelser, Marshall. "The Federalist Period as an Age of Passion." *American Quarterly* X (Winter, 1958): 391–419.

――――. "Jacobin Phrenzy: The Menace of Monarchy, Plutocracy, and Anglophobia, 1798–1799." *Review of Politics* XXI (1959): 239–58.

Sterling, David. "A Federalist Opposes the Jay Treaty: The Letters of Samuel Bayard." *William and Mary Quarterly,* Third Series XVIII (July, 1961): 408–24.

Stewart, Donald. "The Press and Political Corruption During the Federalist Administration." *Political Science Quarterly* LXVII (September, 1952): 426–46.

Stryker, Helen Boudinot. "Elias Boudinot." *The Pennsylvania Magazine of History and Biography* III (1879, no. 2): 191–93.

Swords, Robert. "Memoir of the Life and Character of John

Rutherfurd." *Proceedings of the New Jersey Historical Society*, Second Series II (1872): 197–204.

Thatcher, Harold. "Comments on American Government and on the Constitution by a New Jersey Member of the Federal Convention." *Proceedings of the New Jersey Historical Society* LVI (October, 1938): 285–303.

―――. "The Political Ideas of New Jersey's First Governor." *Proceedings of the New Jersey Historical Society* LX (July, 1942): 184–99.

Thompson, Robert. "Transportation Combines and Pressure Politics in New Jersey." *Proceedings of the New Jersey Historical Society* XVII (January, 1939): 1–15.

Turner, Edward Raymond. "Women's Suffrage in New Jersey, 1790–1807." *Smith College Studies in History* I (July, 1916): 165–87.

Wallace, Michael. "Changing Concepts of Party in the United States: New York, 1815–1828." *American Historical Review* LXXXIV (December, 1968): 453–91.

Ward, John. "An Account of the Steamboat Controversy Between the Citizens of New York and the Citizens of New Jersey." *Proceedings of the New Jersey Historical Society* IX (May, 1962): 118–34.

Weiss, Harry. "A Graphic Summary of the Growth of Newspapers in New York and Other States, 1704–1820." *Bulletin of the New York Public Library* LII (April, 1948): 182–96.

Wesley, Charles. "Negro Suffrage in the Period of Constitution —Making, 1787–1865." *The Journal of Negro History* XXXII (April, 1947): 143–68.

Whitehead, William. "The Origin, Practice, and Prohibition of Female Suffrage in New Jersey." *Proceedings of the New Jersey Historical Society* VIII (January, 1858): 101–5.

Wilson, James Grant. "John Bayard, A Colonial Soldier and Statesman." *Proceedings of the New Jersey Historical Society*, Third Series II (1897): 100–15.

―――. "Judge Bayard of New Jersey and His London Diary of 1795–1796." *Proceedings of the New Jersey Historical Society*, Second Series VIII (1884): 205–16.

―――. "A Memorial of Col. John Bayard." *Proceedings of the New Jersey Historical Society*, Second Series V (1877): 141–60.

————. "Sketch of the Life of Andrew Kirkpatrick." *Proceedings of the New Jersey Historical Society,* Second Series II (May, 1870): 79–97.

Woodhull, Anna. "Memoir of Brig. Gen. Anthony Walton White." *Proceedings of the New Jersey Historical Society,* Second Series VII (1882): 107–12.

Wright, Marion. "Negro Suffrage in New Jersey, 1776–1875." *The Journal of Negro History* XXXIII (April, 1948): 168–224.

————. "New Jersey Laws and the Negro." *Journal of Negro History* XXVIII (1943): 159–99.

Unpublished Studies

Beckwith, Robert Russell. "Mahlon Dickerson of New Jersey, 1770–1853." Ph.D. diss., Columbia University, 1964.

Broussard, James. "The Federalists in the South Atlantic States." Ph.D. diss., Duke University, 1969.

Cranmer, H. Jerome. "The New Jersey Canals: State Policy and Private Enterprise, 1820–1832." Ph.D. diss., Columbia University, 1955.

Deshler, Charles D. "Governor Joseph Bloomfield of New Jersey." Paper presented at the New Brunswick Historical Club, New Brunswick, New Jersey, February 20, 1896.

————. "New Jersey and the Whiskey Rebellion." Paper presented at the New Brunswick Historical Club, New Brunswick, New Jersey, October 25, 1894.

Egerton, Cecil B. "Rufus King and the Missouri Question: A Study in Political Mythology." Ph.D. diss., Claremont Graduate School, 1967.

Ershkowitz, Herbert. "New Jersey Politics During the Era of Andrew Jackson, 1820–1837." Ph.D. diss., New York University, 1965.

————. "The Origins of the Whig and Democratic Parties in New Jersey." Paper presented at the Second Annnual New Jersey History Symposium, Trenton, New Jersey, December 5, 1970.

Fallow, Walter Robert. "The Rise of the Whig Party in New Jersey." Ph.D. diss., Princeton University, 1967.

Hanson, Frederick B. "The Interior Architecture and Household Furnishings of Bergen County, New Jersey, 1800–1810." M. A. thesis, University of Delaware. 1963.

Johnson, Marilynn Ann. "Clockmakers and Cabinetmakers of

Elizabethtown, New Jersey in the Federal Period." M.A. thesis, University of Delaware. 1963.

Keesey, Ruth. "Loyalty and Reprisal: The Loyalists of Bergen County, New Jersey and Their Estates." Ph.D. diss., Rutgers University, 1957.

Knox, Wendell. "Conspiracy in American Politics, 1787–1815." Ph.D. diss., University of North Carolina, 1965.

Pasler, Rudolph. "The Federalist Party in Burlington County, New Jersey." M.A. thesis, University of Delaware, 1964.

Pole, J. R. "The Reform of Suffrage and Representation in New Jersey, 1774–1844." Ph.D. diss., Princeton University, 1953.

Prince, Carl. "The Leadership of New Jersey's First Party System." Paper presented at the Second Annual New Jersey History Symposium, Trenton, New Jersey, December 5, 1970.

_____. "New Jersey's Democratic Republicans, 1790–1817: A Study of Early Party Machinery." Ph.D. diss., Rutgers University, 1963.

Rodgers, Robert M. "Some Phases of New Jersey History in the Jeffersonian Period." M. A. thesis, University of Chicago, 1931.

Rosenberg, Leonard Boyne. "The Political Thought of William Paterson." Ph.D. diss., New School for Social Research, 1967.

Sabine, Julia. "Antecedents of the Newark Public Library." Ph.D. diss., University of Chicago, 1946.

Sher, Paul. "Party Battles in Middlesex County, 1789–1824. M.A. thesis, Rutgers University, 1937.

Thompson, Robert T. "The New Jersey Merchant, 1790–1830." Paper presented at the New Brunswick Historical Club, New Brunswick, New Jersey, January 19, 1933.

Turner, Kathryn. "The Judiciary Act of 1801" Ph.D. diss., University of Wisconsin, 1959.

Venza, James. "Federalists in Congress, 1800–1812." Ph.D. diss., Vanderbilt University, 1967.

INDEX

Abolitionism, 20, 152. *See also* Slavery
"Adams and Liberty," 85, 108 n50
Adams conventions, New Jersey, 154, 155
Adams, John, 78, 79, 89 n28, 104 n12
Adams, John Q., New Jersey Federalist support for, 153–55, 170 n65, 172 n72
Alien Act, 84–85, 91 n59
Aliens in New Jersey, 32 n27; voting by, 99, 109 n54. *See also* Foreigners
Amalgamation, New Jersey Federalist party and, 167 n49
Anderson, William T., 154
Anti-Junto, 27–29 *passim*
Antimasonry, ex-New Jersey Federalists and, 174 n88
Anti-Missouri Crusade, 151–52, 169 n55, 169 n58
Anti-slavery. *See* Abolitionism; Anti-Missouri Crusade; Slavery
Appointments to office: ex-New Jersey Federalists receipt of, 155, 156; and New Jersey legislature (joint meeting), 42, 57–59, 124, 138 n65, 146–47, 150–51, 168 n51, 168 n52. *See also* Patronage
Aradale, Elias Van, 156
"Aristides" (pseudonym), 118
Armstrong, Robert, 156
Army, New Jersey Federalist support for, 94–95, 105 n19
Assembly, New Jersey, 40–41, 49 n30; Federalist strength in, 1800–1824, 188. *See also* Legislature, New Jersey

Baldwin, Luther, 83
Balloting, New Jersey Federalist party behavior regarding, 107–8
Banks, New Jersey Federalist party and, 60, 123, 137–38 n60, 161 n21
Baptists in New Jersey, 32 n33
Bayard, Jane, 18
Bayard, John, 18, 52, 61, 63; biographical sketch of, 204; and nucleus of future New Jersey Federalist party, 52
Bayard, Samuel, 78, 154, 172 n72, 204–5
Beatty, Erkuries, 14, 205
Beatty, John, 14, 154, 205–6
Beatty, Richard, 154
Bell, Andrew, 206, 171 n69
Bergen County, New Jersey, 30 n2; Dutch of, 32 n31; New Jersey Federalist party and, 97, 115, 140–41 n99, 150, 165 n44, 170 n65; and realignment, 170 n65; state legislative delegations of, 1800–1824, 178; vote of, for Federalist candidate for Council, 1796–1822, 189–90
Bible societies, New Jersey Federalists and, 152, 170 n61
Biographical sketches of New Jersey Federalists: Bayard, John, 204; Bayard, Samuel, 204–5; Beatty, Erkuries, 205; Beatty, John, 205–6; Bell, Andrew, 206; Boudinot, Elias, 206; Boudinot, Elisha, 206; Colefax, William, 206–7; Coxe, Richard, 207; Coxe, William, Jr., 207; Dayton, Elias, 207; Dayton, Jonathan, 207–8; Davenport, Franklin, 208; Elmer,

and XYZ affair, 79
Stockton, Robert, 154, 156, 172 n72
Suffrage, 68 n27; New Jersey Federalist party and, 113. *See also* Franchise
Sussex County, New Jersey: and Federalist party, 125, 127, 140–41 n99, 150, 166 n45; liberty cap deposed in, 81; state legislative delegations of, 1800–1824, 186–87; vote of, for Federalist candidate for Council, 1796–1822, 199; and XYZ affair, 80
Swedes in New Jersey, 23

Third partyism, 126–27
Thompson, Jacob R., 154
Times, New Brunswick, New Jersey, 170 n65
Township, in New Jersey Federalist party organization, 101
Towns of New Jersey, 21, 22
Trenton, New Jersey, 21, 33 n42; anti-Genêt meeting held in, 63; and Anti-Missouri Crusade, 151; and New Jersey Society for Suppression of Vice and Immorality, 152; and Washington Benevolent Society, 144–45, 159 n4; XYZ affair meeting held in, 80
True American, 38, 103, 114, 125; on New Jersey Federalist-Republican alliance, 126
Tucker, Ebenezer, 114, 131–32 n11

Union tickets, 150. *See also* "Quidism"

Van Aradale, Elias. *See* Aradale, Elias Van
Violence and politics, 114, 128, 132 n11, 132 n12
Virginia, Federalists of, 170 n63
Virginia and Kentucky Resolutions, 85–86
Voter participation in New Jersey elections, 189–99, 202
Vroom, Peter D., 154, 156, 214

Wall, Garret D., 19, 31 n10, 156; biographical sketch of, 214; Jacksonian,

154, 155, 156; and politically motivated physical violence, 114; and Washington Benevolent Society, 159 n15
Wallace, Joshua, 35 n58, 129, 214–15
War of 1812, 47 n5; and New Jersey Federalist party, 142, 147–48, 171 n24
Washington Benevolent Society, 144–45, 158–59 n13, 159 n14, 159 n15
Washington, Bushrod, 144
Washington, George, 18, 61, 65; New Jersey Federalist party and, 51, 52, 62, 145, 159 n16
Washingtonians, 140 n93
Washington Whig Society, 159–60 n16
West Jersey, 18–19, 21, 31 n20; and Congressional election of 1789, 27–30; ethnic and religious groups in, 22–24, 25; and hard money policy, 25–26
West Jersey ticket. *See* Junto ticket of 1789
Whigs, ex-New Jersey Federalists among the, 156, 171 n69, 172 n72
Whiskey Rebellion, 47 n5, 61–62, 71 n69, 72 n74
White, Anthony Walton, 77, 81, 94; biographical sketch of, 215; and the Whiskey Rebellion, 62, 72 n75
Williamson, Isaac, 36–37, 38, 161 n24, 215
Wilson, James J., 114, 124–25, 132 n12
Women, voting by, 99, 109 n54
Woodbury, New Jersey, 151
Woodruff, Aaron, 65, 141 n104
Woods, John, 61
Woods' Newark Gazette and Paterson Advertiser, 61
Wurts, Alexander, 172 n72

XYZ affair, 79–81

Young Federalists, New Jersey, 117, 133–34 n27, 139 n87, 159 n15; party role of, in 1808, 141 n101. *See also* New-style Federalism
"Yorick," 134 n33